George Gillanders Findlay

The Epistles to the Thessalonians

with introduction, notes and map

George Gillanders Findlay

The Epistles to the Thessalonians
with introduction, notes and map

ISBN/EAN: 9783337728922

Printed in Europe, USA, Canada, Australia, Japan

Cover: Foto ©Lupo / pixelio.de

More available books at **www.hansebooks.com**

:he Cambridge Bible for Schools and Colleges.

General Editor:—J. J. S. PEROWNE, D.D.
Bishop of Worcester.

THE EPISTLES TO THE

THESSALONIANS,

WITH INTRODUCTION, NOTES AND MAP

BY THE

REV. GEORGE G. FINDLAY, B.A.

PROFESSOR OF BIBLICAL LANGUAGES IN THE WESLEYAN COLLEGE,
HEADINGLEY.

STEREOTYPED EDITION.

Cambridge:
AT THE UNIVERSITY PRESS
1898

PREFACE

BY THE GENERAL EDITOR.

THE General Editor of *The Cambridge Bible for Schools* thinks it right to say that he does not hold himself responsible either for the interpretation of particular passages which the Editors of the several Books have adopted, or for any opinion on points of doctrine that they may have expressed. In the New Testament more especially questions arise of the deepest theological import, on which the ablest and most conscientious interpreters have differed and always will differ. His aim has been in all such cases to leave each Contributor to the unfettered exercise of his own judgment, only taking care that

PREFACE.

mere controversy should as far as possible be avoided. He has contented himself chiefly with a careful revision of the notes, with pointing out omissions, with suggesting occasionally a reconsideration of some question, or a fuller treatment of difficult passages, and the like.

Beyond this he has not attempted to interfere, feeling it better that each Commentary should have its own individual character, and being convinced that freshness and variety of treatment are more than a compensation for any lack of uniformity in the Series.

PREFATORY NOTE.

THE care of this volume of the *Cambridge Bible for Schools and Colleges* was intrusted in the first instance to the Rev. W. F. Moulton, D.D., Headmaster of the Leys School, Cambridge, who was compelled by the pressure of other duties to relinquish the work. This he did (as he permits me to say) with very great reluctance and regret. It is a loss to all who may have occasion to use this book, that it is prepared by other hands than those of the original Editor.

I am happy to state, however, that Dr Moulton has not only favoured me with most valuable counsels and suggestions in the preparation of the Commentary, but has, under conditions of peculiar difficulty, found time to revise the proof-sheets; and the following pages, however defective in other respects, will bear some traces of his extreme accuracy, his admirable judgement and finished scholarship.

GEO. G. FINDLAY.

HEADINGLEY, *January*, 1891.

CONTENTS.

			PAGES
I.	INTRODUCTION.		
	Chapter I.	The City of Thessalonica	9—12
	Chapter II.	How the Gospel came to Thessalonica	13—16
	Chapter III.	The Gospel of Paul at Thessalonica	16—22
	Chapter IV.	The Occasion of the Two Epistles	22—27
	Chapter V.	The Genuineness of the Two Epistles	27—31
	Chapter VI.	The Style and Character of the Two Epistles	32—37
	Chapter VII.	Analysis and Digest of the Epistles	37—43
II.	TEXT AND NOTES		45—169
III.	APPENDIX. On the Man of Lawlessness		170—180
IV.	INDEX		181—183
	MAP		*facing Title.*

⁎⁎⁎ The Text adopted in this Edition is that of Dr Scrivener's *Cambridge Paragraph Bible.* A few variations from the ordinary Text, chiefly in the spelling of certain words, and in the use of italics, will be noticed. For the principles adopted by Dr Scrivener as regards the printing of the Text see his Introduction to the *Paragraph Bible,* published by the Cambridge University Press.

"The Apostolic Letters, which made glad
The young and foe-girt Churches of the Lord."
AUBREY DE VERE.

ART THOU THE CHRIST, THE SON OF THE BLESSED?—AND JESUS SAID, I AM: AND YE SHALL SEE THE SON OF MAN SITTING AT THE RIGHT HAND OF POWER, AND COMING WITH THE CLOUDS OF HEAVEN.

INTRODUCTION.

CHAPTER I.

THE CITY OF THESSALONICA.

MOST of the ancient cities in which St Paul laboured have in the course of ages either perished or sunk into insignificance. Rome still remains, "the eternal city," holding a unique place amongst the world's great capitals. And along with Rome, though in a far inferior position, Thessalonica has retained its identity and its importance throughout the immense changes of the last two thousand years.

The town first appears in Greek history under the name of *Therma*,—so called from the warm mineral springs in its vicinity. Its later designation was given to it by Cassander, who on seizing the vacant throne of Alexander the Great in Macedonia married his sister *Thessalonica*. Her name was, no doubt, a memorial of some victory gained by her father Philip of Macedon over his neighbours in Thessaly.

Founding a new city upon this site in 315 B.C., the usurper called it after his highborn wife. Cassander's foundation rapidly grew into a place of commercial and political consequence. After the Roman conquest of Macedonia (168 B.C.), Thessalonica was made the head of one of the four districts into which the kingdom was divided, and on their subsequent reunion became the capital of the whole province. It was declared a "free city," with important rights of self-government, after the civil war which ended with the defeat of Brutus and Cassius at Philippi (42 B.C.), having fortunately sided with the victors. Hence the Thessalonian magistrates are correctly designated "politarchs" in Acts xvii. 6. At the same time, it was the seat of the Roman proconsular administration of Macedonia, and an important military station.

The geographer Strabo (about 24 B.C.) describes Thessalonica as the most populous town of Macedonia; a contemporary author speaks of it as "the mother of all Macedonia." It is referred to in similar terms by Lucian in the second century, and by Theodoret in the fifth. At the beginning of the tenth century it is computed to have held a population of above 200,000. To-day, under the Turkish rule, Saloniki (or Salonica) numbers perhaps 100,000 souls, and is rapidly increasing. In size it is the third, and in importance quite the second, city of Turkey in Europe. The Jews still flourish here, even more than in the Apostle's time; they form a third or more of the population. The remainder are chiefly Greeks, mixed with Turks and Bulgars. The city is now, as it was in the first century, the emporium of Macedonia and one of the chief ports of the Ægean. Saloniki is moreover the terminus of the great trunk line of railway recently completed, running south through the heart of the Balkan peninsula, which will give it largely the command of the trade of Central Europe with the Levant. It is destined still to play, in all probability, an important part in the political and religious history of South-Eastern Europe.

The city owes its importance to its geographical position. It stands in a remarkably fine and picturesque situation, on a hill sloping down to the sea, and guarded by high mountain ridges on both sides. Below the city there stretched far to the south-west the broad and well-sheltered *Thermaic Gulf* (now *Gulf of Saloniki*), with the snowy heights of Mount Olympus, the fabled home of the Greek gods, bounding the horizon. This bay forms the north-western corner of the Ægean Sea, occupying the angle which the Greek peninsula makes with the mainland. It lies moreover near the mouth of the chief passes leading down from the Macedonian uplands, with the wide Danubian plains spread beyond them in the north. And in Roman times the city held a special importance from its situation midway between the Adriatic and Hellespont along the *Via Egnatia*, the great military road which formed the main artery linking Rome to her eastern provinces: *posita in gremio imperii nostri*, says Cicero.   See the *map* facing the title-page.

Cicero spent some months in Thessalonica during his exile from Rome in 58 B.C., and again in Pompey's winter camp, pitched here before the fatal battle of Pharsalus (48 B.C.); here he also halted on his way to and from Cilicia, his province in the East (51—50 B.C.); and from Thessalonica he wrote a number of characteristic letters, which it would be interesting to compare with those of the Apostle Paul addressed to the same place.

St Paul visited Macedonia a second time, on his way from Ephesus to Greece during the third missionary journey (Acts xx. 1, 2), spending doubtless considerable time at Thessalonica; and we find two Thessalonians, *Aristarchus* and *Secundus* (Acts xx. 4), attending him on his subsequent voyage to Jerusalem. Aristarchus remained with the Apostle a long while, and is honourably mentioned in Col. iv. 10, as "my fellow captive," during his imprisonment at Rome. It was from Macedonia (the *subscription* states, conjecturally, "from Philippi") that St Paul addressed, in 58 (or 57) A.D., his second Epistle to the Corinthians (2 Cor. ii. 13, vii. 5, viii. 1). Writing to the Philippians (c. 63 A.D.) from his Roman prison, the Apostle "trusts in the Lord" that he will "come" to see them "shortly" (Phil. ii. 24). And we find him some time after his release fulfilling this intention: "on my way to Macedonia" (1 Tim. i. 3). The last reference found in the N. T. to Thessalonica is in 2 Tim. iv. 10, and is an unhappy one: "Demas hath forsaken me, having loved the present world; and is gone to Thessalonica." If Demas wished to make a fortune, Thessalonian trade would have more attraction for him than the company of a doomed and penniless prisoner in Rome. Perhaps he was a Thessalonian. Singularly enough, Thessalonica claims another Demetrius (*Demas* is probably short for *Demetrius*), a martyr of the Diocletian persecution (c. 303 A.D.), as her patron saint.

INTRODUCTION.

In Church history Thessalonica bears an honourable name. It was a bulwark of the Catholic faith and of the Greek Christian Empire in the early middle ages, when it bore the title of "the orthodox city[1]." It was also an active centre of missionary evangelism amongst the Gothic, and afterwards the Slavonic invaders of the Balkan peninsula. In its energetic zeal for the cause of Christ the Church of Thessalonica nobly sustained the character given to it by St Paul in these Epistles. This city was the scene of a memorable tragedy, when in the year 390 the Emperor Theodosius, in revenge for some affront, ruthlessly massacred 15,000 of its inhabitants. For this act St Ambrose, the great Bishop of Milan, compelled the Emperor to do abject penance, refusing him communion for eight months until he submitted. Amongst the Bishops of Thessalonica, only one name is recorded of the first rank, that of *Eustathius* (died 1198 A.D.), who was the most learned scholar of his age and an active Church reformer. During the decay of the Byzantine empire, the city was for a time under Latin and later under Venetian rule. It underwent three memorable sieges,—having been captured by the Saracens in 904; by Tancred of Sicily, the Norman Crusader, in 1185; and finally, by the Turkish Sultan Amurath II., in 1430 A.D.

Thessalonica possesses three ancient and beautiful Greek Churches turned into mosques, those of St Sophia[2], St George, and St Demetrius; as well as a few very valuable and interesting remains of Roman antiquity. It is now the seat of an influential Greek archbishopric.

---

[1] It should be said, however, that Tafel (*De Thessalonica ejusque agro*, Berlin, 1839), our chief authority on the history of the city, conjectures that this epithet was conferred on Thessalonica because of its stubborn defence of *Image-worship* against the Iconoclastic Emperors of Constantinople in the eighth and ninth centuries.

[2] In the disastrous fire of September 4th, 1890, the mosque of St Sophia was destroyed—a heavy and irreparable loss. As a monument and treasury of Byzantine art, this once Christian cathedral stood second only to St Sophia of Constantinople itself.

CHAPTER II.

How the Gospel came to Thessalonica.

It was in the course of his *second* great missionary expedition that the Apostle Paul planted the standard of the Cross in Europe, in the year of our Lord 53 (or 52). He had slowly traversed Asia Minor from the south-east to the north-west, and was detained in Galatia by sickness for a considerable time; a circumstance which gave him the opportunity of preaching to that interesting people, amongst whom he founded at this time important Churches (Acts xvi. 6, xviii. 23; Gal. iv. 13—15). Twice again were his plans frustrated during this journey. His chief intention seems to have been to evangelize the Roman province of Asia (Acts xvi. 6), where he afterwards spent three fruitful years (Acts xx. 31). This region, with its capital city Ephesus, was for the Apostle's mission probably the most important district between Jerusalem and Rome. But for the present he was "prevented by the Holy Spirit." A similar mysterious intimation arrested him when afterwards he was entering the northerly province of Bithynia: "the Spirit of Jesus suffered them not" (Acts xvi. 7). So St Paul and his companions (Silas and Timothy) found themselves at the port of Troas, fronting Europe and the West, where St Luke also joined them; for just at this point (ver. 10) the narrator of the Acts passes from the third to the first person plural. It was here that the true goal of the Apostle's journey disclosed itself, and the reason of God's repeated interference with His servant's designs. "A vision by night appeared to Paul. There was a man of Macedonia standing, beseeching him: Come over to Macedonia, and help us!" In Macedonia the Gospel was to find a congenial soil and a people prepared for the Lord.

We need not repeat the story of the missionaries' voyage across the Ægean, their journey inland to Philippi, their success and their sufferings in that city, all so graphically related by St Luke, who writes Acts xvi. 10—40 as an eye-witness. One reference in these Epistles the Apostle makes to his experience at Philippi: he writes in 1 Ep. ii. 2, "Though we had already suffered and endured violence in Philippi, we were bold in our God to speak to you the good news of God." The pleasanter side of his connection at this time with Philippi is intimated when, addressing the Philippians many years later, he recalls how "even in Thessalonica ye sent to supply my need, both once and twice" (Phil. iv. 16).

Thessalonica lies a hundred miles west of Philippi along the Via Egnatia, a distance of three days' journey. "Amphipolis and Apollonia" are mentioned in Acts xvii. 1 as the chief towns and halting places on the way. But these places the three evangelists "travelled through." Thessalonica was their objective point. This city attracted the Apostle of the Gentiles on several accounts; and he was resolved to occupy it for Christ.

We have already, in Chap. I., described the position of Thessalonica and its growing importance as a centre of trade and population. There was an additional circumstance which gave the missionaries a vantage-ground here. At Philippi the Jews were not numerous or wealthy enough to boast a synagogue; only they had a *proseucha*, or retired oratory "by the riverside," probably open to the air (Acts xvi. 13). In Thessalonica "there was a synagogue of the Jews" (Acts xvii. 1). It was not that St Paul expected to gain many converts from the synagogue itself; but round the Jewish synagogue there was usually gathered a circle of devout and enlightened Gentiles, in various stages of proselytism, weary of heathen superstition and philosophy, and instructed more or less in the Old Testament, but not prepossessed by the ingrained prejudice, the pride of religion and of race, and the scorn of a crucified Messiah which closed the ears of the Jews themselves against the truth of the Gospel. In this outlying circle of proselytes and synagogue-hearers, distinguished frequently by the presence of a number of the more refined and intelligent Greek women of the upper classes, St Paul was accustomed to find his best audiences. Here he gathered the nucleus of his Gentile Churches. At Thessalonica while "some" of the Jews "were persuaded and consorted with Paul and Silas," a "great multitude of the devout Greeks" did so, "and of the chief women (*the ladies*, as we should say, *of the city*) not a few" (Acts xvii. 4). Such people could best be reached through the synagogue, and the Apostle felt it his duty to address himself to his own countrymen in the first instance ('to the Jew first'), however often they might repel him; so "according to Paul's custom he went in unto them, and for three sabbaths discoursed with them from the Scriptures, expounding and explaining that the Christ was bound to suffer and to rise from the dead, and that *this* is the Christ, —this Jesus whom I preach to you" (Acts xvii. 3). After three weeks of this discussion the synagogue appears to have been closed against Paul and Silas. They only carried a small minority of their compatriots with them. But they must have continued for some time longer in the city, at least a month we should imagine, to have gathered and formed into a Church so large a community as the Epistles indicate, and to have carried them so far in Christian knowledge and discipline.

Before long, however, the jealousy of "the unbelieving Jews" at their success found means to arrest the work of the Apostles. They roused the city mob against them. The rioters attacked the house of Jason (his name is probably equivalent to *Jesus*), a Jew of property who had accepted the faith of Christ and invited the missionaries to lodge with him. Not finding the two leaders, they seized Jason and some other Christians and "dragged" them before the magistrates, on the remarkable charge (1) of being *revolutionaries*—"turning the world upside down," and (2) of *rebellion against the Roman Emperor*, in "saying that there is another king, one Jesus" (*vv.* 5—7). These charges, scattered broadcast, alarmed the "politarchs" as well as the common people (ver. 8); but they could not be sustained, and the accused were dismissed, security being taken for their good behaviour (ver. 9). The accusations brought against Paul and Silas were, however, a distortion of what they had actually preached, and may help us to understand the special character and drift of the Apostolic teaching in this city. The outbreak made it evident that St Paul's unscrupulous enemies were determined, at any cost, to drive him from Thessalonica. He was now, as so frequently, in deadly "peril from his own countrymen" (2 Cor. xi. 26). "The brethren" insisted on his leaving them, and "sent Paul and Silas away by night immediately to Berœa" (ver. 10),—an inland Macedonian town situated forty miles or more from Thessalonica, in the direction of Achaia.

CHAPTER III.

THE GOSPEL OF PAUL AT THESSALONICA.

Now we may ask, *What was the gospel brought to Thessalonica?* Can we give to ourselves any precise account of the "good news" which "Paul and Silvanus and Timotheus" announced in this city, and which produced so powerful and enduring an effect? Further, was there anything special to the place and the occasion in the form which the Apostle's message assumed, and which will serve to explain the peculiar tone of Christian feeling, the style of thought and cast of doctrine, that distinguished the faith of this great Macedonian Church in its first beginnings? To these questions the indications of the two Epistles, compared with the story of the Acts, enable us to give a tolerable answer.

(1) The foundation of St Paul's teaching was laid in *the proof of the Messiahship of Jesus*, drawn from the prophecies of Scripture, compared with the facts of the life, death and resurrection of the Saviour. The method of this proof, briefly indicated in Acts xvii. 3, is set forth at length in the report of his discourse at the Pisidian Antioch given by St Luke in the thirteenth chapter of the Acts.

(2) *The purpose of Christ's death and its bearing on human salvation* must have been abundantly explained by the Apostles. So we infer not only from the central position of this subject in St Paul's later Epistles, and from the prominence given to it in Acts xiii. 38, 39, where the announcement of *forgiveness of sins* and *justification by faith* forms the climax of St Paul's

whole sermon; but the language of 1 Ep. v. 8—10 leaves us in no doubt that the same "word of the cross" was proclaimed at Thessalonica which St Paul preached everywhere. Here "salvation" comes "through our Lord Jesus Christ, who died for us"—a salvation from "the anger of God," a salvation in part received already, in part matter of "hope," and which belongs to those who "have put on the breastplate of *faith* and love." This salvation was the great need of the Gentile world, which "knew not God," and was enslaved to idolatry and shameful lusts (1 Ep. i. 9; iv. 5; 2 Ep. i. 8).

Now we can understand all this in the light of Rom. i. 16—25, iii. 23—26, v. 1—11, and as touching Him "whom God set forth in His blood a propitiation through faith"; but without such knowledge the Apostle's language would have been equally unintelligible to the Thessalonians and to ourselves. Still it must be admitted, and it is remarkable, that very little is said in these two letters on the subject of the Atonement and Salvation by Faith. Evidently on these fundamental doctrines there was no dispute at Thessalonica. They were so fully accepted and understood in this Church, that it was unnecessary to dilate upon them; and the Apostle has other matters just now to deal with.

(3) The Church at Thessalonica being chiefly of heathen origin, St Paul and St Silas had said much to them of *the falsity and wickedness of idolatry*, completing the lessons which many of their disciples had already received in the synagogue. Their faith was emphatically a "*faith toward God*—the living and true God," to Whom they had "turned from their idols" (this seems to imply that many Thessalonian Christians had been converted directly from paganism), and Whom they knew in "His Son" (1 Ep. i. 9, 10). And this living and true God, the Father of the Lord Jesus, they had come to know and to approach as "our Father" (1 Ep. i. 3; iii. 11, 13; 2 Ep. ii. 16), Who was to them "the God of peace" (1 Ep. i. 1; v. 23; 2 Ep. i. 2), Who had "loved them and given them eternal comfort and good hope in grace," had "chosen" them and "called them to enter His kingdom and glory," Who "would count them

worthy of their calling and accomplish in them all the desire of goodness and the work of faith," Who had "given them His Holy Spirit," Whose "will" was their "sanctification," Whose "word" was ever "working in" them, Who would "comfort and strengthen their hearts" in every needful way and would reward them with "rest" from their afflictions in due time, Whose care for His beloved was not limited by death, for He was pledged at Christ's coming to restore those whom death had snatched away (1 Ep. i. 4; ii. 12, 13; iv. 3, 7, 8, 14; v. 18; 2 Ep. i. 5, 7, 11; ii. 13, 16, 17). Such a God it must be their one aim to love and to please; St Paul's one desire for them is that they may "walk worthily" of Him (1 Ep. ii. 12; iv. 1; 2 Ep. iii. 5). The good news the Apostle had brought he speaks of repeatedly as "the gospel *of God*," while it is "the gospel of our Lord Jesus Christ" (2 Ep. i. 8), since He is its great subject and centre: comp. Rom. i. 1, 3, "the gospel of God—concerning His Son."

It is important to note the prominence of *God* in these Epistles, and the manifold ways in which the Divine character and relationship to believing men had been set forth to the Thessalonian Church. For such teaching would be necessary, and helpful in the highest degree, to men who had just emerged from heathen darkness and superstition; and these letters afford the best example left to us of St Paul's *earliest* instructions to Gentile converts. The next report we have of his preaching to the heathen comes from Athens (Acts xvii. 22—31), where his discourse bore principally on two subjects—*the nature of the true God*, and *the coming of Jesus Christ to judge the world*.

(4) So we come to that which was the most conspicuous and impressive topic of the Thessalonian gospel, so far as we can gather it from the echoes audible in the Epistles, viz. *the coming of the Lord Jesus in His heavenly kingdom*. These letters compel us to remember, what we are apt to forget, that the second advent of Christ is an important part of the Christian gospel, the good tidings that God has sent to the world concerning His Son. In 1 Ep. i. 9, 10 the religion of Thessalonian believers is summed up in these two things:

"serving a God living and true, and waiting for His Son from the heavens." It was in the light of Christ's second coming that they had learned to look for that "kingdom and glory of God" to which they were "called," and "for which" they were now "suffering" (1 Ep. ii. 12; 2 Ep. i. 5, 10—12). "The coming of our Lord Jesus with all His saints" was an object of intense desire and fervent anticipation to the Apostle himself, and he had impressed the same feelings on his disciples at Thessalonica to an uncommon degree. His appeals and warnings thoughout these Epistles rest on the "hope in our Lord Jesus Christ" as their strongest support. It was, moreover, upon this subject that the misunderstandings arose which the Apostle is at so much pains to correct—the first appearing in 1 Ep. iv. 13, touching the share of departed Christians in the return of the Lord Jesus; and the second in 2 Ep. ii. 1, 2, concerning the imminence of the event itself.

What may have been the train of thought and feeling in the Apostle's mind that led him to dwell upon this theme with such especial emphasis at this particular period, we cannot tell. But there were two conditions belonging to his early ministry in Europe which naturally might suggest this line of preaching. In the *first* place, the Christian doctrine of final judgement was one well calculated to rouse the Greek people from its levity and moral indifference; and it had impressive analogies in their own primitive religion. It was for this practical purpose that St Paul advanced the doctrine at Athens: "Having overlooked the times of ignorance, God now commands men that all everywhere should repent; *because He has appointed a day* in which He will judge the world in righteousness, by the Man whom He ordained" (Acts xvii. 30, 31). To the busy traders of Corinth and Thessalonica, just as amongst the philosophers and dilettanti of Athens, the Apostle made the same severe and alarming proclamation. The message of judgement was an essential part of St Paul's good tidings. "God shall judge the secrets of men, *according to my gospel*, through Jesus Christ" (Rom. ii. 16). But the declaration of Christ's coming in judgement involves the whole doctrine of the Second Advent.

On this matter St Paul tells us he had abundantly enlarged in the Thessalonian Church (1 Ep. v. 2; 2 Ep. ii. 6).

In the *second* place it should be observed, that the Apostle, in entering Europe by the Via Egnatia, was brought more directly under the shadow of the Roman Empire than at any time before. Philippi, a Roman colony, and a memorial of the victory by which the Empire was established; Thessalonica, a great provincial capital of European aspect and character; the splendid military road by which the missionaries travelled, and along which troops of soldiers, officers of state with their brilliant retinues, foreign envoys and tributaries were going and coming—all this gave a powerful impression of the "kingdom and glory" of the great world-ruling city, to which a mind like St Paul's could not but be sensitive. He was himself, it must be remembered, a citizen of Rome and by no means indifferent to his rights in this capacity; and he held a high estimate of the prerogatives and functions of the civil power (Rom. xiii. 1—7).

But what he saw of the great kingdom of this world prompted in his mind larger thoughts of that mightier and Diviner kingdom, whose herald and ambassador he was. He could not fail to discern under the majestic sway of Rome signs of moral degeneracy and seeds of ruin. He remembered well that it was by the sentence of Pontius Pilate (1 Tim. vi. 13) that his Master was crucified; and in his own outrageous treatment by the Roman officials at Philippi and the sufferings of the Christian flock at Thessalonica he may well have seen tokens of the inevitable conflict between the tyranny of secular rule and the authority of Christ. If such thoughts as' these coloured the speech of Paul and Silas at Thessalonica, we can understand the charge made against them in this city: "These all do contrary to the decrees of Cæsar, saying that there is another king, even Jesus" (Acts xvii. 7). It was in principle the charge alleged against Jesus Himself before Pilate, compelling the Roman governor to pronounce his fatal sentence: "If thou let this man go, thou art *not Cæsar's friend:* whosoever maketh himself a king, speaketh *against Cæsar.*" So the

Jews "cried out" (Jo. xix. 12); and at the bottom, the accusation was true; the sharp-sighted enmity of the Jews rightly discerned that the rule of Jesus was fatal to Cæsarism. If the Apostles preached, as they could do without any denunciation of the powers that be, a universal, righteous and equal judgement of mankind approaching, in which Jesus (crucified by the Roman State) would be judge and king; if they taught that "the fashion of this world passeth away" (1 Cor. vii. 31), and that an atheistic world-wide despotism would one day culminate in a huge disaster, to be "consumed by the breath of the Lord and the brightness of His coming" (2 Ep. ii. 3—11), there were grounds plausible enough for accusing them of treasonable doctrine, even though no express political offence had been committed. That such a judgement was impending was "good news" indeed; but it was of deadly import to the imperial tyranny of Caligulas and Neros, and to the social and political fabric of the existing pagan world of which the deified Cæsars were the top-stone. In this consequence lies the most significant and distinctive, though not the most obvious, feature of the gospel of Thessalonica.

It may be further added, that the hope of Christ's return in glory was the consolation best suited to sustain the Church, as it sustained the Apostle himself, in the great fight of affliction through which they were passing.

(5) *The moral issues* of the Gospel inculcated by St Paul at Thessalonica, the new duties and affections belonging to the new life of believers in Christ, are touched upon at many different points; but not developed with the fulness and systematic method of subsequent Epistles. Most prominent here are the obligation to *chastity*, as belonging to the sanctity of the body and the indwelling of the Holy Spirit (1 Ep. iv. 1—8); and the claims of *brotherly love*, with the good order, the peace, and mutual helpfulness that flow from it (1 Ep. iv. 9, 10; v. 12—15; 2 Ep. iii. 14, 15). What is singular in these Epistles is the repeated and strong injunctions they contain on the subject of *diligence* in labour and attention to the ordinary duties of life (1 Ep. iv. 10—12; 2 Ep. iii. 6—15).

A striking moral feature of the gospel proclaimed at Thessalonica is manifest in *the conduct of the missionaries of Christ* themselves,—their incessant labour, their unbounded self-denial, the purity and devoutness of their spirit, and their fearless courage (1 Ep. i. 6, 7; ii. 1—12; 2 Ep. iii. 8, 9).

CHAPTER IV.

The Occasion of the Two Epistles.

1. ST PAUL had been absent no long time from Thessalonica—the "season of an hour" (1 Ep. ii. 17). He had been at Athens in the interval (1 Ep. iii. 1), and is now engaged at Corinth (Acts xviii. 1, 5). He had left Thessalonica very unwillingly (1 Ep. ii. 17; Acts xvii. 10: "The disciples *sent away* Paul and Silas"), promising and fully expecting to come back quickly. He had set his heart on returning to his persecuted flock, and had twice attempted to do so, but insuperable and malicious hindrances came in his way (1 Ep. ii. 17, 18: "Satan hindered us"). After the failure of his second attempt, when the Apostle had now arrived at Athens and his anxiety for the Thessalonians was unendurable, he resolved to send Timothy in his place, the only companion now left to him (ch. iii. 1, 2), in order to comfort and strengthen this infant Church. From Acts xvii. 14, 15 we learn that Silas and Timothy had in the first instance both stayed behind at Berœa, with instructions to follow their chief as soon as they found it possible. This direction Timothy was able speedily to obey; and on his return St Paul despatched him forthwith from Athens to Thessalonica (see notes on 1 Ep. iii. 1, 2). Timothy had now once more rejoined the Apostle (Silas too, at or about the same time, and coming from the same quarter), who had meanwhile removed from Athens to Corinth.

Timothy brought a report which greatly relieved and gladdened the heart of the much-tried Apostle. It was a very "gospel" to him. The Thessalonians were "standing fast in the Lord." The expectations he had formed of them were in no way disappointed. Their faith had endured without flinching the fiery test of persecution. Their love to each other and to their absent father in Christ was devoted and sincere. They were mindful of the Apostle's teaching, maintaining a consistent walk and by their faithfulness and zeal commending the gospel with powerful effect throughout Macedonia and Achaia. "What fitting thanks," St Paul asks, "can we render to God for all the joy with which we rejoice over you before our God?" (1 Ep. iii. 6—10; i. 2—8; iv. 1, 9, 10; v. 11). St Paul's Epistles contain nowhere a more earnest or unqualified commendation than that which he bestows on the fidelity of the Thessalonian Church.

What the Apostle hears from his assistant increases his longing to see them again; for this he is "praying night and day with intense desire" (ch. iii. 10). Indeed his primary object in writing the First Epistle is *to express his great desire to revisit Thessalonica* (ch. ii. 17; iii. 11). Associated with this wish there are two other purposes that actuate his mind. On the one hand, he finds it necessary *to explain his continued absence*, and in doing so *to justify himself from aspersions* thrown upon him by his opponents. This self-defence is the first subject on which he enters, in ch. ii. 1—12. We gather from it that there were certain enemies of the Christian cause in Thessalonica (Jewish enemies, as the denunciation of *vv.* 14—16, together with the general probabilities of the situation, strongly suggests), who had taken advantage of the absence of the missionaries to slander them[1]. They had insinuated doubts of their courage (ch. ii. 2), of their disinterestedness and honesty

---

[1] It is necessary to observe that the opponents St Paul has in view in 1 Ep. ii. (see esp. *vv.* 15, 16) are *unconverted Jews*, altogether hostile to the gospel Paul preached. The Jews of Thessalonica drove him from this city, and following him to Beræa attacked him there; and their compatriots at Corinth imitated their example, though happily not with the same success (Acts xvii. 5, 13; xviii. 12—17). Of the *Jewish Christians* opposed to Paul and his Gentile mission, the "false brethren" who afterwards "troubled" him at Corinth and in Galatia, we find in these Epistles no trace whatever.

(*vv.* 3, 6, 9), and of their real affection for their Thessalonian converts (*vv.* 7, 8, 11, 12). They had said: "These so-called 'Apostles of Christ' are self-seeking adventurers. Depend upon it, their real object is to make themselves a reputation and to fill their own purse at your expense. They have beguiled you by their flatteries and pretence of sanctity into accepting their new-fangled faith; and then, as soon as trouble arises and their mischievous doctrines bring them into danger, they creep away like cowards, leaving you to bear the brunt of persecution. And likely enough, you will never see them again!" Chapter ii. is a reply to innuendoes of this kind, which are such as unscrupulous Jewish antagonists would be sure to make. And considering the short time that Paul and Silas had been in this city, and the influence which the synagogue-leaders had formerly possessed over many members of their flock; considering also the disheartening effect that continued persecution was likely to have upon a young and unseasoned Church, one cannot wonder at the danger there was lest confidence in the absent missionaries should be undermined by these insidious attacks. On the whole, that confidence had not been shaken. "You have good remembrance of us at all times" (ch. iii. 6); so Timothy had assured St Paul. But the Apostles show themselves, in ch. ii. 1—12, most anxious to increase and strengthen this good remembrance.

On the other hand, and looking onward to the future, St Paul writes in order *to carry forward the instruction of his converts* in Christian doctrine and life, "to perfect what is lacking in your faith" (ch. iii. 10). With his entrance into Europe the Apostle's mission has entered upon a new stage. He is no longer able quickly to revisit his Churches, which are now numerous and widely separated, and to exercise a direct pastoral oversight amongst them. The defect of his presence he must supply by messenger and letter. When he describes himself as "longing to see you and to complete the deficiencies of your faith," in explaining this earliest of his apostolic letters, we see how the necessity of such Epistles arose and to what conditions we owe their existence.

The "deficiencies" which St Paul has to correct or supplement, are chiefly of a practical nature. They concern—(1) on the *moral* side, the virtue of *chastity*, sadly wanting in Greek city-life, in respect of which the former notions of Gentile converts had commonly been very lax; and *brotherly love*, with which, in the case of this Church, the duty of *diligent labour* was closely associated (ch. iv. 1—12). (2) On the *doctrinal* side, a painful misunderstanding had arisen touching *the relation of "them that sleep" to Christ on His return*, which Timothy was not able altogether to remove; and there was in regard to this event generally a restlessness of mind and over-curiosity unfavourable to sober and steadfast Christian life (ch. iv. 13—v. 11). (3) With this we may connect symptoms of *indiscipline* in one party, and of *contempt for extraordinary spiritual manifestations* in another, which the closing verses of the Epistle indicate (ch. v. 12—22).

Respecting these needs of the Church, as well as concerning its loyalty and earnestness of faith, Timothy, doubtless, had given the Apostle a full report.

II. After writing the First Epistle St Paul received further tidings from Thessalonica, which moved him to write a *Second*. The situation of the Church remained, for the most part, the same, but accentuated in its leading features. We gather from the opening Act of Thanksgiving (ch. i.) that the storm of persecution was still more violent and the fidelity of the Church even more conspicuous than when the Apostle wrote a few months before. "Your faith grows exceedingly, and your love multiplies. We make our boast in you amongst the Churches of God, because of your faith and endurance in persecution" (ch. i. 3, 4). The Apostle says nothing further, however, of his intention to return; his hands were by this time tied fast at Corinth (Acts xviii. 5—18): he commends them to "the Lord, Who will stablish them and keep them from the Evil One" (ch. iii. 3—5). Nor does he enter on any further defence of his conduct toward the Thessalonians. That was now unnecessary.

There are two things which he is wishful to say. First and chiefly, *about the Second Advent*—"the coming of our Lord Jesus Christ and our gathering together unto Him" (ch. ii. 1). A report was circulated, claiming prophetic origin, and alleged to have St Paul's authentication, to the effect that "the day of the Lord had arrived" and He must be looked for immediately (ver. 2). This the Apostle declares to be a deception (ver. 3). And he gives reasons, partly derived from his original teaching, why so speedy a consummation was impossible. This gives occasion to his memorable prediction of the advent of "the Man of Sin" (or "Lawlessness"), whose appearance and exaltation to supreme power will be, he announces, the signal for Christ's return in glory (*vv.* 3—12). This prophecy is the one great difficulty which meets the student of these Epistles. It is amongst the most mysterious passages in the Bible. See the *Appendix*.

The other object the Apostle has in writing 2 Thessalonians is *to reprove the disorderly fraction of the Church* (ch. iii. 6—15). The First Epistle intimated the existence of a tendency to idleness and consequent insubordination (ch. iv. 11, 12; v. 12—14), to which he there alluded in a few words of guarded and kindly censure. His gentle reproof however failed to check the evil, which had now assumed an aggravated and persistent form and endangered the Church's peace. It was connected with the prevalent excitement on the subject of Christ's advent. This expectation furnished an excuse and incentive to the neglect of ordinary labour. The Apostle now takes the offenders severely to task, and directs their brethren to refuse support from the funds of the Church to such as persisted in idleness, and to avoid their company.

That this letter is the *second* of the two, and not the first (as Grotius, Ewald, F. C. Baur, and some other critics have conjectured), is evident from the course of affairs and the internal relationship of the Epistles, as we have just examined them. 2 Thessalonians bears on its face the character of a sequel and supplement to 1 Thessalonians. It deals more fully and urgently with two important points raised in the former letter, as they present themselves in their further development. The disturbing influences whose presence is only indicated in 1 Thessalonians, have now reached their crisis. And the Apostle's thanksgiving (ch. i. 3—12) implies an advance both in the severity of persecution, and in the growth and testing of Thessalonian faith; for which faith he gives thanks in terms even stronger than before. The personal recollections and explanations, so interesting a feature of the other Epistle, are eminently suited to the Apostle's *first* communication of the kind with this beloved Church. The absence of such references in the shorter Epistle marks it as virtually an appendix to the other, following it after a brief interval. The expression of ch. ii. 2, "neither through word, nor *through letter* as on our authority," is most naturally explained as alluding to some misquotation or misunderstanding of the language of 1 Thessalonians on the subject in question.

The two Epistles were written, as we have seen, *from Corinth;* not from Athens, as it is stated in the concluding note, or "subscription," attached to the Epistles in the MSS followed by the Authorised English version. They were both composed during the Apostle's residence of eighteen months in Corinth (Acts xviii. 11), extending from Autumn 53 to Spring 55 A.D. (possibly, 52—54). They belong therefore, as nearly as we can judge, to *the winter of* 53—54 A.D.,—the last year of the Emperor Claudius; being 23 years after our Lord's Ascension, two years after the Council at Jerusalem, four years before the Epistle to the Romans, thirteen years, probably, before the death of St Paul and the outbreak of the Jewish War, and seventeen years before the Fall of Jerusalem.

CHAPTER V.

THE GENUINENESS OF THE TWO EPISTLES.

THAT these two letters were written by the author whose name they bear, has never been doubted by anyone until the present century. No writings of the N. T. are more strongly and unanimously supported by the testimony of the Early Church. The German writer Christ. Schmidt first raised suspicions against 2 Thessalonians in the year 1801, and Schrader against 1 Thessalonians in 1836. The objections of these scholars were further developed by Ferdinand C. Baur, the founder of what is called the Tendency School of N. T. Criticism, who gave them currency in his influential work on "Paul the Apostle of Jesus Christ" (1845: Eng. Trans., 1873). Baur supposed the Epistles to have been written by some disciple of Paul, with the Apocalypse of John in his hand, who wished to excite renewed interest amongst Pauline Christians in the Second Advent. He dates them therefore in the reign of Vespasian, subsequently to the Fall of Jerusalem (70 A.D.).

I. The authenticity of *the First Epistle* has been amply vindicated, and is now acknowledged even by the leading sceptical critics of the school of Baur, such as Holtzmann and Pfleiderer. If any one expressed doubts on the subject, it would be sufficient to point (1) to *the picture the Apostle gives of himself* and his relations to this Church in chaps. i.—iii. It is an exquisite piece of self-portraiture, bearing all the marks of circumstantial truth and genuine feeling, harmonizing with what we learn of St Paul from other sources, and free from anything that could make us suspect imitation by another hand. One feels the beat and throb of Paul's heart in every line of these chapters. *Nemo potest Paulinum pectus effingere* (Erasmus).

(2) The same air of reality belongs to *the aspect of the Thessalonian Church*, as it is delineated in these letters. It exhibits the freshness, the fervour and impulsive energy of a newborn faith, with something of the indiscipline and excitability that often attend the first steps of the Christian life, so full at once of joy and of peril. The Church of Thessalonica has a character of its own. It resembles the Philippian Church in the frankness, the courage, and the personal devotion to the Apostle, which so greatly won his love; also in the simplicity

and thoroughness of its faith, which was untroubled by the speculative questions and tendencies to intellectual error that beset the Corinthian and Asiatic Churches. These characteristics agree with what we know of the Macedonian temperament. At the same time, there was at Thessalonica a tendency to morbid excitement and to an unpractical and over-heated enthusiasm, that forms a peculiar feature in the portrait the Epistles furnish of this Christian Society.

(3) *The attitude of St Paul toward the parousia* is such as no disciple or imitator, writing in his name, could possibly have attributed to him after the Apostle's death. He is made to write as though Christ were expected to come *within his own lifetime:* "we the living, those who survive till the coming of the Lord," 1 Ep. iv. 15, 17. These words, taken in their plain sense, leave it an open question whether the Lord Jesus would not return while the writer and his readers yet lived. That a later author, wishing to use the Apostle's authority for his own purposes, should have put such words into his master's lips is inconceivable. For then *St Paul had died, and Christ had not returned.*

(4) Observe, too, the manner in which the writer speaks in the same passage of "those falling asleep" (present tense: see note *ad loc.*), in such a way as to show that the question concerning the fate of believers dying before the Lord's return was a *new* one, that had arisen in the Thessalonian Church for the first time. If this be the case, the letter can only have been written within a few months of this Church's birth. For it is never long in any large community before death has made its mark.

II. The suspicions cherished against *the Second Epistle* have been more persistent; but they are equally ill-founded. Baur rightly maintained that the two letters are from the same source, and that both must be regarded as spurious, *or both authentic.* The Second is closely bound to the First, alike in language and in matter; and the two chief and distinctive passages of the former (ch. ii. 1—12; iii. 6—15) are based on the corresponding paragraphs of the latter. If we ascribe the

Second Epistle to an imitator of the Apostle, we must suppose that another writer, at least 20 years later[1], taking up 1 Thessalonians and adding this sequel to it, has reproduced the Apostle's manner to perfection, and has carried his thoughts and his line of exhortation forward precisely where he left them off; and that in doing so he has escaped detection by skilfully avoiding every kind of reference to intervening events and to the circumstances of his own time. We have no reason to believe that any post-Apostolic writer had either the skill or cunning to execute such a feat. And no adequate motive for the forgery is adduced.

It is alleged that the purpose of the supposed inventor was to introduce into the Pauline theology Apocalyptic ideas, similar to those found in the Revelation of St John, and to disseminate them amongst Gentile Christians. There is manifestly a relation between the Johannine and the Pauline Apocalypse; but as we shall endeavour to show (*Appendix* on "The Man of Lawlessness"), it is St John who has derived from St Paul, not *vice versa*. The brief and enigmatic sketch of this Book is developed and filled out in larger proportions and with glowing dramatic colours by the Seer of Patmos. Moreover, it is impossible to point to any time subsequent to the year 70, at which there existed an expectation of the immediate coming of Christ so intense and overpowering as is indicated in 2 Ep. ii. 2, and which needed to be qualified and checked in the manner of this Epistle. John's Apocalypse, on the contrary, is designed *to quicken a flagging faith* in the parousia.

Add to this, amongst the details of St Paul's Apocalyptic sketch, the expression of ver. 1, "our gathering together unto Him," which accords with 1 Ep. iv. 13—18, and indicates a time when in the first freshness of Christian hope it was natural to think that the Lord would return to find the body of His people still living on the earth; "the temple of God," ver. 4, pointing to the Jewish Temple yet standing (see note *ad loc.*); and the description of "the Adversary" as "exalting himself

---

[1] Recent hostile critics, such as Hilgenfeld and Pfleiderer, would say, 60 *years later*, "in the closing years of Trajan"!

against every one called God,"—"seating himself in the temple of God, showing off himself as God," which is quite intelligible if written when the blasphemous freaks of the Emperor Caligula and his attempt to set up his statue in the Temple at Jerusalem (40 A.D.) were still vividly remembered. At a later period these incidents were effaced by other and yet more portentous developments of "the mystery of lawlessness," such as have left their trace on the pages of the Book of Revelation, but are not indicated here.

There is said to be, after all, a contradiction between 1 Ep. iv. 13—v. 10 and 2 Ep. ii. 1—12, the First Epistle representing the parousia as *near and sudden*, the second as *more distant and known by premonitory signs*. But the latter modifies and corrects an erroneous inference drawn from the former statement. The premonitory sign of the coming of Antichrist shews that the end, though it might be near, is *not immediate*. On the other hand, no date is given for the advent of Antichrist in 2 Ep. ii.; and the "times and seasons" still remain uncertain, as in 1 Thessalonians. The same contrast is found in Christ's own predictions—e.g. between Matt. xxiv. 33 (*a preparatory sign*) and ver. 36 (*uncertainty of date*).

Outside ch. ii. 1—12 there is nothing to lend a colour to the theory of a later origin for the Second Epistle. The directions given respecting the treatment of the "brother walking disorderly" belong to quite the incipient stage of Church government and discipline. To suppose this passage written in the second century, or even in the last quarter of the first, is to attribute to the author an extraordinary power of ignoring the conditions of his own time, and a power exercised in a quite gratuitous fashion. But these directions harmonise well enough with those addressed to the Corinthians (1 Cor. v.) respecting the extreme case of disorder occurring in that Church.

CHAPTER VI.

The Style and Character of the Two Epistles.

In Style the two Epistles are as nearly as possible identical. The characteristic features of St Paul's dialect and manner as a writer are very apparent; but they have not yet taken the bold and developed form which they present in the Epistles of the second group (Romans, Corinthians, Galatians). In wealth of language, in force of intellect and spiritual passion, these letters do not reach the height of some of the later Epistles. Nor should we expect them to do so. The Apostle's style is the most natural and unstudied in the world. It is, as M. Renan says, "conversation stenographed." In Galatians and 2 Corinthians, where he is labouring under great excitement of feeling, face to face with malignant enemies and with his disaffected or wavering children, his language is full of passion and grief, vehement, broken, passing in a moment from rebuke to tenderness, from lofty indignation to an almost abject humility: now he "speaks mere flames"—but the sentence ends in pity and in tears; "yea, what earnestness, what clearing of himself, what indignation, what yearning, what jealousy, what avenging!" In Romans and Galatians, again, you watch the play of his keen and dexterous logic—large and massive generalisation, bold inference, vivid illustration, swift retort, and an eagerness that leaps to its conclusion over intervening steps of argument indicated only by a word or turn of phrase in passing. But these Epistles afford little room for such qualities of style. They are neither passionate, nor argumentative; but practical, consolatory, prompted by affection, by memory and hope. Hence they represent, as it has been aptly said, "St Paul's normal style," the way in which he would commonly write and talk to his friends.

In their general character, in simplicity and ease of manner, in the rarity of those involved periods and abrupt transitions which distinguish the polemical Epistles, these letters resemble that to the Philippians. But it is remarkable that the Epistle to the Philippians contains twice as many *hapax legomena* to the chapter (i.e. words used nowhere else in the N. T.), as do our Epistles[1]. For Philippians was written nearly ten years later; and it will be found that as time went on the Apostle's vocabulary constantly enlarged, and the habit of using new and singular words grew upon him.

Ch. i. 2—5; ii. 14—16 in the First Epistle; ch. i. 6—10; ii. 8—10 in the Second, are good examples of St Paul's characteristic practice of extending his sentences to an indefinite length in qualifying and explanatory clauses, by the use of participles and relative pronouns and conjunctions. Later Epistles (*Ephesians* especially) show how this habit also gained upon the writer. In 1 Ep. i. 8; ii. 11; iv. 4, 14; 2 Ep. i. 9; ii. 7; iii. 6 we find instances of *ellipsis* and *anacoluthon*—of those altered and broken sentences, and dropped words left to the reader's understanding, to which the student of St Paul is accustomed. 1 Ep. ii. 14, 15 (the *Jews*—who killed the Lord Jesus, &c.); v. 8, 9 (*salvation*—for God did not appoint us to wrath, &c.); 2 Ep. i. 10 (that *believed*—for our testimony was believed) illustrate St Paul's curious fashion of "going off upon a word," where some word suddenly suggests an idea that draws him away from the current of the sentence, which he perhaps resumes in an altered form. In 1 Ep. ii. 4, 19—20; iii. 6—7; iv. 2 and 6; v. 4—5; 2 Ep. ii. 9 and 11, 10 and 12 we see how expressions of the Apostle are apt *to return upon and repeat themselves* in a changed guise. 1 Ep. iii. 5; v. 23; 2 Ep. iii. 2—3; iii. 11 (read in the Greek) exemplify the fondness, shared by St Paul with many great writers, for *paronomasia*, that is for playing on the sound of the words he uses.

There is *not a single quotation from the O. T.* in these Epistles. St Paul is addressing Gentile converts, and in such a way that Scriptural proof and illustration are not required. But there are a number of evident allusions in that direction, show-

---

[1] By counting *verses* instead of chapters, we find this statement somewhat modified. Philippians contains not quite two *hapax legomena* in every five verses; 1 and 2 Thess. exactly one in every four. For the number of *hap. leg.* see Grimm-Thayer's *N. T. Lexicon*, Appendix IV.

ing how the writer's mind was coloured by the language of the Old Testament. Compare

 1 Ep. ii. 4 with Ps. xvii. 3, &c.;
  ii. 16 with Gen. xv. 16;
  iv. 5 with Ps. lxxix. 6;
  v. 8 with Isai. lix. 17;
 2 Ep. i. 8 with Isai. lxvi. 15;
  i. 9, 10 with Isai. ii. 10, 11, 17, 19—21;
  ii. 4 with Dan. xi. 36;
  ii. 8 with Isai. xi. 4;
  ii. 13 ("beloved by the Lord") with Deut. xxxiii. 12.

More remarkable, and quite unusual in St Paul, are the repeated *echoes of the words of Jesus* that occur in the passages relating to the Judgement and Second Coming. Compare

 1 Ep. ii. 15, 16 with Matt. xxiii. 29—39, Luke xi. 45—52,
  xiii. 33, 34;
  iv. 16, 17 with Matt. xxiv. 30, 31;
  v. 1—6 with Matt. xxiv. 36—44, Luke xii. 38—40, 46;
 2 Ep. ii. 2 with Matt. xxiv. 6.

In their CHARACTER these oldest extant Epistles of the Apostle Paul can now be easily described. They are *the letters of a missionary*, written to an infant Church but very recently brought from heathen darkness into the marvellous light of the Gospel. They lie nearer, therefore, to the missionary preaching of the Apostle of the Gentiles, as we find it, for instance, in Acts xiv. 15—17; xvii. 22—31, than do any of the later Epistles. This accounts for their simplicity, for the absence in them of controversy, and the elementary nature of their doctrine[1].

They are addressed to a Macedonian Church, and they exhibit in common with the Epistle to the (Macedonian) Philippians' a peculiar warmth of feeling and mutual confidence between writer and readers. They are singularly *affectionate letters*. From 2 Cor. viii. 1, 2; xi. 9 we gather that the generosity which endeared the Philippians to St Paul (Phil. iv. 14—17) distin-

---

[1] But compare what is said of *the character of the Macedonians* in Chapter IV. above.

guished the Macedonian Churches generally. The Apostle can scarcely find words tender enough or images sufficiently vivid to express his regard for the Thessalonians (1 Ep. ii. 7, 11, 17, 19, 20; iii. 9). He feels his life bound up with them (ch. iii. 8). He boasts of them everywhere (2 Ep. i. 4; 2 Cor. viii. 1, 2). If he exhorts them, his warnings are mingled with commendations, lest they should think he has some fault to find (1 Ep. iv. 1, 9, 10; v. 11; 2 Ep. iii. 4). Again and again he repeats, more than in any other letters, "You yourselves know," "Remember ye not?" and the like,—so sure he is that they have understood and bear in mind his teaching, and are altogether one with him. In like fashion, writing to the Philippians (ch. i. 5), the Apostle gives thanks to God "for your fellowship in the gospel, from the first day until now."

Further, these two are especially *cheering and consolatory letters*. The Apostle sent Timothy to "comfort" the Thessalonians "concerning their faith" (1 Ep. iii. 2), and in writing he pursues the same object. Persecution was the lot of this Church from the beginning (1 Ep. iii. 4; Acts xvii. 5—9), as it continued to be long afterwards (2 Cor. viii. 2; comp. what was written to Philippi ten years later, Phil. i. 28, 29). So the Apostle bends all his efforts to encourage his distressed and suffering friends. He teaches them to glory in tribulation. He makes them smile through their tears. He reveals the "weight of glory" that their afflictions are working out for them, till in comparison they seem light indeed. He shows them—and to a generous Christian heart there is no greater satisfaction—how much their faithful endurance is furthering the cause of Christ and of truth (1 Ep. i. 6—8; 2 Ep. i. 3, 4), and how it comforts and encourages himself and his fellow-labourers (1 Ep. iii. 5—7).

Lastly, these are *eschatological Epistles*: that is, in the language of theology, they set forth "the Last Things" in Christian doctrine,—the second coming of Christ, the raising of the dead and transformation of the living saints, and the Judgement of the world; they announce the advent of Antichrist as the forerunner and Satanic counterpart of the returning Christ (2 Ep. ii. 1—12). The latter passage is called the Pauline Apocalypse; since it holds in St Paul's Epistles, in regard to its teaching and import, the place of the Book of Revelation in the writings of St John. We have suggested, in Chapter III. of the Introduction, some circumstances that may have led St Paul to dwell at this time especially upon this subject. The persecutions under which the Thessalonians laboured served to incline their thoughts in the same direction,—toward the heavenly kingdom that they hoped would soon arrive to put an end to the miseries of "this present evil world."

By their eschatological views and teachings these letters are linked to ch. xv. of 1 Corinthians, which was probably the next of St Paul's Epistles in order of time to these. Afterwards the subject of the *parousia* retreats into the shade in the Apostle's writings. For this two causes suggest themselves. Between the writing of 1 and 2 Corinthians St Paul suffered from a severe sickness (2 Cor. i. 8—10; iv. 7—v. 8), which brought him to the gates of death, and profoundly affected his spiritual experience: from this time he anticipated that death would end his earthly career (Phil. i. 20, 21; Acts xx. 24; 2 Tim. iv. 6—8, 18). And again, the disturbing effect of the thought of the Parousia in the Thessalonian Church and the danger of a morbid pre-occupation of mind with this idea such as he had seen there, may have led him to make the subject less prominent in his later teaching. In St Paul's last letters, however, written at the close of life to his helpers Timothy and Titus, he reverts frequently and fondly to "that blessed hope and appearing of the glory of our great God and Saviour Jesus Christ" (Tit. ii. 13). Long ago had he reconciled himself to the fact that he must first indeed be "absent from the body" in order to be "present with the Lord." Yet still *the coming of the Lord Jesus* was the goal of his labours and longings. It was in his eyes the summit of all Christian hope. And these two fervent Epistles, with their bright horizon of promise crossed by lurid thunder-clouds, breathe throughout the constant desire of the Church with which the Book of Scripture closes,—

AMEN. COME, LORD JESUS!

CHAPTER VII.

ANALYSIS AND DIGEST OF THE EPISTLES.

I. IN the First Epistle there are two clearly marked sections. CH. I.—III. are *personal*; CH. IV. and V., *moral and doctrinal*.

(1) The first and chief part of the letter is an outpouring of the Apostle's heart to his readers. He tells them *what he thinks of them*, how he prays for them and thanks God for what they are, for all they have attained and all they have endured as Christian believers. Then he talks about *himself and his fellow-missionaries*, reminding his readers of their work and life at Thessalonica, and informing them of his repeated attempts to return to them, of the circumstances under which he had sent Timothy in his place, and the inexpressible delight given to him by Timothy's good report of their state and of their love for the absent Apostles.

(2) In *v*. 1 of CH. IV. the writer begins to preach, and passes from narrative and prayer to exhortation. His homily bears chiefly on *Christian morals*,—"how you ought to walk and to please God." In the midst of this condensed and powerful address is introduced the great passage relating to the Second Coming (CH. IV. **13**—V. 11), explaining to the Thessalonians *what they should believe* on this vital matter of faith, to them so profoundly interesting. The misunderstandings and the agitation existing in this Church affected its "walk;" they were injurious to the Church's peace and disturbing to its soberness and joy of faith. Hence the introduction of the doctrinal question at this stage and in this form.

II. The Second Epistle contains very little personal matter. After the Thanksgiving, which occupies the first chapter, St Paul proceeds at once to the questions of *doctrine* and *discipline* which called for this further deliverance from him. CH. II. and III. of 2 Ep. therefore correspond to CH. IV. and V. of 1 Ep. But the scope of St Paul's exhortations is here more limited. He deals (1) in CH. II. **1**—**12**, with *the false alarm about the parousia*, which was just now producing a demoralising excitement; (2) with the case of certain *idlers and busybodies*, whose obstinate indiscipline compels him to take stern measures for their correction (CH. III. **6**—**14**). The intervening part of the

Epistle (Ch. II. **13**—III. **5**) is taken up with thanksgiving, prayer, and exhortation of a general character.

The following is the scheme of exposition pursued in the Notes upon these two Epistles:—

1 Epistle.   Address and Salutation. Ch. i. 1.
 § 1. The Thanksgiving and the Reasons for it. Ch. i. 2—10.
 § 2. The Apostle's Conduct at Thessalonica. Ch. ii. 1—12.
 § 3. (Parenthetical) Jewish Persecutors of the Church. Ch. ii. 13—16.
 § 4. St Paul's Present Relations to the Thessalonians. Ch. ii. 17—iii. 13.
 § 5. A Lesson in Christian Morals. Ch. iv. 1—12.
 § 6. The Coming of the Lord Jesus. Ch. iv. 13—v. 11.
 § 7. Rules for the Sanctified Life. Ch. v. 12—24.
  Conclusion. Ch. v. 25—28.

2 Epist. § 1. Salutation and Thanksgiving. Ch. i. 1—4.
 § 2. The Approaching Retribution. Ch. i. 5—12.
 § 3. The Revelation of the Lawless One. Ch. ii. 1—12.
 § 4. Words of Comfort and Prayer. Ch. ii. 13—iii. 5.
 § 5. Discipline for the Disorderly. Ch. iii. 6—15.
  Conclusion. Ch. iii. 16—18.

It may be convenient to give in conclusion a digest of the Epistles, in the shape of a running paraphrase:—

THE FIRST EPISTLE TO THE THESSALONIANS.

Ch. I. PAUL and his colleagues wish the Thessalonian Church "Grace and Peace." (*v.* 2) They constantly remember them in their prayers, and thank God for the rich fruit which their faith and love and hope in Christ are bearing. (*v.* 4) They are sure that God in His love has chosen them for His own. (*v.* 5) They had proof of this in the confidence, wrought by the Holy Spirit, with which they at first addressed them and in the powerful effect which the gospel had upon them. With joyful courage these young disciples encountered persecution, following the path marked out by the Apostles and their Lord. (*v.* 7) They were indeed a pattern to their fellow-believers; and the

INTRODUCTION. 39

story of their conversion from idolatry to the service of the true God and hope in Christ had spread even beyond Macedonia and Achaia, and bore signal witness to the truth and power of the Divine message.

CH. II. "I need scarcely remind you," he continues, "of the way in which our ministry amongst you began. You know what we suffered at Philippi, and you remember the boldness with which we proclaimed God's message to you. (*v.* 3) There was no delusion or trickery, no impure motive in our work. We felt that we had a solemn trust committed to us by God, and we spoke and acted accordingly. (*v.* 5) You know that we never flattered you; and God knows we sought no gain or glory for ourselves. We might, in our apostolic quality, have charged you with our maintenance; (*v.* 7) but rather we treated you like a mother nursing her children, ready to give you, with the gospel, our very lives. So much had we learnt to love you! (*v.* 9) We toiled night and day to save you expense, while we preached to you the gospel. To yourselves we can appeal whether our conduct towards you did not in every way commend our message. (*v.* 11) As our children, with fatherly counsel and encouragement we strove to make you worthy of your calling and your hopes.

(*v.* 13) "And, thank God, our labour was not in vain. It was *God's* word, not man's, you received in our message; and in you it has its due effect. You are following in the steps of the Judean Churches and sharing their persecutions. Your fellow-countrymen treat you as they were treated by their fellow-Jews—the *Jews*, (*v.* 15) murderers of the Lord Jesus as they were of the prophets! Enemies of mankind, offensive to God, they chase us from city to city and would prevent our preaching to the Gentiles. But His wrath is upon them, and their doom is near!

(*v.* 17) "As for ourselves, compelled to leave you for a while (our hearts indeed still with you), we counted on coming back again to see you. We made determined efforts, more than once, to do this; but Satan stood in the way. (*v.* 19) For you verily will be our glory and crown at Christ's coming, as you are already! CH. III. And so, on our second failure, finding ourselves at Athens, we thought it best to send Timothy, just then our only companion. We were fearful lest you should have been overpowered by affliction; and we sent him to cheer you and sustain your faith. We had told you, as you will remember, what conflicts you might expect; and so the event proved.

(*v.* 6) "But now Timothy has returned; and how shall I relate the joy his tidings give me! how thank God sufficiently for His grace manifest in you! To hear of your steadfast faith and abounding love, of your affection for us and great desire to see us—all this is an unspeakable comfort; it is new life to me. (*v.* 11) May God our Father and Christ our Lord grant me soon the delight of seeing you, and helping you onward in your faith! May the Lord quicken yet more your love, as ours is kindled towards you! May He give you confidence of heart, and the holiness which will fit you for His coming!

Ch. IV. "Before we close this letter, we have some requests to make, which we urge upon you in the name of the Lord Jesus. In general, that you follow the rules of life we gave you. You *are* doing this, we know; but there is room for progress. (*v.* 3) In particular, be free from all taint of unchastity. Be masters of your bodily passions. In this lies great part of your sanctification. Lust, with its dishonour, is the mark of Gentile godlessness. (*v.* 6) This sin brings wrong and injury on others, while it degrades the man himself. The Lord is the avenger of every offence against social purity. By such offence you set *Him* at defiance, and outrage His Holy Spirit given to you.

(*v.* 9) "As to brotherly love, God Himself is your teacher; and all your brethren in Macedonia benefit by your proficiency. Still, in this grace increase is always possible. We desire to see in you a quiet spirit, (*v.* 12) and that honourable labour and independence be your ambition!

(*v.* 13) "Death has been busy amongst you. And your sorrow is deepened by a strange fear lest your sleeping friends should have lost their part in the hope of Christ's return and their place in His heavenly kingdom. Be comforted. His resurrection from the dead is a pledge of theirs. God will restore them at His return. (*v.* 15) *They* will have indeed the first and foremost share in His glorious advent. At His trumpet's call they will rise from their sleep; (*v.* 17) we who live on the earth will rejoin them; and together, in one body, we shall ascend to meet our returning Lord. With Him we and they shall then dwell for ever!

Ch. V. 1. "But *when* this will be, and what train of events will precede the Advent, remains a secret. We are told that the day of the Lord comes 'as a thief in the night.' (*v.* 3) So it will prove for the wicked and unbelieving. Just when they are most secure—like men asleep at night or drunken—then ruin falls upon them! But *you* surely are not in the dark; (*v.* 5) you live in the daylight, as sober, wakeful men. And when the end comes, it will not find you unprepared. But take heed that it be so. (*v.* 8) Be ready, like soldiers on the watch, clad in the armour of steadfast faith and love, and a high Christian hope. Well may you hope for salvation in the dread Day, knowing that God has chosen you for this, (*v.* 10) and that Christ has died to the end that in life or death you may live evermore with Him.—With such thoughts comfort and edify each other.

(*v.* 12) "But further, we must ask you to appreciate the labours of those who hold rule and office amongst you. Their work is difficult; give them your confidence and love. Avoid all contention. (*v.* 14) Let each take his part in the work of brotherly admonition, of consolation, of sympathy and patient help in dealing with weak or troublesome members of the flock. Never must evil be retaliated; do nothing but good to others for your part.

(*v.* 16) "Let your life be filled with joy, prayer, thanksgiving: this is the Christian life; it is God's will for you. Beware of quenching the influence of the Holy Spirit by disparagement of His prophetic gifts. Put everything to proof indeed; but hold fast what is good, while you shrink from every kind of evil. (*v.* 23) Above all, may God Himself, Source and Giver of peace, accomplish your full sanctification. In the integrity of a consecrated body, soul, and spirit may you be preserved and found without blame at Christ's coming. God has called you for this end; He is faithful: it shall be done!

(*v.* 25) "Have us remembered in your prayers.

"Exchange a holy kiss of salutation as from me.

"I solemnly require you to see that this letter is read to every brother in the Church.

"The grace of our Lord Jesus Christ be with you!"

The Second Epistle.

CH. I. In commencing his second letter, bearing also the names of "Silas and Timothy" with his own, the Apostle repeats his salutation of "Grace and Peace." (*v.* 3) He feels "bound to thank God" for the signal growth of the Thessalonians' faith, and the affluence of their love; and especially for their courageous fidelity under violent and continued persecution. Over this, as he tells them, he boasts everywhere on their account. (*v.* 5) In their steadfastness he sees a token of the rest and heavenly glory awaiting the sufferers, and an omen of fearful import for their enemies. "You and they," he says, "are in the hands of a righteous God. And they will have to pay for all they are inflicting on you now, and for their refusal of the knowledge of God and His gospel, when Christ returns in triumph. (*v.* 9) Eternal destruction will be their doom, into which the terror and majesty of His presence will drive them out; while His glory will shine forth in His saints—in *you* who believed our testimony of Him. (*v.* 11) And so we pray for you, that you may prove worthy of your calling, that all may be fulfilled in you that goodness can desire and faith effect; that so Christ may find in you His glory, you in Him! For this is the design of grace."

Ch. II. The Apostle has one principal and urgent purpose in writing now. It touches "the coming of our Lord Jesus Christ," in regard to which he desires to remove a dangerous and disturbing impression existing in Thessalonica, to the effect that "the day of the Lord was close at hand!" (*v.* 2) How this rumour originated, it was hard to say,—whether through supposed prophetic intimation, or the ordinary teaching of the Church, or from some misunderstanding or abuse of the Apostle's written words. But its disastrous effect was manifest, and its *falsity*.—"I gave a token," the Apostle writes, "of that which must precede the final coming of Christ: there will be first *the apostasy*, and *the revelation of the Man of Lawlessness*, the great enemy of God. (*v.* 4) He will attempt to annihilate religion, and will seat himself in God's temple as the sole object of human worship. The spirit of atheistic lawlessness, to be incarnated in him, is already actively at work—but for the present *under restraint*, as I pointed out to you. (*v.* 6) One day, however, the restraint will be withdrawn; and then the Lawless One will stand revealed!—whom the Lord Jesus by His breath will consume, and destroy by the splendour of His coming! —(*v.* 9) Satan will instigate the great Opposer, and attest his coming by miracles, suited to deceive those whose hearts are inclined to falsehood. Their deception will be the fit punishment for their rejection of the truth of God, and their love of lies and wickedness.

(*v.* 13) "Far different, brethren, is it with you. God has set His love upon you and made you His own. For this end He sanctifies your spirit, and His truth commands your faith. And from our lips you received salvation,—for which we owe to God continual thanksgiving. (*v.* 15) We bid you stand fast, and hold firmly by all that we have taught you, both by word and letter. May our Lord Jesus Christ Himself be your comforter; may God Who loves you and has given you in His grace eternal hopes and consolations, comfort your hearts and sustain you in all your service both of deed and word!

CH. III. "Let us add, that *we* in turn need your prayers. We would fain see the gospel triumph at Corinth, as it did in Thessalonica. Pray that we may be delivered from evil and unbelieving men. Surely our faithful Lord will be your keeper. (*v.* 4) And we rely on your faithfulness and regard for our injunctions. The Lord lead you still in the way of God's love and Christ's patience!

(*v.* 6) "There is one especial charge we have to lay upon you: we require, in the name and authority of Christ, that you have no fellowship with insubordinate brethren, with any who act in defiance of the rule of life we prescribed. What that is you know by our example. (*v.* 8) Far were we from eating the bread of idleness, from burdening others with our maintenance and insisting on our right to live at their cost. (*v.* 10) And we always said, *Let the idler suffer hunger.* (*v.* 11) Yet we hear that there are men of this kind in your Church—unruly, neglecting their own business, meddling with that of others. In the name of Christ we solemnly charge them to be quiet, and to earn an honest living. And none of you must be discouraged by their misconduct. (*v.* 14) If any of the offenders still refuses correction, let him be a marked man,—have no company with him. Perhaps he will then be ashamed. Still you must not regard him as an enemy, but as a brother needing admonition.

(*v.* 16) "Now may peace be with you, from the Lord of peace! May He be with you all!

"I add this greeting with my own hand, and sign it, PAUL. Note the signature: you will in future know my letters by it.

"The grace of our Lord Jesus Christ be with you all!"

THE FIRST EPISTLE OF PAUL THE APOSTLE

TO THE

THESSALONIANS.

PAUL, and Silvanus, and Timotheus, unto the church 1
of the Thessalonians *which is* in God the Father and

TO THE THESSALONIANS I. So the title runs in the oldest copies. St Paul's Epistles were at first gathered into a single volume by themselves, entitled "the Apostle." Within this volume the Epistles were distinguished simply by the names of those to whom they were addressed. The order of this earliest collection was the same as appears in our English Bibles (except that the position of the Epistle to the *Hebrews* varied—now fourth, now tenth, and then last of the fourteen). The Thessalonian letters came last in the second group, which consisted of five smaller Epistles addressed to Churches—*Ephesians to 2 Thessalonians*. This was not the order of time (see *Introd.* p. 27), but of magnitude and supposed importance.

THE ADDRESS AND SALUTATION. CH. I. 1.

This being the earliest of St Paul's extant letters, let us note with care the form of his address and introduction, for it is that from which he never departed. But his greetings were enlarged as time went on, and varied with every variation in the circumstances of his readers and in his relations to them.

The ordinary address of an ancient letter ran thus: "X. to Y. greeting." The greeting was, in Latin, a wish of "Health"; in Greek, of "Joy"; in Hebrew, "Peace to thee!" The Apostle's salutation, adopted by the Church, combined the Hebrew and Greek (Jewish and Gentile, Eastern and Western) forms of courtesy, transforming the latter by a verbal change (*chairein* becoming *charis*)—slight indeed to the ear, but great in its significance—into the devout and Christian "Grace to you!" On *grace* and *peace* see note below.

The Address is usually followed by an Act of Thanksgiving (*vv.* 3 ff.).

1. *Paul*] Here and in 2 Ep. St Paul introduces himself without the title *Apostle*, or any personal designation. Similarly in his much

in the Lord Jesus Christ: Grace *be* unto you, and peace, from God our Father, and the Lord Jesus Christ.

later Epistles to the Philippians, and to his friend Philemon. For in these cases he has no need to stand on his dignity. He is "gentle among them, as a nurse with her children" (ch. ii. 6—8); and prefers, as in writing to Philemon (ver. 9), to merge the Apostle in the friend. For a further reason comp. note on *Apostles*, ch. ii. 6.

Paul, and Silvanus, and Timotheus] "Silvanus and Timotheus" had been Paul's companions at Thessalonica, see *Introd.* chap. II. The Apostle was accustomed to associate with himself in writing to the Churches any of his helpers present with him and known to his readers. This was courteous, and promoted mutual sympathy.

Silvanus (so in 2 Ep. i. 1; 2 Cor. i. 19; 1 Pet. v. 12) is the **Silas** of Acts xv.—xviii.; comp. *Lucas* (Luke) for *Lucanus*. The name (English, *Sylvan*: comp. our surname *Wood*, or *Woods*) is Latin, like that of Paul himself (*Paulus*). Both were Roman citizens, as we learn from Acts xvi. 37. Silas was notwithstanding a Jew—a leading member of the Church at Jerusalem, and an inspired man (a "prophet": Acts xv. 22, 23). Silas shared with the Apostle Paul the honour of planting the gospel and first suffering for Christ in Europe; and his name worthily stands at the head of these earliest books of the N. T. The association of St Silas with St Paul terminated with the Second Missionary Journey of the Apostle. But he is probably the "Silvanus" of 1 Pet. v. 12, and his name is, along with that of Mark, a link between the Apostles Peter and Paul.

Timotheus (on whom see further ch. iii. 1, 2) is our familiar **Timothy**, as the name is uniformly given in the R. V. He shares in the addresses of 2 Corinthians, Philippians, Colossians, and 1 and 2 Thessalonians; and St Paul toward the close of his life wrote two inspired letters to this most constant and beloved of his companions, his "dear child Timothy." He joined the Apostle in the course of this Second Missionary Expedition (Acts xvi. 1—3), and remained in his service to the end of St Paul's life. At this time Timothy must have been very young; for he is referred to as a "young man" in 1 Tim. iv. 12 and 2 Tim. ii. 22, twelve years later. In the narrative of the Acts at this time he stands quite in the background; while Silas took a leading part in the common work, Timothy acted as their youthful attendant and apprentice, just as John Mark was "minister" (or "attendant," R. V.) to Barnabas and Paul at an earlier period (Acts xiii. 5).

These three names—*Paul, Silas, Timothy*—are typical of the mixed state of society in Apostolic times, and the varied material of which the Church was at first composed. It was built on a Jewish basis, with a Græco-Roman superstructure. Paul and Silvanus were *Jews*, with *Roman* name and citizenship. Timotheus had a *Greek* name and father, with a *Jewish* mother (Acts xvi. 1—3).

So much for the authors of the letter: the readers are designated **the Church of Thessalonians in God the Father and the Lord Jesus Christ** (R. V.). This remarkable form of address, used in both Epistles, the

Apostle does not employ again. We may expand it thus: "To the assembly of Thessalonians, gathered in the twofold Name, confessing God as Father and Jesus Christ as Lord."

Observe the two parts of this description: (1) the *local* qualification, "church *of Thessalonians*." Nearest to this is the phrase "churches of Galatia" (Gal. i. 2), named however from the district, not the people. In 1 and 2 Corinthians the address runs, "To the church of God that is in Corinth"; afterwards, "To the saints that are in Ephesus, Philippi," &c. The change from "church *of* Thessalonians" to "church *in* Corinth" is significant; it indicates an enlargement during the four years intervening of the conception of the Church, now no longer constituted by the local assembly, but thought of as one and the same Church here or there, in Corinth, Rome, or Jerusalem. Comp. note on ch. ii. 14, "churches of God which are in Judæa."

(2) The *spiritual* definition: "the assembly...*in God the Father*," &c. *Church* is in the N. T. *ecclesia* (French *église*), the common Greek word for "assembly," or legal meeting of citizens, "called out" by the herald; which in the LXX (the Greek rendering of the O. T.) is applied frequently to the solemn religious assemblies of the people of Israel. The Apostle distinguishes this "assembly of Thessalonians" from both those gatherings. The Christian *ecclesia* is "in God the Father,"—therefore a religious assembly marked off from all that is pagan, having "one God, the Father"; also "in the Lord Jesus Christ," and thus distinguished from everything Jewish and Pagan alike, by its confession of "one Lord Jesus Christ" (1 Cor. viii. 5, 6). The creed of the Thessalonian Church is here contained in brief. Its members had been "baptized into the name of the Father, and of the Son"; and all that they believed in and lived for as a Church centred in these two names—two, yet one ("in God the Father and the Lord," not "and *in* the Lord"). "In God as *Father*," they knew and owned themselves His children. "In the *Lord*," they discerned their Saviour's Divine Sonship and glory (ver. 10); "in *Jesus*," His human birth and history (ch. ii. 15; iv. 14, &c.); and "in *Christ*," the living Head and Redeemer of His people. This is His full style and title, "The Lord Jesus Christ."

Grace be *unto you, and peace*] In this earliest Epistle the salutation has its shortest form. The qualifying words, "from God our Father," &c. (see R. V.), are not authentic here; they first appear in 2 Ep. The usage of St Paul's other Epistles naturally led copyists to make the addition here. But the "church" that is "in God the Father and the Lord Jesus Christ," needs not to be told from Whom these gifts come.

Grace is the sum of all blessings that God bestows through Christ. *Peace* is the sum of all spiritual blessing that man receives and experiences; it is Grace in its fruit and realisation. In the wide sense of its Hebrew original (*Shalôm*), Peace is more than the absence of hostility and disorder; it denotes health and harmony of nature, inward tranquillity and wellbeing. And Grace, which in the first instance is God's love and favour to the undeserving, becomes also the inward possession of those who receive it, manifesting itself as the spirit and habit of their lives. The supreme exhibition of God's grace is *the death of*

2 We give thanks to God always for you all, making
3 mention of you in our prayers; remembering without

Christ for sinful men, and the great instrument of peace is *the sacrifice of the cross:* Jesus "by God's grace tasted death for every man," "making peace through the blood of His cross" (Heb. ii. 9; Col. i. 20; Eph. ii. 14—18; &c.).

St Paul's whole gospel is in these two words. GRACE is his watchword, as LOVE is that of St John. For his conversion and Apostolic call were, above everything, a revelation of Divine *grace*: see 1 Cor. xv. 9, 10, "By the grace of God I am what I am"; comp. Eph. ii. 7; iii. 2—8; 1 Tim. i. 12—15. See additional note on *grace*, 2 Ep. i. 12.

SECTION I. THE THANKSGIVING AND THE REASONS FOR IT.
CH. I. 2—10.

In every Epistle, except *Galatians*, the Apostle's first words are of thanks and praise to God for the fruits of God's grace found in his readers, according to his own maxim (ch. v. 18), "In everything give thanks." And his thanksgiving is expressed here in the fullest and warmest terms. Its special grounds and reasons lie (1) in *the earnest Christian life* of the Thessalonians, ver. 3; which gave assurance (2) of *their Divine election*, ver. 4; already manifest (3) in *the signal character of their conversion*, which took place under the most trying circumstances, *vv.* 5, 6; and which (4) had greatly furthered *the progress of the gospel, vv.* 7, 8; for (5) *everywhere the story was told* of how the Thessalonians had forsaken idolatry in order to serve the true God, and to await from heaven the return of Jesus, *vv.* 9, 10.

This long sentence is a good example of St Paul's manner as a writer. His thought flows on in a single rapid stream, turning now hither, now thither, but always advancing towards its goal. His sentences are not built up in regular and distinct periods; but grow and extend themselves like living things under our eyes, "gaining force in each successive clause by the repetition and expansion of the preceding" (Jowett). See *Introd.* pp. 32, 33.

2. *We give thanks to God always for you all*] "We," i.e. the three above named. Here, as in Phil. i. 4, he has thankfulness and joy over them "all;" no other Churches seem to have been so much to the Apostle's mind as these two. And everything dear to him or useful to others in his friends moves him to gratitude toward God on their account. This St Paul felt that he "owed to God" (2 Ep. i. 3), the Source of all goodness in men; and it was the best and safest way of commending them.

making mention of you in our prayers] i.e. **when engaged in prayer**. As often as the Apostle and his companions prayed, the Thessalonian Church came to their mind; and with supplication praise on their behalf constantly mingled. For the connection of *prayer* and *thanksgiving*, see notes on ch. v. 17, 18.

3. *remembering without ceasing...in the sight of God and our Father*] Standing ever in the presence of God, the witness of all his thoughts,

ceasing your work of faith, and labour of love, and pa-

St Paul bears with him unceasingly the remembrance of what he had beheld in the Christian life and spirit of his Thessalonian brethren. The adjunct comes in with solemn emphasis at the end of the verse. Comp. ch. iii. 9: " What fitting thanks can we render for all the joy with which we rejoice over you *before our God?*" and the frequency with which the writer appeals to "God" as "witness" of his feelings and his behaviour (ch. ii. 4, 5, 10); similarly in Rom. i. 9, "God is my witness...how unceasingly I make mention of you, always in my prayers beseeching," &c.; and in the thanksgiving of Phil. i. 8, "God is my witness, how I long after you all!" We are reminded of Elijah's protestation, " As the LORD liveth, before Whom I stand!" (1 Kings xvii. 1, &c.)

He says **before our God and Father** (R.V.): for it is in the character of *Father* that St Paul approaches God in prayer (comp. ch. iii. 11; 2 Ep. ii. 16; and *the Lord's prayer*: "After this manner pray ye, Our Father"); and "in God" as "Father" (ver. 1) the Thessalonians became a "church," and had received the blessings for which the Apostle now gives thanks.

remembering...your work of faith, and labour of love, and patience of hope in our Lord Jesus Christ] " Remembering," i.e. " how active and fruitful your faith has shown itself to be, how devoted and unwearied your love, and what fortitude your hope in the Lord Jesus has inspired." **Faith, Love,** and **Hope** are the essence of practical Christianity. *Fides, amor, spes—summa Christianismi* (Bengel); comp. 1 Cor. xiii. 13. **Work, Labour, Patience** are their threefold expression; comp. the "works and labour and patience" of the Ephesian Church, in Rev. ii. 2, 3.

There was a remarkable vigour, a moral courage and activity in the life of this Church, over which the Apostle rejoiced even more than he did in the eloquence and knowledge of the Church of Corinth (1 Cor. i. 5). *Warmth of heart and practical energy* were the distinguishing features of Thessalonian Christianity (see *Introduction*, chap. IV.):

"Whose faith and work were bells of full accord."

The *work of faith* includes the two expressions that follow. It embraces the whole practical issue of a Christian life, denoting *that which faith effects*, its outcome and result in the doings of life; expressed from the Divine side in "the fruit of the Spirit" (Gal. v. 22), and "fruit of the light" (Eph. v. 9, R. V.). This expression the Apostle uses once more, in 2 Ep. i. 11. This first appearance of the word "faith" in St Paul's Epistles, conjoined with "work," shows how far he was removed from antinomianism, from approving either a merely theoretical, or sentimental faith. In his later Epistles, especially in Galatians and Romans, we find "faith" contrasted with "works,"—i.e. Pharisaic " works of law," supposed to be meritorious and to earn salvation by right and as matter of debt on God's part (see Rom. iv. 1—4, ix. 32; Gal. ii. 16, iii. 10—14). No such notions had as yet troubled the simple-minded Thessalonians. But in the later as in the earliest

tience of hope in our Lord Jesus Christ, in the sight of

Epistles faith is always with St Paul an operative principle of life, a working power. He quite agreed with St James (ch. ii. 17) that "faith, if it have not works, is dead." Hence in Gal. v. 6 he writes of "faith working through love."

The Thessalonians' *work of faith* was manifest especially in the two forms of **toil of love and endurance of hope**. Similarly in 2 Ep. i. 3, 4, *faith* is joined with *love* (the "charity" of 1 Cor. xiii.) on the one side, and with *patience* on the other. These are the two chief branches of Christian work—loving service to the brethren and our fellow-men (comp. ch. iv. 9, 10; v. 13), and fearless testimony for Christ before the world, with endurance of the loss and suffering this may entail (*vv.* 6, 7; ii. 13, 14; iii. 2—4)—"the good fight of faith" (1 Tim. vi. 12). So we see the Christian life in its simplest elements: "a faith that had its outward effect on your lives; a love that spent itself in the service of others; a hope that was no transient feeling, but was content to wait for the things unseen, when it should be revealed" (Jowett).

We must distinguish "work" from "labour" (or *toil*). The former points to *the thing done*, as matter of achievement: the latter to *the pains spent* in doing it, as matter of exertion. Under this latter word the Apostle refers to his own manual labour (ch. ii. 9; 2 Ep. iii. 8), also to his labours as a minister of Christ (ch. iii. 5; 2 Cor. x. 15 &c.; see besides 1 Cor. iii. 8, "Each shall receive his reward according to his own toil"). *Work* may be easy and delightful: *labour* is toilsome; no selfish man will endure it for another's good. Hence *labour* is the test of *love*. How will a mother toil and weary herself for her child! So St Paul, to whom with his many infirmities his work must often have been a heavy task.

"True love is humble, thereby it is known;
Girded for service, seeking not its own."

"*Patience* of hope" is not all the Apostle means. The Greek word implies active endurance—*perseverantia* and *tolerantia*, as well as *patientia* or *sustinentia* (Vulgate); the constancy of blind Milton, that both "bears up, and steers right onward." It is not the resignation of the passive sufferer, so much as the fortitude of the stout-hearted soldier, which carries him in the hope of victory through the long day's march and conflict. In Rom. ii. 7 the first and last of these expressions meet, and this word is rendered "*patient continuance in* good *work*" (see Trench's *N. T. Synonyms*, on *patientia*). Christian *hope* inspired this courage: "hope is the balm and life-blood of the soul." So Jesus Himself "for the joy that was set before Him endured the cross" (Heb. xii. 2). And the Thessalonians were "imitators of the Lord" (ver. 6), following the patience of Christ (2 Ep. iii. 5). Being the embodiment of Hope, Patience takes its place in 2 Ep. i. 4; and elsewhere.

This was the climax of Thessalonian virtue, tried from the first by fierce persecution (ver. 6; iii. 2—6). For their "endurance" the Apostle gloried in this Church, and Christ was glorified in them (2 Ep. i. 4—12); such conspicuous courage gave powerful testimony to the Gospel

God and our Father; knowing, brethren beloved, your 4

(*vv.* 7, 8). Observe that here Hope inspires Patience: in Rom. v. 4, "Patience worketh hope." Both are true.

Their hope was *in our Lord Jesus Christ*. This adjunct might, grammatically, be applied to the three foregoing phrases—to *faith, love,* and *hope* alike; but less suitably, as we think. Faith and love are subsequently conceived in a wider sense: *God* is the Object of faith in ver. 8, and love embraces *brotherly love* in ch. iv. 9, v. 13, &c.; whereas "our Lord Jesus Christ," in His final coming, is frequently, and with concentrated emphasis, represented as the Object of the Thessalonians' hope (see ver. 10; ii. 12, 19; iii. 13; iv. 14—v. 11; 2 Ep. i. 7—10; ii. 1—8. The Second Advent and the Last Judgement had been leading themes of St Paul's preaching at Thessalonica, and had taken powerful hold of his hearers' minds (see *Introd.* pp. 18—21). In this expectation lay the peculiar strength, and at the same time the danger and temptation of their faith, as we shall afterwards see. "If Joy is the key-note of the Epistle to the Philippians, Hope is that of the present Epistle" (Ellicott).

in the sight of God, &c.] Connected most suitably with "remembering" (see note above); though the clause might grammatically be attached to the "faith, hope, and love" just preceding, and would so give a good sense.

4. *knowing, brethren beloved, your election of God*] Better, following the A. V. *margin* and R. V., **knowing, brethren beloved by God, your election**: comp. 2 Ep. ii. 13, "brethren beloved by the Lord."

The Apostle thinks of his readers as *brethren*, for he has just been carrying them in his thoughts in prayer "before our God and *Father.*" The knowledge that God their Father loves them and has chosen them for His own, gives confidence to the Apostle's prayers for them and inexpressible joy to his thanksgivings. Comp. 2 Ep. ii. 13: "We are bound to give thanks always for you, brethren beloved by the Lord, because God from the beginning chose you," &c.; and Eph. i. 3—5, "Blessed be God..., Who blessed us in every spiritual blessing,...according as He chose us in Christ," &c.

The participle "beloved" is not however present in tense, as though the Thessalonians were simply loved now, in consequence of their newly-acquired Christian worth; it is in the Greek perfect tense, signifying a love existing in the past and realised in the present, the antecedent and foundation of their goodness. So in 1 John iii. 1: "Behold what manner of love the Father *hath given* us, that we should be called sons of God!"

The Christian excellence of the Thessalonians, therefore, moved the Apostle and his companions to thanksgiving (*vv.* 2, 3), not simply on its own account, but because it marked them out as *the objects of God's loving choice*. The word **election**, here occurring for the first time in St Paul's Epistles, and expressing one of his most important doctrines, needs to be carefully studied. The N. T. use of the word originates in the O. T. idea of Israel as God's "peculiar possession," "the

5 election of God. For our gospel came not unto you in
people whom He chose for His inheritance" (see Ps. xxxiii. 12, cxxxv. 4; Deut. xiv. 2; Isai. xliii. 1—7; &c.). Such "election" implies two things—(1) *selection out of others*, nations or men, who are not thus chosen—"the rest" (ch. iv. 13, v. 6); and (2) *appropriation by God* for His own love and service. Since Israel as a people now rejected Christ, St Paul was compelled to distinguish between national Israel and the true "election," the spiritual kernel of the chosen people, who were the real objects of God's favour: "the election obtained what Israel seeks after, but the rest were hardened" (Rom. xi. 7). With this true election, through Christ all believing Gentiles are identified—"wild olive shoots, grafted into the good olive-tree" (Rom. xi. 17—24). So the national gives place to a *spiritual election*—the "Israel of God" (Gal. vi. 16); and the Apostle Paul applies the term, as in this place, to Jewish and Gentile members of the Church indiscriminately. This transference is strikingly expressed in 1 Pet. ii. 9: "You (who believe in Christ) are a chosen race, a royal priesthood, a holy nation." God's election no longer marks out a nation or body of men as such, but it concerns *individuals*, each believer in Christ being the personal object of this loving choice—the "election of grace" (Rom. xi. 5). The *end* for which God in His grace so chooses men, appears in 2 Ep. ii. 13, "God chose you unto salvation," i.e. final deliverance from death and all evil, to be brought about by the return of Christ from heaven (ver. 10): the same end is set forth in the words of 1 Ep. ii. 12 and v. 9, 10—"God calleth you to His own kingdom and glory;" He "appointed you not to wrath, but to obtain salvation through our Lord Jesus Christ, that whether we wake or sleep, we should live together with Him." And the *means* toward this end are stated in 2 Ep. ii. 13,—"in sanctification of spirit and faith in the truth" (see note *ad loc.*). Similarly in Eph. i. 4, "He chose us to be holy and without blemish before Him." In later Epistles (Rom. viii. 28—30; Eph. i. 4, 5) St Paul's teaching on this subject receives two further extensions: (1) it is to *sonship* toward God that Christian believers are predestined; and (2) their election is carried back *to eternity*, "before the foundation of the world." It is questionable whether "from the beginning" in 2 Ep. ii. 13 points back so far as this (see note *ad loc.*) The "election" of Thessalonian believers goes back at any rate as far as the Divine love of which they are the objects—"beloved by God." But the Apostle's mind is occupied with the event of the conversion of his readers, when God's love to them and choice of them were practically manifest.

God's choice of men for His purposes must, of course, precede *their* choice of Him and of His salvation; but it in no way precludes human choice and freedom of will—nay rather anticipates and prepares for our free volition (comp. Rom. viii. 28—30), and invites us to be "workers together" with it for our salvation: "work out your own salvation, ...for it is God that worketh in you" (Ph. ii. 12, 13). It rests on the Divine *foreknowledge* of men ("whom He foreknew, He foreordained"), and seeks from their coming into life its destined objects (see Gal. i. 15,

word only, but also in power, and in the Holy Ghost, and

16). But "Prescience, as prescience, hath in itself no causing efficacy" (Hooker). Observe that Scripture does not speak of any *choice of men to believe in Christ*, but of *the choice of* (assumed) *believers to receive salvation*. The consistency of man's free-will with God's sovereignty forms an insoluble mystery, which does not belong to the doctrine of election alone, but runs through the whole of life and religion.

The Apostle writes "*knowing* your election," not that he is absolutely sure of the final salvation of every one to whom he writes—ch. iii. 5 speaks otherwise; but from what he knows and remembers of them, he is practically certain that the circle of his readers belongs to God's elect and that they will attain Christ's heavenly kingdom (see ch. ii. 12; v. 8—11, 24).

The evidence of this to his mind was twofold, lying (1) in *the power* given to himself and his companions in preaching at Thessalonica (ver. 5), and (2) in *the zeal and devotion* with which the Thessalonians had embraced the gospel (ver. 6).

5. *For our gospel came not unto you in word only, but also in power*] The R. V. reads, **how that our gospel**, &c.; better perhaps, **in that**; the difference is slight: in any case the conversion of the Thessalonians, described in *vv.* 5, 6, was not that wherein their election *consisted*, but wherein it was *evidenced*. Paul and Silas were conscious in declaring their message of a power beyond all words attending it, which made them sure at the time that it would not be in vain. It was evident to them that God "had much people in this city."

our gospel is God's good news about Jesus Christ, proclaimed by His servants. See Rom. i. 1—5. Hence it is both God's gospel (ch. ii. 2, &c.), and "our" gospel.

and in the Holy Ghost] The peculiar "power" in which St Paul and his helpers spoke at Thessalonica was not their own: their message **came in the Holy Spirit**, accompanied by the supernatural energy of the Spirit of God and of Christ. To this, as the N. T. teaches, the efficacy of the Gospel is always due. "He," said Jesus, "the Spirit of truth, shall testify of Me; and ye also do testify" (John xv. 26, 27). *Power* is an idea constantly associated with *the Holy Spirit*, according to the words of Christ in Acts i. 8, "Ye shall receive power, when the Holy Spirit has come upon you;" so in 1 Cor. ii. 4, "My message was not in persuasive words of wisdom, but in demonstration of the Spirit and of power," &c.,—

"that mighty Breath
From heaven's eternal shores."

in the Holy Spirit, and much fulness (R.V. *margin*), or **abundant fulfilment**. The preposition "in" is not repeated in the Greek, so that the third adjunct is closely identified with the second (Holy Spirit).

The same Greek word is used in the phrase "*full-assurance* of the understanding" in Col. ii. 2; "of hope," "of faith" (Heb. vi. 11; x. 22). But the "fulness" of this passage is ascribed to the "gospel" as it "came to" its Thessalonian hearers. It had its *full effect* upon them.

in much assurance; as ye know what manner of *men* we
6 were among you for your sake. And ye became followers
of us, and of the Lord, having received the word in much

Comp. 2 Tim. iv. 17, where the corresponding verb is used,—"that through me the message might be fulfilled" (R. V.)—*fully proclaimed*. This "fulfilment" has been shown in ver. 3; comp. ch. ii. 13; 2 Ep. ii. 13.

The *power* is in the gospel preached, the *fulfilment* in the hearers, and the *Holy Spirit* above and within them inspires both.

as ye know what manner of men *we were among you for your sake*] The R.V., more accurately, **even as ye know...we shewed ourselves toward you**. The Apostle appeals to *the knowledge of his readers* to confirm what he has just said respecting the powerful effect of the Gospel upon them. This result in the experience of the Thessalonians accorded with the spirit and behaviour of the apostles towards them. "It was a mutual influence: so we preached, and so ye believed," 1 Cor. xv. 11 (Jowett). In ch. ii. 1—12 (see the remarks introductory to ch. ii.) the Apostle draws a vivid portrait of himself and his colleagues as they were at Thessalonica.

They so lived and laboured **on your account**—out of love to their Thessalonian hearers (comp. ch. ii. 8), to those whom they felt sure God in His love had chosen for Himself (ver. 4) and was calling by their means "to His own kingdom and glory" (ch. ii. 12). Comp. 2 Tim. ii. 10, "I endure all things because of the elect."

"In the background," behind "the purpose of the Apostle and his colleagues," there was "the purpose of God," Who for the Thessalonians' sake gave this power to His servants (Alford).

6. *And ye became followers of us, and of the Lord*] **imitators of us** &c. (R.V.); comp. ch. ii. 14; 2 Ep. iii. 9, where the same correction is made. An "imitator" not only accepts the teaching of another, but copies his example. This *imitation* consisted (1) in the joyful endurance of suffering for the Gospel's sake, as the following words show (comp. ch. ii. 2, 14, 15, &c.); but (2) also in the vigour which marked the life of this Church, corresponding to that of the Apostle's ministry amongst them (ver. 4). See note on "work of faith" (ver. 3).

Thus imitating their apostles, the Thessalonian believers were walking in the steps of *the Lord*, Who Himself "received" from the Father "the word in much affliction," and "with joy of the Holy Spirit:" "The words that Thou gavest Me," He said to the Father, "I have given them;" men "persecuted Me, and they will persecute you," He promised His disciples; and He too "rejoiced in the Holy Spirit" (John xvii. 8; xv. 20; Luke x. 21). Accordingly, in Col. i. 24 the Apostle writes of himself as "filling up what is left behind of the afflictions of Christ."—Observe two things here: (1) How inspiring to the Thessalonians to be told they were walking in the very steps "of the Lord;" this makes toil welcome, and shame glorious. (2) How bold in the Apostle, and what a good conscience he kept, that he could

affliction, with joy of the Holy Ghost: so that ye were 7 ensamples to all that believe in Macedonia and Achaia.

identify following himself with following *Christ*. Comp. 1 Cor. xi. 1, "Be imitators of me, even as I also of Christ."

Ver. 6 is parallel to ver. 5, both serving to establish ver. 4. St Paul was satisfied that God had set His love upon these Thessalonians and chosen them to salvation, in the first instance by the extraordinary power and effect upon them of his preaching, as they will remember (ver. 5); and further by their joyous endurance of persecution, proving the thoroughness of their conversion, to which everyone is witness (*vv.* 6—10). "We give thanks to God for you...being well assured of your Divine election, in that our message to you was attended with the manifest power of the Holy Spirit, and you gladly consented to the sufferings that it brought upon you" (*vv.* 3—6).

having received the word] On "receive" see note to ch. ii. 13.

"The word" (*par excellence*) stands alone for "the word of the Lord" (ver. 8), or "of God" (ch. ii. 13), the same as "our gospel" (ver. 5).

in much affliction] This **great affliction** (or *tribulation*: same Greek word, ch. iii. 4; 2 Ep. i. 4, 6) is described in Acts xvii. 5—9, and referred to frequently in the Epistles: see *Introd.* pp. 15, 35. Persecution marked out the path in which the Thessalonians were called to follow Christ, and gave them an immediate opportunity of showing the genuineness of their faith. So with the kindred Philippian Church: "To you it was granted as a favour on Christ's behalf, not only to believe in Him, but also to suffer for His sake" (Ph. i. 29).

with joy of the Holy Ghost] i.e. **coming of** (or *inspired by*) **the Holy Spirit**. Joy constantly attends suffering for the truth's sake, and for the word of God. Of this St Paul was an eminent example— "sorrowing, yet alway rejoicing" (2 Cor. vi. 10, &c.); and Christ Himself, Who promises His disciples "My joy" amidst the sorrows of His passion (John xv. 11); the Thessalonians were "imitators." At a later time the Apostle notes in the Macedonian Churches, "in much proof of affliction, the abundance of their joy" (2 Cor. viii. 2). All such joy is *from the Holy Spirit*, and is a sign of His indwelling,—

"Whose blessed unction from above
Is comfort, life, and fire of love!"

The same Spirit Who enabled the apostles to preach with *power* in spite of all opposition, enabled the Thessalonians to believe with *joy* in spite of all persecution.

The Apostle introduces the Holy Spirit in *vv.* 5 and 6 as One whose presence and attributes were well known to his readers. They had been "baptized into the name of the Holy Spirit," as well as "of the Father and the Son:" see notes on ver. 1, "in God the Father &c." In these first few verses the whole doctrine of the Trinity is implied.

7. *so that ye were ensamples to all that believe in Macedonia and Achaia*] Rather, **ye became an ensample** (R.V.),—or **example**, or **pattern** (as the same word—naturalized as "type" in English—is

8 For from you sounded out the word of the Lord not only in Macedonia and Achaia, but also in every place your faith

rendered in Tit. ii. 7, Heb. viii. 5). The Apostle applies this expression to himself in 2 Ep. iii. 9; also in Ph. iii. 17; and to Timothy, in 1 Tim. iv. 12.

"Those that believe" (that is, "in God," or "Christ") equivalent to **believers**—is a frequent designation of Christians with St Paul. See ch. ii. 10, 13; 2 Ep. i. 10; &c. Similarly, "they that are of faith" (Gal. iii. 7, 9), "him that is of faith in Jesus" (Rom. iii. 26); for *faith* is the root and essence of all that makes a man a Christian.

The example of the Thessalonians affected all believers **in Macedonia and in Achaia** (according to the true reading). These were distinct provinces, and the influence of Thessalonian faith had extended from the one to the other. The Apostle was now in Corinth, the capital and centre of *Achaia* (a Roman province, covering nearly the area of the present Kingdom of Greece), and could judge of the effect of the conduct of the Thessalonian Church in that district. And Timothy, with Silas, had lately returned from the northern province, traversing various Macedonian towns on his way, and would be able to report of the influence of this example there (ch. iii. 6; Acts xviii. 5). On the relation of Thessalonica to *Macedonia* see *Introd.* pp. 9, 10, and the *map*. In 2 Cor. viii. 1—5 St Paul brings these two provinces into competition, in a sort of generous rivalry.

St Paul imitated Christ, the Thessalonians him (ver. 6), and all neighbouring Christians took pattern by them. So good example spreads.

8. *For from you sounded out the word of the Lord*] Better, **hath sounded out**, or **resounded**. The Greek word suggests a clear ringing note, "as of a trumpet" (Chrysostom); and the tense (perfect) implies no transient sound, but a continuing effect: see note on *beloved*, ver. 4.

"The word of the Lord" is the standing O. T. designation for God's revealed will,—all that, as *the Lord*, He says to men. But "the Lord" is now *Christ* in His Divine authority and glory; and this title of Christ is notably frequent in our two Epistles. Only in them is this expression applied by St Paul to the Gospel (comp. ch. iv. 15; 2 Ep. iii. 1). Afterwards he calls it "the word of God," or "of Christ"— "not men's word, but as it is in truth, God's word" (ch. ii. 13). The fullest declaration of the authorship and purport of this "word" is from the lips of St Peter, in Acts x. 36: "The word which God sent,—in good tidings of peace through Jesus Christ: He is Lord of all."

Ver. 8 gives proof of the earnestness with which the Thessalonians had embraced the Gospel, as set forth in *vv.* 6 and 7. For they had so received it as to echo it far and wide. The violent persecution directed against them, failing to shake their faith, had served to advertise it.

"Truth, like a torch, the more 'tis shaken shines."

not only in Macedonia and Achaia] Now the two provinces are united, in contrast with the rest of the world.

to God-ward is spread abroad; so that we need not to speak any *thing*. For they themselves shew of us what manner of 9

but also in every place your faith to God-ward is spread abroad] Lit., **hath gone out**: the Apostle keeps up the metaphor with which he began the sentence. Ps. xix. 4, quoted also in Rom. x. 18, seems to be running in his mind: "Their sound went forth into all the earth" (LXX). For the *tense*, see note on "hath sounded out."

The conversion of the Thessalonians, taking place under such remarkable circumstances, had made a great sensation, the news spreading even beyond the limits of Greece. [For a view of the importance of Thessalonica and its commanding geographical position, see *Introd*. Ch. I.] Aquila had lately come to Corinth from Rome (Acts xviii. 2), and may have brought word that the news was current there. The charge of treason against Cæsar recorded in Acts xvii. 6, 7, would almost certainly be reported in Rome. "In every place" is a natural hyperbolé, used like our *everywhere*, *everybody* and the French *tout le monde*, of that which is widely and generally current. The Thessalonian believers in Christ were

"bravely furnished all abroad to fling
The wingèd shafts of truth."

With "in every place" the sentence of ver. 8 is complete; but as the writer extends his statement, it alters its shape in his mind, and the assertion with which he set out (*the word...hath sounded forth*) is now repeated in another way: **your faith that is unto** (*is directed to*) **God, hath gone out**. This mobility is characteristic of St Paul's style (see *Introd*. Ch. VI.). The same thing appears in a double aspect: the fame of the gospel spread by the Thessalonians and the fame of their faith in it travelled together.

"Faith *toward* God" is a rare and distinct expression. It indicates the new *direction*, or *attitude* of the heart and life, which the next verse vividly depicts. Comp. 2 Cor. iii. 4 and Philem. 5: "toward the Lord Jesus."

so that we need not to speak any thing] Lit., **have no need**,—a phrase used three times in this Epistle (ch. iv. 9, v. 1), and nowhere else by St Paul.

Read this in close connection with the next verse. It is as much as to say, "No need for us to tell the story. We hear of it from all sides; everywhere people are talking about your conversion and your brave testimony for Christ."

9. *For they themselves shew of us*] Rather, **report concerning us** (R.V.) "They" points to "those in Macedonia and Achaia" and "in every place,"—any whom the Apostle visited, or to whom he had thought of sending the news. "Instead of waiting to be told by us, we find them spreading the joyful news already!" And this self-diffusing report concerned not the Thessalonians alone, but *Paul and his colleagues*. It published their success at this great city, and helped their further progress: **they report...what kind of an entrance we had unto you**.

entering in we had unto you, and how ye turned to God
from idols to serve the living and true God, and to wait for

The "manner" of this "entering in" is not to be found in the kind of reception given to the evangelists at Thessalonica, but in the way in which they presented themselves and entered on their ministry here: comp. ver. 5, and ch. ii. 1, 2. The reports that told of the heroic faith of the Thessalonians, told also of the wonderful energy and success with which Paul and Silas had preached to them.

and how ye turned to God from idols to serve the living and true God. Lit., **from the idols, to be bondmen to a God living and true.** This explains the "faith toward God" of ver. 8. "How" implies not the fact alone, but the *manner* of their conversion—"with what decision and gladness" (vv. 5, 6), parallel to "what manner of entrance." The Thessalonian Christians had been mainly Gentiles and heathen: comp. ch. ii. 14.—Also Acts xvii. 4, 5, from which it appears, however, that there was a sprinkling of Jews among them, and "a great multitude" of proselytes, already more or less weaned from idolatry.

The "faith toward God" defined in this verse, is the faith of the whole Bible, in which from first to last God asserts Himself as "the Living and True" against the ten thousand forms of human idolatry. The word [Greek], Greek *eidōlon*, means properly an *appearance*, a mere *image*, or *phantom*. Homer, e.g., applies the term to the phantoms of distant persons by which his gods sometimes impose on men (*Iliad* v. 449; *Odyssey* iv. 796). Comp. Lord Bacon's *idola tribus, specus, fori, theatri*, in the *Novum Organum*. This word is the equivalent in the Septuagint Version of Hebrew designations for heathen gods and their images of like signifiance—*teraphim, vanities, nothings*. To all these the Name of the God of Israel—Who "is the true God, and the living God" (Jer. x. 10—is the constant, tacit antithesis: "I am Jehovah" (more strictly *Yahveh*, or *Yahweh*, commonly "the Lord" in the English O. T.)—"he HE IS" see Exod. iii. 13, 14 for its interpretation; and for its use in argument against idolatry, such passages as Isai. xli. 4; xliv. 6, 8; xlv. 21, 22. Like the Prophets and Psalmists e.g. in Ps. xcv. 4—8; Isai. xliv. 9—20; Jer. x. 1—10, St Paul was powerfully impressed with the illusion and unreality of heathen religions. He defines idolatry in two passages, 1 Cor. viii. 4 and x. 19, 20, as being *self*-ism, *self*-deceit; and in the horrible immorality then existing in the Gentile world he saw its natural consequence and judicial punishment, Rom. i. 18—32.

"True" signifies *real, of that we word: "one God" is the "very God" of the Nicene Creed, *the real God*; comp. John xvii. 3—"that they should know Thee, the only true God;" and 1 John v. 20. "This is the true God, and life eternal."

The service to this "living and true God" which the Thessalonians had embraced, was that of *bondmen*, acknowledging themselves His property and at His absolute disposal. St Paul habitually calls himself "Christ's" more "God's." This is "bondman." In Gal. iv. 8 he

his Son from heaven, whom he raised from the dead, *even* Jesus, which delivered us from the wrath to come.

speaks of heathenism as *bondage to false gods*; in Rom. vi. 15—23 he shows that to become a Christian is to exchange the *bondage of sin* for *bondage to righteousness* and *to God, bondage under grace*. The full conception of the Christian relationship to God is formed by the combination of the idea of *sonship* (in respect of affection and privilege with that of *bond-service* (in respect of duty and submission), to Him "Whose service is perfect freedom."

On the relation of this passage to St Paul's general teaching see *Introd.* pp. 17, 18. So far, in *vv.* 8, 9, St Paul has related the conversion of the Thessalonians in the language and spirit of the O. T., and as an acceptance of Hebrew faith. In the next verse he advances to that which was distinctively Christian in their new creed:—

10. *and to wait for his Son from heaven...even Jesus*] Lit., from **the heavens**: comp. 2 Cor. xii. 2, "the third heaven;" and Heb. iv. 14, "Jesus....Who (in ascending) hath passed through the heavens." *Heaven* is a plural word in Hebrew, and its conception was manifold, implying the existence of successive regions and stages, like the Courts and Chambers of the Tabernacle, leading up to the innermost, immediate presence-chamber of the Most High.

This expectation separated the Church of Thessalonians from the Synagogue. It involved the belief in Jesus as *the Christ* (Acts xvii. 3); and if Christ, then *Son of God* and *King of His kingdom* amongst men. "The kingdom and glory of God to" which "He is calling" the Thessalonians (ch. ii. 12), will be inaugurated by the return of their Deliverer from heaven; and this they are awaiting. Jesus, God's Son, had come already, to suffer affliction and to die for men's salvation (ver. 6; ch. ii. 15; v. 9). He had gone to heaven, "that He might receive His kingdom and return" (Luke xix. 12; comp. Acts iii. 21).—return as Judge to reward God's faithful servants and to render to oppressors and persecutors their due (2 Ep. i. 5—10). Such, we gather, had been the line of Paul and Silas' teaching at Thessalonica: see *Introd.* Ch. III. Hence their readers were possessed with the idea of the *parousia*, or second advent of Christ. This formed a chief part of their religion. They were in truth "like men looking for their Lord, when He should return from the wedding" (Luke xii. 36). Comp. note on "patience of hope," ver. 3; also ch. iv. 13, 17, v. 1; 2 Ep. ii. 1, 2, 16.

From *vv.* 9 and 10 we may draw a definition of religion, as consisting of two things—*serving* and *waiting*, seen in its present and future, its practical and its ideal aspect: the first springing out of *faith*, the second out of *hope*, while both gain through *love* their Christian character and spirit.

his Son...whom he raised from the dead] "The palmary argument in proof of the Divine sonship of Jesus" (Bengel): comp. Rom. i. 4, "declared to be the Son of God with power, according to the spirit of holiness, by the resurrection of the dead." And Christ's resurrection was equally the warrant of faith in His future kingdom and judgeship,—

2 For yourselves, brethren, know our entrance in unto you,

"whereof God hath given assurance, in that He hath raised Him from the dead" (Acts xvii. 31). Indeed it was the seal of the whole Apostolic message (read 1 Cor. xv. 3, 14; 1 Pet. i. 3—5, 21; Acts ii. 32—36; iii. 13—21). Raised from the dead, Jesus was exalted as God's Son, and man's Saviour, and Lord of all things, to the highest heaven (Eph. i. 20—22); and in this character He will return, as He said, "with His Father's glory and with the holy angels," to "render to every man according to his deeds" (Matt. xvi. 27; Mark viii. 38). The Resurrection was the first step in Christ's glorification, the pledge of all the rest.

even *Jesus, which delivered us from the wrath to come*] *delivered* should be **delivereth** (R.V.). The Greek participle is *present* ("the One delivering"); and such a participle, with the definite article, approaches the force of a substantive (see note on "all that believe," ver. 7), denoting a continued work, or perpetual office. Reference to 2 Cor. i. 10, or 2 Tim. iv. 17, 18, where the same verb is used, will show that it signifies *rescue* rather than *redemption*, indicating the greatness of the peril, and the sympathy and power of the Deliverer.

This deliverance is not yet complete: see Rom. v. 9, 10, "having been justified by His blood,—reconciled to God through the death of His Son, we *shall be saved* from God's wrath,—saved in His life." It is a rescue "from the wrath *to come*" (comp. Matt. iii. 7),—more strictly, **the wrath that is coming**; as in Eph. v. 6; Col. iii. 6. For God's anger against sin is never quiet; it is *on the way*, like a tide that rises till it reach its full height. Comp. 2 Ep. ii. 11, 12; Rom. i. 18, 28. As against the Jewish nation, the Apostle sees that its term is now reached: "His wrath is come upon them to the uttermost" (ch. ii. 16). For others its recompenses are preparing, who "in their hardness and impenitence of heart" are "laying up for themselves a store of wrath" (Rom. ii. 4—6), comp. 2 Ep. i. 7—10 and notes.

How Jesus "delivers us" from the wrath impending over sinful men, St Paul does not tell us here; he had certainly taught the Thessalonians. In ch. v. 8—10 he opposes to God's "wrath" "*salvation* through our Lord Jesus Christ, Who died for us;" and this shows that he had proclaimed at Thessalonica the same doctrine of reconciliation through the Cross which he expounds in the next group of his Epistles, and which was the core of his gospel from the beginning. On this most important point, see once more *Introd.* pp. 16, 17.

SECTION II.

THE APOSTLE'S CONDUCT AT THESSALONICA. CH. II. 1—12.

Analysis. The ministry of Paul and his colleagues at Thessalonica had been unmistakably genuine, ver. 1. This appeared (1) by *their boldness* in the conflict amid which their work began, ver. 2; (2) by *their sincerity and freedom from personal ambition*, *vv.* 3—6; (3) by *their gentleness and tender affection* toward the Thessalonians, *vv.* 7, 8; (4) by *their extreme and self-denying labours*, ver. 9; (5) by *the purity of*

that it was not in vain: but even after that we had suffered 2
before, and were shamefully entreated, as ye know, at Phi-

their life, ver. 10; and (6) by *the fidelity and high spiritual aim* of their teaching, *vv.* 11, 12. Four words resume the whole: *courage, purity, love, fidelity*. Here is a mirror for ministers of Christ, and an ideal for all His servants. The service of Christ called into exercise in Paul and his companions the highest and finest qualities of manly character. And this is still the case, especially on missionary fields of labour, where similar dangers are encountered and the same powers of leadership required.

This section is of the nature of a *self-defence*, called forth (see *Introd.* pp. 23, 24) by the calumnies of St Paul's enemies at Thessalonica. But there blends with his self-defence the lofty strain of *thanksgiving* in which the letter commenced, and which breaks forth again distinctly in ver. 13 and is pursued to the end of ch. iii.; so that this paragraph grows naturally out of the last.

The Apostle continues to identify Silas and Timothy with himself, writing in the plural,—

1. *For yourselves, brethren, know our entrance in unto you*] **entering in** (R.V.), same word as in ch. i. 9; see note. And the "For" of this verse is parallel to the "for" of ch. i. 9: what "*they* themselves (other people, strangers in different places) report of us" is confirmed by what "*you* yourselves know" of the successful entrance the Gospel had won at Thessalonica. Both these *fors*, and all that the Apostle has written since ver. 4 of ch. i., go to sustain his assurance of God's loving "choice" of the Thessalonian believers. We must not allow the artificial division of chapter and verse to break the thread of the writer's thoughts.

The appeal made to the recollections and experience of the readers is characteristic of these letters, see *vv.* 2, 5, 10, 11; ch. i. 5, &c.; and comp. *Introd.* p. 35.

Concerning the "entrance" of the missionaries amongst them the Thessalonians know better than anyone else, **that it hath not been found vain** (R.V.). The Greek perfect tense (see note on ch. i. 8) implies *a settled result:* not merely did the coming of Christ's servants produce a striking impression at the time; their work has proved thoroughly successful. Its fruit is permanent.

Vain is lit. **empty**, void of substance and power. So the apostles' "labour" would "turn out," if "the Tempter" should destroy the Thessalonians' faith (ch. iii. 5); so his "preaching" and his hearers' "faith" at Corinth, if Christ's resurrection were not a fact (1 Cor. xv. 14). "Not empty" echoes the "power" and "much fulness" of ch. i. 5.

This verse might be rendered somewhat more freely in English idiom: **For you know of yourselves, brethren, that our coming amongst you has not proved vain.**

2. *but even after that we had suffered before, and were shamefully entreated, as ye know, at Philippi*] More exactly, **having suffered before,**

lippi, we were bold in our God to speak unto you the gospel

and been shamefully entreated (R.V.), or **though we had already suffered and were shamefully treated at Philippi**. "Entreated" is older English for *treated*, as in Matt. xxii. 6 and Luke xviii. 32 (*spitefully entreated*). *Shamefully treated* is one word in the Greek,—*outraged*. It implies insult and injury combined, such as constituted a legal crime. This accords with the protest of Paul and Silas against the Philippian magistrates (Acts xvi. 37): "They have beaten us, publicly, uncondemned, being Romans!" Such indignities the Apostle felt keenly; they added a distinct element to his sufferings.

As to the circumstances of the missionaries' visit to Philippi and their experience there, read carefully Acts xvi., and comp. *Introd.* Chap. II. "As ye know," for the Apostle had doubtless told his Thessalonian friends of his treatment at Philippi. Moreover, this town was but three days' journey east of Thessalonica along the Via Egnatia, and news of all kinds readily passed between them (*Introd.* Chap. I.).

Instead of being daunted by the violence they suffered, Paul and Silas at Philippi "sang praises to God at midnight, with their feet fast in the stocks." And God there signally vindicated His servants and turned their shame to honour. So we are not surprised to read of the holy confidence with which they declared their message at Thessalonica: **we waxed bold** (R.V.)—or, **took courage in our God to speak unto you the gospel of God amid much conflict**.

The last words of the clause explain the first, on which the emphasis rests. The "conflict" that broke out at Philippi continued under another form at Thessalonica, and the apostles needed all their courage and faith in God to sustain them in entering on their ministry in this new city. Throughout this first European mission it required a hard struggle to win for the Gospel a footing anywhere. There was *much conflict*.

The Greek verb (*waxed-bold*) implies the undaunted bearing and address of the missionaries, the *outspokenness* with which they faced their opposers in the delivery of God's message. This was more than natural courage: "we waxed bold *in our God*." God's presence and the consciousness that His Spirit was with them (ch. i. 5, see note) made them fearless. "It is not ye that speak," said Jesus, "but the Spirit of your Father that speaketh in you...Fear them not therefore" (Matt. x. 16—32). Besides, it was "the gospel *of God*" which they proclaimed: God had put the message into their lips. This is the secret of St Paul's heroism. The highest moral courage, such as that of President Lincoln or General Gordon in modern times, springs from faith in God.

The evangelists addressed themselves to their work at Thessalonica with a high degree of confidence, and under the fullest sense of Divine direction. Contrast with this the "weakness and fear and much trembling in" which the Apostle shortly afterwards "was with" the Corinthians (1 Cor. ii. 3—5). St Paul's mood as a preacher was not always the same; circumstances depressed or elated him.

of God with much contention. For our exhortation *was* 3 not of deceit, nor of uncleanness, nor in guile: but as we 4 were allowed of God to be put in trust with the gospel,

3. *For our exhortation* was *not of deceit, nor of uncleanness, nor in guile*] Read **error** for *deceit;* and supply the Greek ellipsis by **is not** (R.V.) rather than *was not*. The Apostle is setting forth the habit and spirit of his ministry: "We behaved in this fearless way at Thessalonica, for our ministry is free from all that is false and impure." It is *true* men that make *brave* men. In ver. 5 Paul returns to his conduct at Thessalonica; *vv.* 3, 4 speak of his general policy.

"Exhortation" hardly conveys his full meaning,—**our appeal** is perhaps better; it is the practical "appeal," or "address," which "the gospel of God," as the missionaries of Christ preach it everywhere, makes to its hearers. Comp. note on "comfort," ch. iii. 2.

This appeal "is not of error" (*deceit*, A.V., is incorrect)—not the product of illusion or deception; for it is "the gospel of God" (ver. 2), "the word of *the truth* of the gospel" (Col. i. 5). This was amongst Paul's constant and uppermost convictions. The heavenly Form that met him on the road to Damascus, the Voice that said, "Depart, for I will send thee far hence unto the Gentiles,"—these were no phantasy. "I know Him whom I have believed" (2 Tim. i. 12).

As the Apostle was sure of the genuineness of his message, so he was conscious of *the purity of his motives:* "nor of uncleanness." This epithet commonly denotes bodily defilement, and is a synonym for *unchastity*, as in ch. iv. 7, &c. But there is a "defilement of spirit" as well as "of flesh" (2 Cor. vii. 1). Self-seeking (ver. 5) in the witness of truth makes his testimony corrupt. So *truth and purity* go together; each promotes and guards the other. Comp. 1 Pet. i. 22, "Ye have purified your souls in obeying the truth." On the other hand, the Apostle speaks of the "deceit of unrighteousness" (2 Ep. ii. 10), and of "men corrupt in mind and bereft of truth, supposing that godliness is a way of gain" (1 Tim. vi. 5).

So much for his motives: of his *method* St Paul will only say, "nor in guile;" as he puts it more at large in 2 Cor. iv. 2, "not walking in craftiness, nor handling the word of God deceitfully, but by the manifestation of the truth commending ourselves to every man's conscience in the sight of God." The servant of truth should use only the weapons of truth. "Guile" was doubtless imputed to St Paul by his slanderers in Thessalonica, as it was subsequently at Corinth: "being crafty (as they say), I caught you with guile" (2 Cor. xii. 16).

To sum up the verse: *Our doctrine is true; our motives pure; and our conduct straightforward.*

4. *but as we were allowed of God to be put in trust with the gospel, even so we speak*] Again the A.V. misses the force of the Greek perfect: better, **as we have been approved by God to be entrusted.** "Allow" in older English bears the stronger sense of *accept, approve* (comp. Rom. xiv. 22), but even so falls short of the meaning of St Paul. His word is the same that is rendered in the last clause of the verse as *trieth*

even so we speak; not as pleasing men, but God, which

(R.V., *proveth*); it includes both *proving and approving*, it is *approving on trial*, or *testing:* comp. ch. v. 21 (same Greek verb, "*Prove* all things"); and 1 Cor. iii. 13, "The fire will *prove* each man's work." The Apostle had been tested for his work, and tested by it; God had made proof of him as a minister of Christ, and he was shown to be worthy of his trust: *tried*, then *trusted* (comp. 1 Tim. i. 12). "To be put in trust with the gospel" is the highest conceivable responsibility; the sense of it is enough to exclude every base motive and deceitful practice (ver. 3). On Paul's *trust*, read 1 Tim. i. 12—17 and Acts ix. 15, 16: "He is a chosen vessel unto Me."

so we speak] under the sense of this solemn trust, with the sincerity and self-abnegation that our charge demands.

not as pleasing men, but God, which trieth our hearts] R.V., **proveth** (see previous note): more precisely, **pleasing God—Him who proves our hearts**. This last is an O.T. expression, a standing attribute of God: see Ps. xvii. 3, Jer. xi. 20, &c.; also Acts i. 24, "Thou, Lord, which knowest the hearts of all." "Unto whom all hearts be open, all desires known, and from whom no secrets are hid" (Book of Common Prayer).

The "heart," in the language of the Bible, is not the seat of the feelings alone; it is "the inner man," the real self, the centre and meeting-point of all our thoughts, feelings, and resolves. It is there that God proves us: "The LORD looketh upon the heart." No impure motive or crafty expedient, such as might deceive men, escapes Him. The sense of this continual and omniscient scrutiny makes any kind of dishonesty impossible to the Apostle. Read 1 Cor. iv. 1—5; 2 Cor. v. 9—12: "He that judgeth me is the Lord."

It is *God's* gospel that Paul and Silas have to preach; *God* had trusted them with it, and given them strength and courage to proclaim it (ver. 2); to *God's* approval, therefore, they must look, and to that alone. "Men," such as the magistrates of Philippi and the populace of Thessalonica, would be pleased only if the messengers of Christ were silenced. So the authorities of Jerusalem "charged Peter and John not to speak at all nor teach in the name of Jesus;" but they answered: "If it be right in the sight of God to hearken unto you rather than unto God, judge ye" (Acts iv. 18, 19). This sense of the sovereignty of God gives religion its invincible power; it is the conviction that makes martyrs. It is finely expressed in the *Antigone* of Sophocles (ll. 450—460), where the heroine replies to the tyrant Creon:

> "Nor could I think thine edict of such might,
> That one who is mortal thus should overrule
> The infallible, unwritten laws of heaven."

St Paul tells us elsewhere, and by way of example, that he "pleased all in all things for their good, unto edification" (1 Cor. x. 33; Rom. xv. 2). To please men in that which displeases God, is to injure them: "If (in such circumstances) I pleased men, I should not

trieth our hearts. For neither at any time used we flattering 5
words, as ye know, nor a cloke of covetousness; God *is*
witness: nor of men sought we glory, neither of you, nor 6

be Christ's slave" (Gal. i. 10). That is, to be the slave of public
opinion,—often an ignorant, sometimes an unprincipled master.

Vv. 3 and 4 are then a general disclaimer of unworthy motives on the
part of the missionaries. Their bold testimony at Thessalonica (*vv.* 1
and 2) was due to two things—their *sincerity of heart*, and their *loyalty
to God*. Now we resume the account of the Apostle's relations to the
Thessalonians, confirming these professions:—

5. *For neither at any time used we flattering words*] **were we found
using words of flattery** (R.V.: same verb as in ver. 1, "*found* vain");
or, **did we fall into the use of flattering speech**. "Found" might
suggest *detection*, which is not in the Apostle's mind. Lit., **word
of flattery**, referring to the tenor and general style of the apostles'
speech. He adds a third time (see note on ver. 1) "as ye know."
St Paul, as his friends well knew, was not one to

"crook the pregnant hinges of the knee,
Where thrift may follow fawning."

In repudiating **the cloak of covetousness** he appeals to "God" as
"witness" (comp. Rom. i. 9, "God is my witness, whom I serve in
my spirit in the gospel of His Son;" also ii. 15, ix. 1),—"God, Who
proveth our hearts" (ver. 4). The "cloak" signifies the *pretext* of
an affected self-devotion, such as might be used to conceal the
"covetousness" of a selfish heart. "God is witness," he says, "that no
secret avarice was hidden behind our zeal for your salvation."

The Greek word for "covetousness" denotes *greed* of any kind,
—oftenest, but not always or necessarily, *for money;* it is the spirit of
self-aggrandisement, selfishness as a ruling passion. (Comp. the note
on "defraud," ch. iv. 6.) Such a motive in the servant of God would
constitute the "uncleanness" denied in ver. 3.

This verse gives double evidence of the pure zeal for God professed in
vv. 3 and 4—the one *outward* and of the lips, the other *inward* and
known only to God in the heart. Contrast the opposite description of
Ps. xii. 2: "A flattering lip, and a double heart."

6. *nor of men sought we glory, neither of you, nor yet of others*] This
clause continues ver. 5, and is so construed in the R.V.: **nor** (were we
found) **seeking glory of men, neither from you, nor from others**.
"*Of* men" points to the general source of such "glory," indicating its
character; "*from* you," &c., to the particular quarter whence, conceivably, it might have been sought.

The motive of *ambition*—"that last infirmity of noble minds"—rises
above the *selfishness* just disclaimed; but it is just as warmly repudiated,
for it is equally inconsistent with the single-mindedness of men devoted to the glory of God. Our Lord finds in superiority to human
praise the mark of a sincere faith: "How can ye believe," He asks,
"which receive honour one of another, and the glory that cometh from
the only God ye seek not?" (John v. 44).

yet of others, when we might have been burdensome, as *the*

when we might have been burdensome, as the *apostles of Christ*] Lit., **as apostles of Christ,** without the definite article. St Paul is speaking for himself and Silas and Timothy; and the latter were not of *the* Apostles, but they were, in common with himself, "*apostles* of Christ."

"Apostle" signifies by derivation *emissary*, or *envoy*,—one "sent out" by authority with some message or commission. The term was probably in current use amongst the Jews, when Jesus adopted it for His chosen Twelve. But it obtained in the early Church a wider application, concurrently with its stricter reference to the Twelve (including Paul, afterwards recognized as being of the same order, 1 Cor. ix. 1; Gal. i. 1, 17, ii. 7, &c.). Of this we have examples in *Barnabas and Paul*, Acts xiv. 4, 14; *Andronicus and Junias*, "amongst the apostles," Rom. xvi. 7; *Titus and others*, "apostles of the churches," 2 Cor. viii. 23; *Judean emissaries*, "false apostles," 2 Cor. xi. 13; *Epaphroditus*, sent from the Philippian Church to Paul in prison at Rome, Ph. ii. 25; also in Rev. ii. 2; Heb. iii. 1 (Christ Himself is "the Apostle," being sent forth from God), John xiii. 16. In John xvii. 18; xx. 21 we find the fundamental idea of the word and the basis of its larger application: "As Thou didst send Me forth into the world, even so I have sent forth them." In this more general use, *apostle* did not differ much from our word *missionary*. The title belonged to men who were sent out in Christ's name by particular Churches—either with a specific and limited mission, or with a general commission to preach the gospel—as well as to those directly appointed by Jesus Himself and charged with His full authority. But after N.T. times the designation came to be reserved, with slight exceptions, to the Twelve and Paul. See Bishop Lightfoot's detached note on the *Name and Office of an Apostle* in his Commentary on *Galatians*, pp. 92 ff.; and Huxtable's very valuable *Dissertation* in the Pulpit Commentary on *Galatians*, pp. xxiii.—l. St Paul certainly possessed the lower apostleship (see Acts xiii. 1—3), and there was no need for him in this letter to claim the higher, nor to distinguish himself from his missionary companions. His friend Luke puts the Apostle, in the early stage of his ministry, on a level with Barnabas (Acts xiv. 4, 14). The time came when he was compelled to assume the highest Apostolic powers and to assert his equality with Peter and the Twelve (Gal. i. 1; ii.; 1 Cor. ix. 1, 2, xv. 7—11; 2 Cor. xii. 11—13, xiii. 3—10); but it was not yet.

"Burdensome" is lit. **in** (or in our idiom, **of**) **weight**—an ambiguous phrase, whose sense is interpreted by ver. 9: "that we might not burden any of you." These "apostles of Christ"—according to Paul's maxim, "They which preach the gospel should live of the gospel" (1 Cor. ix. 14)—might have claimed their maintenance from the Thessalonian Church. Had they been "seeking glory of men," they would certainly have done so; it was both the easier and the more dignified course. "Weight" suggests the secondary sense of *honour, glory:* R.V. margin, **claimed honour** (comp. 2 Cor. iv. 17, "weight of glory": *weight* and *glory* are one word in Hebrew). Not because they were *apostles* (as though this were a privilege peculiar to the name), but "as

apostles of Christ. But we were gentle among you, *even* as 7
a nurse cherisheth her children: so being affectionately de- 8
sirous of you, we were willing to have imparted unto you,

Christ's apostles"—sent on His errand, preaching His word: "so hath the Lord ordained" (1 Cor. ix. 14; Luke x. 7). We find that the Apostle, while in Thessalonica at this time, did receive help twice over from his Philippian friends, and gratefully remembered it (Phil. iv. 15, 16). So afterwards, at Corinth, he allowed contributions to be sent him "from Macedonia" (2 Cor. xi. 9).

7. *But we were gentle among you*] Lit., and more graphically, **in the midst of you** (R.V.); also, **were found gentle**—same verb as in ver. 1, and ch. i. 5 (*shewed ourselves toward you*, R.V.).

Instead of *gentle*, **babes** is the reading of "most of the ancient authorities" (R.V., margin), including the Vulgate (*parvuli*): the difference in the Greek lies only in the repetition or omission of a single letter. The modern editors (with the weighty exception of Westcott and Hort: see the Note in their *New Testament in Greek*, vol. II., p. 128), decide in favour of the received reading,—(1) because "gentle" better suits the context; and (2) because this Greek word occurs only once besides in the N.T. (1 Tim. ii. 24), for copyists are prone to change an unfamiliar into any familiar word resembling it that gives a tolerable sense, and "babes" is a favourite expression of St Paul. If *babes* be the genuine reading—and it is difficult to resist the evidence in its favour—then it must be explained as it is by Origen and Augustine, endorsed by Westcott: *like a nurse amongst her children, talking in baby language to the babes.*

The gentleness of these apostles of Christ stands in tacit contrast with the airs of authority and the exactions of selfish and vain-glorious men in like circumstances (*vv.* 5, 6). The behaviour of the "false apostles" who appeared at Corinth affords us an example of that which St Paul and his comrades avoided. See 2 Cor. xi. 20, 21, xii. 13—18.

We note the union of *gentleness* and *courage* (ver. 2) in the missionaries: a mark of the true hero, like Wordsworth's 'Happy Warrior,'—

"who though endued as with a sense
And faculty for storm and turbulence,
Is yet a soul whose master-bias leans
To homefelt pleasures and to gentle scenes."

(We were gentle in the midst of you) **as though a nurse were cherishing her own children.** The "nurse" is *mother* at the same time—a mother with the babe at her breast, the perfect image of fostering love. Comp. Christ's picture in Matt. xxiii. 37.

8. *so being affectionately desirous of you*] R.V., **even so.**

The rare and peculiar Greek verb (one word) rendered "being affectionately desirous" implies the *fondness* of a mother's love—**yearning over you.**

With this mother-like affection, he continues, **we were well pleased to impart unto you, not the gospel of God only, but also our own**

not the gospel of God only, but also our own souls, because ye were dear unto us. For ye remember, brethren, our

souls (R.V.). The apostles were not merely *willing* (A.V.) to bestow themselves on the Thessalonians, they actually *did so*, and with the glad consent of a mother nourishing the babe from her own life. The same verb is rendered "thought-good" in ch. iii. 1; and the corresponding noun is "good-pleasure" in 2 Ep. i. 11 (see note).

For "souls" we might read "lives" (*psyché* is never the soul in general, but the individual soul, the personality)—**our lives, our very selves**. The Apostle sacrificed all personal aims and private interests—"what things were gains to me"(Phil. iii. 7)—to the cause of the Gospel; his life was put in continual hazard in behalf of the Church; and for such people as the Macedonian Christians he did this with cordial satisfaction. "If I am made a libation over the sacrifice and service of your faith, I joy and rejoice with you all" (Phil. ii. 17). Even to the thankless Corinthians he says, "I will most gladly spend and be spent for your souls" (2 Cor. xii. 15). This is the true way to "impart the gospel of God," to give our own heart and soul with it. For it is to impart the Gospel in the spirit in which it came from God, "Who spared not His own Son, but gave Him up for us all" (Rom. viii. 32); and in the spirit of Christ, "Who gave Himself up for us" (Gal. i. 4; ii. 20), Who "poured out His soul unto death" (Isai. liii. 12).

because ye were dear unto us] More adequately, **ye became very dear** (R.V.); lit., **beloved**, the word so often applied to Christ (in the Gospels) by the Father: "My Beloved," "My Son, the Beloved" (comp. Eph. i. 6, "accepted in the Beloved"). This Church had won upon St Paul's affections in an especial degree. They were lovable people, dear to God and to the servants of God. Comp. ch. i. 3, 4; 2 Ep. ii. 13, 16; see also *Introd.* pp. 34, 35, and notes on *vv.* 19, 20.

9. *For ye remember, brethren, our labour and travail*] In ch. i. 3 (see note) the Apostle spoke with thankfulness of his readers' "labour of love;" this laborious spirit they had learnt from himself: comp. 2 Ep. iii. 8, 9, where it appears that to some of them his example was a reproof.

"Travail" is added to "labour," as in 2 Ep. iii. 8; 2 Cor. xi. 27 (the reference being in each case to *manual* labour), to indicate the *difficulty*, as labour the *toilsomeness* of the Apostle's work.

St Paul was a "tentmaker by trade" (Acts xviii. 3). Jewish fathers, even if wealthy, had their sons taught some mechanical craft as a remedy against poverty or idleness; and Paul had learnt in his youth at Tarsus the business of cutting out and stitching the coarse goats' hair cloth used in Cilicia for making tents. He found this skill in his wandering apostleship a great resource. An irksome kind of labour, to be sure, and but ill paid. It was a pathetic sight when the Apostle held up "these hands" to the Ephesian elders, hard and blackened with their rough task (Acts xx. 34). But he thus earned for himself the necessaries of subsistence, and avoided burdening the infant Churches with his maintenance. In this way he was free to direct his own move-

labour and travail: for labouring night and day, because *we* would not be chargeable unto any of you, we preached unto you the gospel of God. Ye *are* witnesses, and God *also*, 10 how holily and justly and unblameably we behaved our-

ments, and raised himself above mean suspicions. At the same time, he did not refuse occasional aid from a Church like the Philippian, in which he had full confidence, and whose affection would have been hurt by refusal. On this subject read 1 Cor. ix. 1—19; 2 Cor. xi. 7—12; Phil. iv. 10—20; Acts xx. 33—35. Silas and Timothy, who are included in this statement, may have had other means of support. But in Acts xx. 34 the Apostle speaks of "these hands" as "ministering" also "to the needs of those with me."

for labouring night and day] Omit "for," and read this clause in apposition with the last. **Ye remember...our labour and travail: working night and day...we preached**, &c. Busy in teaching and preaching during the daytime, the Apostle often pursued his tentmaking far into the night.

because we *would not be chargeable unto any of you*] St Paul puts it in a more delicate way than this: **that we might not lay a burden on any of you.** It was consideration for his Thessalonian flock, rather than regard to his personal independence, that influenced him. How different was he from the false shepherds who "eat the fat and clothe them with the wool, but feed not the flock" (Ezek. xxxiv. 3). Most of the Thessalonian Christians, doubtless, were poor; while at Philippi there was "Lydia, a seller of purple," and perhaps others of considerable means, who could afford to "send once and again to" Paul's "necessity" (Phil. iv. 15, 16). Yet Jason of Thessalonica, in whose house the apostles lodged, seems to have been a man of substance (Acts xvii. 5—9); and there were "of the first women" of the city "not a few" amongst Paul's adherents in this place.

Thus "making the gospel without expense," as later at Corinth (1 Cor. ix. 18),—*we preached unto you the gospel of God*] "Preached" is *proclaimed*, **heralded.** St Paul refers to the circumstances of his "entrance" (ver. 1) and the manner in which he and his companions then bore themselves. The Herald, or Town Crier, in ancient cities was commonly a salaried official.

A third time the Apostle writes "the gospel *of God*" (comp. *vv.* 2, 4, 8)—a phrase occurring only thrice in all the other Epistles. It suggests in ver. 2 the greatness of the charge entrusted to Paul; here, *the greatness of the boon gratuitously bestowed* on the Thessalonians.

10. *Ye* are *witnesses, and God* also] In ver. 5 the witness of man and of God (to the outward and inward respectively) were distinguished; here they are combined: **You are witnesses, and so is God.**

how holily and justly and unblameably we behaved ourselves among you that believe] R.V. more correctly, **toward you**: also **righteously** instead of *justly*. Concerning "you that believe," as a designation of Christians, see note to ch. i. 7.

For *holily* we might substitute **religiously.** The Greek adverb does

11 selves among you that believe: as you know how we exhorted and comforted and charged every one of you, as a
12 father *doth* his children, that ye would walk worthy of God,

not represent the ordinary N.T. word for "holy" (*hagios*, i.e. *saint*), but another adjective (*hosios*), which is frequent in the O.T. and in common Greek. The former denotes Holiness as a relationship to God; the latter, as a condition or disposition of the man: they differ as *consecrated* from *religious* or *pious*. For the combination of Holiness (in this latter sense) with Righteousness, see Eph. iv. 24; Tit. i. 8; also Luke i. 75; in the O.T., Deut. xxxii. 4; Ps. cxlv. 17 (applied to God), &c. The terms are not mutually exclusive, but may apply to the same acts and persons. The "holy" man has regard to the sanctities, the "righteous" man to the duties of life; but duty is sacred, and piety is duty. They cover the whole field of conduct, regarded in turn from the religious and moral standpoint, while "unblameably" affixes the seal of approval both by God and man.

Unblameably reappears in the "blameless" of ch. iii. 13 and v. 23.

11. *as you know how we exhorted and comforted and charged every one of you, as a father* doth *his children*] The R.V. recasts the verse, restoring the order and emphasis of the Apostle's words: **how we dealt with each one of you, as a father with his own children, exhorting you, and encouraging you, and testifying**, &c. "Dealt with" is not in the Greek, but English idiom requires some such verb to sustain the participles that follow. The writer intended to complete the sentence with some governing verb, but the intervening words carried his thoughts away. See the observations on St Paul's style in the *Introd*. Chap. VI.

The Apostle compared himself to *a nurse-mother* (ver. 7) in his tender, gentle affection; now he is *a father* in the fidelity and manly strength of his counsels. Comp. 1 Cor. iv. 14—21, where he gives a different turn to the figure.

"Exhorting" is the general term for animating address: comp. notes on ver. 3, and ch. iii. 2. "Encouraging" (as in ch. v. 14, John xi. 19, 31; rendered uniformly in A.V., "comforting") is the calming and consoling side of exhortation, as addressed to the afflicted or the weak. "Testifying" (same word as in Gal. v. 3; Eph. iv. 17; Acts xxvi. 22) supplies its solemn, warning element. The Thessalonian Church was both suffering and tempted, and the Apostle's ministry to them had been at once *consolatory* and *admonitory*. So are his two Epistles.

every one] Lit., **each single one**, as in 2 Ep. i. 3, indicates St Paul's discrimination and care for individuals. Comp. the "publicly, and from house to house" of Acts xx. 20.

12. *that ye would walk worthy of God*] Better, **in order that ye should**, and **worthily** (R.V.) "Walk" is the common Hebrew and O.T. figure for the conduct of life.

It was *God's* message the apostles of Christ had brought to the Thessalonians (*vv*. 2, 9); "unto *God*, the living and true," they had "turned from their idols to serve" Him (ch. i. 9). They must, therefore, now live a life "worthy *of God*"—worthy of those who have such a God and are

who hath called you unto his kingdom and glory. For this 13

His servants and sons. Nowhere, perhaps, does St Paul lay such continued emphasis on the relation of the Christian believer to God as in these Epistles: see *Introd.* pp. 17, 18.

To "walk worthily of God" is the noblest possible ideal of life; so high that it would appear visionary and impracticable, if it were not for what follows :—

(worthy of God) *who hath called you unto his kingdom and glory*] According to the truer reading, **who calleth**—for it is a call that continues till its purpose is accomplished (comp. ch. iv. 8, "God who giveth His Holy Spirit," R.V.); and **into His own kingdom**, &c.

Such is the confidence of "you that believe" (ver. 10); and this conviction gives the believer will and courage to aspire to the loftiest moral attainments: comp. ch. v. 24 (note). *God's* summons the Thessalonians had heard; His call could not be purposeless or powerless.

The announcement of *the Kingdom of God* was a leading feature of St Paul's preaching at Thessalonica; comp. 2 Ep. i. 5, and see *Introd.* pp. 18—21. It is also designated "the kingdom of the Son," Col. i. 13; "of Christ and God," Eph. v. 5; Rev. xi. 15; "of heaven," in St Matthew. This kingdom is sometimes spoken of as present, sometimes as future—a variation which marks the language of Christ equally with His Apostle. The expression comes in the first place from the Jewish Rabbis, being derived from the predictions of Dan. ii. 44, 45, vii. 13, 14; Mic. iv. 7; and these predictions again had their foundation in the great prophetic declarations respecting the throne and house of David (2 Sam. vii.; Ps. ii. and cx.). It was the popular designation for that perfect Divine rule which the Jews expected to see established on earth by the Messiah at His coming. It was called "the kingdom of heaven" (or "the heavens"), as having its seat and origin in heaven, and in contrast with the existing "kingdoms of this world and their glory," of which the Tempter said to Jesus, in harmony with Jewish ideas, "All this hath been delivered *unto me*" (Luke iv. 6). But God calls men "from the dominion of Satan" (Acts xxvi. 18) into "*His own* kingdom and glory." The difference is, fundamentally, not one of place or time; it is a moral opposition. John the Baptist, and then Christ, in similar terms announced the new kingdom to be "at hand;" in leaving the world Jesus declared that His "Father's kingdom" would be revealed on His return (Matt. xiii. 43, xxvi. 29, 64; Luke xix. 12, &c.). At the same time, He taught that the kingdom already existed in His Person and was constituted by His presence; that in its essence it was set up within His disciples, and therefore its future coming would be the manifestation and unfolding of what they already possessed in the spiritual life received from Him: see Luke xvii. 21; John xviii. 36, 37; Matt. v. 3, 10, xiii. 31—33, 38, &c. Christ's doctrine of the kingdom is virtually contained in the two petitions of the Lord's Prayer: "Thy kingdom come, Thy will be done, as in heaven so also upon earth." This implies that so far as God's will is done on earth, His kingdom is here already; earth being ruled from heaven and by heaven's law. But the

cause also thank we God without ceasing, because, when ye
more it makes its power felt on earth, the more necessary does its
heavenly glory become. St Paul sees the kingdom present and ruling
where there is "righteousness and peace and joy in the Holy Spirit"
(Rom. xiv. 17): but what is now possessed of it he regards as only the
"*earnest* of our inheritance" (Rom. viii. 23; Eph. i. 14); God "is" ever
"calling" His servants onward "to His own kingdom and glory."

The *glory* is God's glory—the splendour of His future revelation as
He will at last, on the return of Christ, be manifested to His saints.
In this glory they will share. "The kingdom and glory of God" are
one, the latter being the full display and consummation of the former.
And in the Apostle's view, "the hope of the glory of God" (Rom. v. 2)
is bound up with the "hope in our Lord Jesus Christ," which the
Thessalonians so earnestly cherished.

Obeying the voice of God that calls them to a place in His glorious
kingdom, St Paul's readers will know how to "walk worthily." This
summons is the ever-renewed incitement of a holy life, and inspires us
with the most exalted of those "mighty hopes which make us men."
So "we were saved by hope" (Rom. viii. 24).

This view of the religion of the Thessalonians agrees with what was
said of them in ch. i. 9, 10. "Walking worthily of God" corresponds
to "serving a living and true God;" and the "call to His kingdom and
glory" invites them to "wait for His Son from the heavens."

SECTION III.

JEWISH PERSECUTORS OF THE CHURCH. CH. II. 13—16.

This short paragraph is of peculiar interest. The Apostle was at the
time exposed in his Gentile mission to the bitterest persecution from
the unbelieving Jews, as we gather from the contemporary narrative
of Acts xvi.—xviii. And he employs against them in *vv.* 15, 16
language more severe than is found in any other of his writings.
Evidently he regarded the Jews as being now, in the counsels of
God, a doomed nation (ver. 16). Accordingly, we find him in Rom.
ix.—xi., a few years later, arguing upon the reprobation of "Israel
after the flesh" as a settled thing. We observe, too, his desire (ver. 14)
to draw the Jewish and Gentile sections of the Church nearer to each
other in sympathy under the stress of persecution. As to the bearing
of this passage on the date of the Epistle, see *Introd.* p. 23, *foot-note.*

Analysis: The Apostle (1) again *thanks God for the reception given
to the Gospel* by his readers, ver. 13; (2) he sees in their *union
with the Judean Churches in persecution* a proof of its efficacy in them,
ver. 14; and (3) this gives him occasion *to denounce Jewish violence*
against the Gospel, whose punishment is now decreed and impending,
vv. 15, 16.

13. *For this cause also thank we God without ceasing*] Revised
reading: **And for this cause we also,** &c. The Apostle has already
given thanks for the Christian worth of the Thessalonians (ch. i. 2 ff.);

received the word of God which *ye* heard of us, ye received *it* not as the word of men, but as it is in truth, the word of God, which effectually worketh also in you that believe.

his thanksgiving is renewed when he considers that this is *the fruit of his own and his companions' labour* amongst them. Hence **we** is emphasized here (in the Greek), but not in ch. i. 2.

"For this cause" looks back over the whole of the last section, *vv.* 1—12. Accordingly he continues :—

because, when ye received the word of God, which ye *heard of us*] Better, (we give thanks) **that** (R.V.), or **in that** : comp. notes on ch. i. 5 and 2 Ep. i. 3. The recollections of the last paragraph prompt the writer to the thanksgiving which takes shape in the words that follow :—

For *ye received the word of God*, &c., R.V. renders : *ye received from us the word of the message* (Greek, *word of hearing*), even the word *of God*. Perhaps the A.V. is nearer to St Paul's meaning: "from us" in the original immediately follows "hearing," and appears to be dependent upon it. We therefore translate, somewhat freely, but after the order of the Greek : **when you received the word you heard from us— God's word.** "Word" is not repeated by the Apostle, nor has it the definite article; English idiom requires both. His joy is that a message heard from his lips, not his own indeed but God's word (see *vv.* 2, 8, 9, and note on the last), had been thus received. For the connection of "hearing" and "from us" comp. 2 Tim. i. 13, ii. 2, "what thou hast *heard from me*"; and 2 Cor. i. 19, "the Son of God proclaimed through me and Silas and Timothy." "Faith comes by hearing"; and hearing requires "a preacher" (Rom. x. 13—17).

ye received it *not as the word of men, but as it is in truth, the word of God*] R.V., **accepted** for *received:* the Greek verb differs from that of the last clause, which might signify the mere outward reception of something "heard"; this term, as in ch. i. 6, denotes a willing, hearty acceptance—a *welcome* given to the "word." It is the expression used in Gal. iv. 14:—"as an angel of God you *received* me"; again in Phil. iv. 18, where Paul speaks of his *welcoming* the timely gift from Philippi; and is the common Greek term for receiving a guest.

Literally the clause reads, **you accepted not men's word, but, as it is truly, God's word.** "*Men's* word" —the mere word of "Paul and Silas and Timothy." The Thessalonians accepted God's word *as God's*, with reverence and faith. They recognised in what they heard from Paul and Silas a higher Voice, the message of the living and true God, calling them to life eternal. The success of religious teaching lies in its power to make God's voice audible through human speech. If the preacher cannot do this, he does nothing. And this accounts for the result, which St Paul next describes :—

which effectually worketh also in you that believe] **which also worketh** (R.V.: read *worketh* with an emphasis), or **is operative, effectual.**

The "work of faith" which the Apostle admired in the Thessalonian Church (ch. i. 3: see note) is the work of God's word in them.

14 For ye, brethren, became followers of the churches of God which in Judea are in Christ Jesus: for ye also have suffered like *things* of your own countrymen, even as they *have* of

In their lives that word takes effect; it puts forth its energy, and does its proper work. "The seed" of all such fruit "is the word of God" (Luke viii. 11).

On "you that believe" see note to ch. i. 7. Here the present tense of the participle makes its force sensible—"you that do believe;" continued faith being the condition of this sustained efficacy of the word of God in the Thessalonians. Mighty as it is, that word can do nothing for us unless we *believe* it (comp. Matt. xiii. 58).

14. *For ye, brethren, became followers of the churches of God which in Judæa are in Christ Jesus*] *Followers* should be **imitators** (R.V.), just as in ch. i. 6: imitators of the apostles and of their Lord, the Thessalonians were imitating the Judæan Churches, and in the same respect, viz. in the willing endurance of suffering for the word's sake. Silas, be it remembered, had been an active member of the Church at Jerusalem (Acts xv. 22, 32), and through him especially the missionary band would be in communication and sympathy at this time with their brethren in Judæa.

More strictly, **which are in Judæa in Christ Jesus** (R.V.). "In Judæa" is the local, "in Christ Jesus" the spiritual *habitat* of these Churches. This latter phrase—an expression characteristic of St Paul and frequent in subsequent Epistles—signifies "in union and communion with Him, incorporated with Him who is the Head" of His Body the Church (Ellicott). It distinguishes the Christian from other Judæan communities which also claimed to be "Churches (assemblies) of God." Comp. note on "Church...in God the Father," &c., ch. i. 1.

Observe the order *Christ Jesus*, a combination almost confined to St Paul, and which he employs when he thinks of Him in His actual Person and official character, as the present Head and Life of His people on earth; whereas *Jesus Christ* is the historical order, and points to His earthly course and exaltation to Messiahship (see Acts ii. 36).

"Church of God" is an O.T. expression, found in the Greek rendering of Neh. xiii. 1; Deut. xxiii. 1—3 (church of the LORD: *congregation*, A.V.); it denotes that the Church *belongs to God*, while it suggests, according to the derivation of *ek-klesia*, that its members are *called out* (of the world) *by God* (comp. ver. 12). In Gal. i. 22 the Apostle writes, more simply, "the Churches of Judæa which are in Christ."

This reference to the Home Churches creates a link between far-off Thessalonica and Judæa. The Thessalonians are not alone in their troubles; they are fighting the same battle as the mother Church and the first disciples of the Lord. Comp. Ph. i. 30, "having the same conflict which ye saw in me." Their union with Christ's persecuted flock in its native land shewed that the Gospel was working in them to purpose (ver. 13), and working everywhere in the same way.

for ye also have suffered like things *of your own countrymen, even*

the Jews: who both killed the Lord Jesus, and their own 15
prophets, and have persecuted us; and they please not God,

as they have *of the Jews*] St Paul says **the same**, not *like things*. And this "for" represents a different word from the previous "for;" it is rather **in that**, not accounting for the Thessalonians imitating Judean example, but explaining wherein the imitation consisted.

The hostility of their fellow-townsmen formed a bitter ingredient in their afflictions (Acts xvii. 5—9). The Apostle tells them that it was the same with the primitive Churches in Judæa—that, indeed, the murder of the Lord Jesus and of the old prophets, and the expulsion of the apostles, were due to feelings precisely similar to those aroused in their own city against themselves. This was a proof that they were in the true succession. Christ had said, "A man's foes shall be they of his own household." Such comfort has often to be given to young missionary churches.

But the Apostle has now to add words of awful severity respecting those whom his readers knew to be the prime instigators of persecution, both against themselves and him—*the Jews:*—

15. *who both killed the Lord Jesus, and their own prophets*] Revised reading, simply **the prophets.**

Christ represented His death as the culmination of the murders of the ancient prophets (Luke xi. 47—52; xiii. 31—33; xx. 9—16); St Stephen had said the same thing in Paul's hearing, with poignant force (Acts vii. 52). Now the Apostle takes up the accusation.

More exactly, **killed the Lord,** (even) **Jesus**; or, changing the grammatical form but retaining the order of the Greek words, **The Lord they slew, Jesus,—as well as the prophets.** This sets the deed in an appalling light. To have killed *the Lord*—Who bears a title that belongs to God, and "Him whom they were bound to serve" (Jowett); (comp. 1 Cor. ii. 8: They "crucified the Lord of glory"); that Lord being *Jesus* their Saviour (comp. Acts iv. 12), and such an one as Jesus was known to be! The double name, emphasized in each part, brings into striking relief at once the Divine authority and the human character of Christ. Comp. Acts ii. 36 ("Him did God make both Lord and Christ—this Jesus whom you crucified!"); also the parable of Luke xx. 9—18, Mark xii. 1—11, "The husbandmen said, This is the heir; come, let us kill him!"

and have persecuted us] Better, **and drave us out** (R.V.), words which echo those of Christ in Luke xi. 49: "I will send them prophets and apostles; and some of them they will kill and persecute." Already Christ, like the prophets, had been killed; and now His apostles were driven out, "fleeing from city to city" (Matt. xxiii. 34) to avoid the like fate. Read the account of Paul's departure from Jerusalem in Acts ix. 28—30; and his later experience there, Acts xxi.—xxiii.; also the narrative of James' death and Peter's escape from Herod's prison, in Acts xii. 1—9. Paul and Silas had now been hunted all the way from Philippi to Corinth by Jewish malignity, and it was only the authority and good sense of the Roman Governor,

16 and are contrary to all men: forbidding us to speak to the

Gallio, that made it possible for him to remain in the latter city. Comp. 2 Cor. xi. 26: "In perils from mine own countrymen."

and they please not God] Omit *they*, and put a comma only before this clause, for it is immediately continuous with the last: more exactly, **and are not pleasing to God.** This is an instance of what the grammarians call *meiosis* or *litotes*, the studiously restrained and smooth expression covering intense feeling; as where the Apostle says, "I praise you not," meaning severe blame (1 Cor. xi. 17, 22). Their unpleasingness to God was due not to these wicked acts alone, but to their whole conduct. Comp., in the O.T., such sayings as Isai. lxv. 5: "These are a smoke in My nostrils;" and Jer. xxxii. 30. By contrast, the Apostle spoke of himself as "not pleasing men, but God" (ver. 4).

and are contrary to all men] At war both with God and men! The sense of God's displeasure often shews itself in sourness and ill-temper towards one's fellows. Unbelief and cynicism go together. The rancour of the Jews against other nations at this time was notorious. Tacitus, the Roman historian, writing in the next generation, remarks on their "*adversus omnes alios hostile odium*" (*Histor.* v. 5). This animosity culminated in the war against Rome (A.D. 66—70), and brought a fearful retribution.

The quarrel between Judaism and the world, alas, still continues, as the *Judenhasse* of Germany and Russia testifies. Jewish hatred has been more than repaid by Christian persecution. The antipathy is powerfully impersonated in Shakespeare's *Shylock*. The Jew says of his debtor, "I hate him, for he is a Christian." And Antonio in turn:

"You may as well use question with the wolf,
Why he hath made the ewe bleat for the lamb;
You may as well do anything most hard,
As seek to soften that (than which what's harder?)
His Jewish heart."

But we may hope that better feelings will prevail in the future on both sides. St Paul is thinking, however, not of the Jewish sentiment in general, but of the opposition of his people to the rest of the world on that one point which concerned him so deeply, viz. *the salvation of men through Christ*.

16. *forbidding us to speak to the Gentiles that they might be saved*] R.V., **may be saved.** As much as to say: "These Jews, if they had their way, would prevent us speaking a single word to you about the Gospel; they would willingly see all the Gentiles perish!" This stamped them as enemies of the human race. They were furious to think that unclean Gentiles claimed a share in their Messiah! Their murderous hatred against Paul was due to the fact that he preached Christ to the heathen and declared God to be the God of Jews and Gentiles equally, saving both alike through faith in Christ. So when in his defence before the Jewish multitude at the Temple he came to the words, "Depart, for I will send thee far hence *unto the Gentiles*," they broke out in uncontrollable rage, "Away with such a fellow from the

Gentiles that they might be saved, to fill up their sins alway: for the wrath is come upon them to the uttermost.

earth, for it is not fit that he should live!" (Acts xxii. 21—23). The Jews of Thessalonica seem to have been especially mean and fanatical (Acts xvii. 5, 11, 13); and the Apostle wishes his readers to see how entirely he is on their side as against his fellow-countrymen.

to fill up their sins alway] After the death of Christ a space for repentance was allowed them, the "forty years" alluded to in Heb. iii. 9, 17. Had they accepted Christ's message of reconciliation through the apostles and become His witnesses to the Gentiles, the judgement would have been averted (Acts iii. 19). The measure allowed to the nation's sins was not yet full; but this last refusal made their cup overflow—slowly filling, as it had been, for many ages. "Fill ye up then the measure of your fathers," Jesus had said to them (Matt. xxiii. 32); and this they had done, beyond all question. The phrase *fill up their sins*, signifying ripeness for judgement, is used in Gen. xv. 16 of the Amorites in Abraham's time—an ominous parallel. "Alway:" comp. Stephen's reproach, "As did your fathers, so do ye" (Acts vii. 51).

for the wrath is come upon them to the uttermost] **but the wrath** (R.V.), not *for*; as though he said, "But the end comes at last: they have always been sowing this harvest; now it has to be reaped." *Whose* wrath this is, goes without saying; so in Rom. v. 9 God's anger is called with impressive emphasis "*the* wrath." It is indeed "the wrath" of ch. i. 10 (see note): there regarded in its final and general manifestation to the world, here in its imminent relation to the people of Israel. There it is "coming;" here it "is come," or **has arrived.**

These words are prophetical; but the announcement goes beyond prediction. The Jews as a people had decisively refused the gospel of Jesus Christ, and their fate was sealed. The nation was moving swiftly and visibly down the inclined plane to ruin. And this calamity was to be *final*. "To the uttermost," says the Apostle; lit., **unto an end.** In former threatenings the Lord had said, "Yet will I not make a full end" (Jer. iv. 27, and often). He does make *a full end* this time— an end of the Old Covenant and of national Israel as the elect people; still it is not "*the* end," as though God had no further dealings with ancient Israel: see on the contrary Rom. xi.

In the year 70 of our Lord Jerusalem fell, after the most dreadful and calamitous siege known in history; and the Jewish people ever since have wandered without a home and without an altar. *Tristis exitus,* says Bengel: *urgebat miseros ira Dei, et* εἰς τέλος (*tandem,* at length) *urbem cum templo delevit.*

SECTION IV.

St Paul's Present Relations to the Thessalonians.

Ch. II. 17—III. 13.

The Apostle had been drawn aside in the last paragraph, by a sudden and characteristic burst of feeling, from the main purpose of his letter.

17 But we, brethren, being taken from you for a short time in presence, not in heart, endeavoured the more abundantly

To this he now returns. Ver. 17 might follow quite naturally upon ver. 12. Having recalled to his readers the circumstances of his arrival at Thessalonica and the manner of his life amongst them, he goes on to speak of the feelings and views which he now entertains in regard to them. And he continues in this vein to the end of ch. iii. He speaks (1) of his *great desire to revisit them* and the attempts he has made to do so, *vv.* 17—20; (2) he relates how *he sent Timothy* with messages and enquiries when he found this impossible, ch. iii. 1—5; (3) he expresses *his satisfaction at the report* Timothy has brought back to him, *vv.* 6—8; and (4) he *repeats his thanksgiving* and his longing to see them, *with prayers* both on this account and for their final acceptance in the day of Christ, *vv.* 9—13.

We may suppose that St Paul's enemies, while they set down the preaching of the missionaries in the first instance to base motives (see note to ver. 3), went on to insinuate that the Apostle's continued absence showed his unconcern for his persecuted followers. (Comp. *Introd.* pp. 23, 24.) Hence the warmth and energy of his protestations.

17. *But we, brethren, being taken from you*] **bereaved of you** (R.V.), or **torn away from you**; lit., *orphaned*—a word employed in Greek with some latitude—the very strongest expression the Apostle could find, occurring only here in the N.T.

for a short time] Lit., **season of an hour**,—as we say, "an hour's time." St Paul expected, when he left Thessalonica, to be able to return very shortly. Meanwhile the apostles felt themselves to be parted from their friends "in presence (or person)—not in heart." The comfort of their parting was the hope of speedy reunion:

"Parting is such sweet sorrow,
That I shall say Good-night, till it be morrow."

We find from Acts xvii. 10 that it was "the" Thessalonian "brethren" who "sent away Paul and Silas by night unto Beroea," in order to secure their safety. Unwilling to go, the apostles were eager to return:—

we...endeavoured the more abundantly] *exceedingly* (R.V.): **we were the more earnest in our endeavours** (because our hearts were so truly one) **to see your face, with great desire.**

"Face" is identical in Greek with the "presence" of the former clause: they were parted in sight, not in affection; but true affection longs for sight. This "great desire" excited and sustained the apostles' endeavours. "We longed for the sight of your dear faces, and did our utmost to get back to you:" so in ch. iii. 10, "Night and day praying exceedingly that we may *see your face.*" Such, too, was the love of St John to his friends: "But I hope speedily to see thee; and we will talk mouth to mouth" (2 John 12; 3 John 14). "The spiritual interest of the Apostle about his converts is never for a moment separate from his tender human love for them" (Jowett).

to see your face with great desire. Wherefore we would 18 have come unto you, even I Paul, once and again; but Satan hindered us.   For what *is* our hope, or joy, or crown 19

18. *Wherefore we would have come unto you*] The true reading is **because**—not "wherefore," due probably to a misunderstanding of the following verb, which is not removed by the rendering of the R.V., "because we *would fain* have come." This but repeats the "great desire" just expressed ; whereas the Greek verb implies *resolution* rather than inclination. The Apostle, as we understand him, is giving the explanation of his strenuous endeavours (ver. 17), lying behind them in his *determined will*—**because we had resolved to come to you**: "we had set our minds upon it."

even I Paul] Better, **I Paul, for my part.** He speaks for himself: Timothy did return after a time (ch. iii. 1, 2); and Silas had been left behind in Macedonia (Acts xvii. 14; xviii. 5). Paul had not come at all; but it was not for want of will.

And the Apostle had made up his mind to this more than once—**both once and twice.** Silas had, no doubt, shared in the wish and endeavour to return *from Berœa;* the second attempt, likewise frustrated, was made by the Apostle alone, *from Athens* (ch. iii. 1). The expression recurs in Ph. iv. 16. Compare with the whole statement Rom. i. 13: "Many times I purposed to come to you, and have been hindered hitherto." The Apostle's prophetic gift did not save him from the discipline of disappointment.

but Satan hindered us] Properly, **and Satan, &c.**: "but" would be the regular conjunction here; there is a slight dislocation of structure in the sentence, due to excited feeling. We may paraphrase the sentence thus: **We strove eagerly to find means of coming to see you; indeed, for my part, I had made up my mind to do it more than once; and our way was blocked, by Satan!** What form the hindrance took we can only guess. Jewish malice doubtless had much to do with it. But behind this baffling and unforeseen combination of circumstances the Apostle discerned the craft of the Arch-enemy.

Satan] i.e. "the Adversary," is the O.T. name of the Leader of evil spirits, the great enemy of God and man—called also "the Devil" (Slanderer), "the Evil One" (2 Ep. iii. 3), and "the Tempter" (ch. iii. 5). Satan is, throughout the New Testament, a real personality, and no figure of speech. See note on 2 Ep. ii. 9; and comp. Rev. xii. 9.

To account for his intense longing to see the Thessalonians, St Paul describes his interest in them in the glowing terms that follow:—

19. *For what* is *our hope, or joy, or crown of rejoicing?*] Not *rejoicing,* but **glorying** (R.V.), or **boasting.** "Crown of glorying" is a Hebrew idiom (Isai. lxii. 3; Prov. xvi. 31, &c.); it is the crown which expresses one's exultation,—not the king's "diadem" (as in Rev. xix. 12), but the wreath of the victor in the games (1 Cor. ix. 24, 25). So he calls the Philippians his "joy and crown—a boast to me in the day of Christ, that I have not run in vain" (Ph. ii. 16, iv. 1). And here: "Who will furnish our crown at Christ's coming—who, indeed, but *you?*"

of rejoicing? *Are* not even ye in the presence of our Lord
20 Jesus Christ at his coming? For ye are our glory and joy.

Are not even ye] This clause is best read, with Westcott and Hort, as a rhetorical parenthesis—**are not even ye?**—then the main question is resumed and completed: "before our Lord Jesus at His coming?"

It is *then* that the Apostle will wear the crown which the Thessalonians furnish for him. His wealth is in hope. He loves them for what they are, but still more for what they will be in the "unveiling of the sons of God" (Rom. viii. 19),—"set faultless before the presence of His glory with exceeding joy" (Jude 24). Then how *proud* (in the just sense of that word) will their Apostle be of them! See the prayers of ch. iii. 13 and v. 23, 24; also Col. i. 28, 29, where the goal of Paul's labours is that he "may present every man perfect in Christ."

our Lord Jesus Christ] should be **our Lord Jesus** (R.V.). On a point like this we should always consult a critical text, such as that of the Revisers. Copyists were peculiarly liable to error in the names of Christ.

Observe the return in glory, and as Judge, of the same *Lord Jesus* Whom the Jews wickedly killed, ver. 15: "I saw in the midst of the throne...a Lamb, as though it had been slain," Rev. v. 6. He had said to His judges: "Ye shall see the Son of Man sitting at the right hand of power and coming in the clouds of heaven" (Matt. xxvi. 64). This title identifies the Divine Judge and Conqueror over sin and death with the historical and human Jesus (comp. John v. 27; Acts xvii. 31). The combination *Lord Jesus* is more frequent in these Epistles than anywhere else in the N.T., a circumstance due to their prevailing reference to the Second Coming. For further notes on the title see ch. i. 10 and 2 Ep. i. 7.

his coming] Lit., *presence*—Greek, **parousia**—i.e. "presence" in its active sense (different from the "presence," or "face," of ver. 17 and 2 Ep. ii. 9)—**His arrival.**

Here is the earliest example of a word, *parousia*, that has passed into the language of theology, denoting the promised Advent of Christ in glory, when He will come to complete His work of redemption and to judge mankind. His own teaching on the subject is recorded in Matt. xxiv., xxv.; Mark xiii.; Luke xii. 35—59; xvii. 20—37; xix. 11—27; xxi. 5—36; John v. 27—29; xiv. 1—3; xvi. 22, &c. Seven times the Apostle uses this solemn word in these two letters—once besides, in 1 Cor. xv. 23. From the three writings we learn nearly all that he has to teach on this mysterious subject. The *parousia* is spoken of by Christ, in answer to His disciples, in Matt. xxiv.; and is referred to also in the Epistles of James, Peter, and John.

20. *For ye are our glory and joy*] Or: **Yea, verily, you are our glory and joy** (Ellicott). Emphasis rests both on "ye" and "are." This delight was not matter of hope alone (ver. 19), but of present *fact.* See ch. i. 2—4, and iii. 9: "The joy wherewith we rejoice on your account before our God"; and 2 Ep. i. 4: "We glory in you in the Churches of God." *Glory* is praise and honour from others; *joy* is one's own delight.

Wherefore when we could no longer forbear, we thought 3
it good to be left at Athens alone; and sent Timotheus, 2

CHAPTER III.

The division of chapters at this point is unfortunate. The import of
ver. 1 lies in its connection with *vv.* 17—20 of ch. ii. We have included
the whole of this chapter in the same section of the Epistle with the
foregoing paragraph. See note introductory to ch. ii. 17.

1. *Wherefore when we could no longer forbear*] **Wherefore** (i.e.
because of our longing to see you) **no longer bearing it** (the frustration
of our attempts to return to Thessalonica). "Bear" is the same word
as in 1 Cor. xiii. 7: "Love beareth all things"—*bears up under, holds
out against.* "This protracted separation and repeated disappointment
was more than we could endure."

to be left at Athens alone] **left behind...alone** (R. V.).

2. *and sent Timotheus*] **Timothy**: see note on this name, ch. i. 1.
The Acts of the Apostles traces St Paul's footsteps from Thessalonica
to Berœa, and on from Berœa to Athens: read Acts xvii. 10—16; and
consult the *map* in regard to the route. But its account of the move-
ments of his companions appears at first sight inconsistent with what
we read here. For in Acts xvii. 14—16 we find Silas and Timothy both
left behind at Berœa, while Paul goes on to Athens, instructing them to
follow and rejoin him there as soon as possible. "Paul waited for them
at Athens;" but they do not seem to have arrived. The two comrades
of the Apostle are not mentioned by St Luke again until he tells us
of their *return together from Macedonia, when they find him at Corinth*
(Acts xviii. 1—5). St Paul interpolates between the time of his leaving
the two at Berœa and of their return in company from Macedonia
reported by Luke a distinct mission *of Timothy by himself to Thessalonica*. There is, after all, no conflict between the Apostle and his
historian and friend. He relates an incident which St Luke in his
general and cursory narrative passed over, either as unimportant for his
purpose, or because he was unaware of it. Since we have good reason to
believe in the accuracy of both, we must adjust their statements to each
other. This may be done in two ways: it is possible that Paul on
arriving at Athens and finding that he could not return to Thessalonica
from that city, sent directions to Timothy to go back in his place to the
Macedonian capital, *instead of coming on to Athens*, while Silas still
remained in Macedonia; and that, after Timothy had made this visit,
they both rejoined their leader at Corinth. Or it may be—and this
agrees better with the words "left behind"—that Timothy *did come to
Athens from Berœa*, and was immediately despatched again to Thessalonica, so that the Apostle was practically alone from the time he
left Berœa until Silas and Timothy rejoined him at Corinth.

The "we" of *vv.* 1, 2, 6 appears to refer to the Apostle himself;
comp. 2 Cor. x. and xiii. for the interchange of "I" and "we" in St
Paul's manner of referring to himself. He may write *we* representa-
tively, where others are joined with him in sympathy, though not in

our brother, and minister of God, and our fellowlabourer in the gospel of Christ, to establish you, and to comfort you 3 concerning your faith: that no *man* should be moved by

act. If Silas was now with Paul at Athens, he also must shortly have returned to Macedonia (see Acts xviii. 5); but the words "left *alone*" would seem in that case to be pointless. It was a trial to St Paul at this time to be "left alone." But his anxiety about the Thessalonians compels him, notwithstanding, to send his young helper to them.

our brother, and minister of God, and our fellowlabourer in the gospel of Christ] This description of Timothy is given in varying forms by the ancient MSS. The Revisers prefer to read, **our brother and God's minister**, &c.; but they say in the margin, "Some ancient authorities read *fellow-worker with God*." Possibly this is what the Apostle wrote: **our brother and a fellow-worker with God**. The other variations can best be explained by it; and copyists would scarcely have substituted by this bold expression the easy phrase "minister of God," which occurs in other Epistles, had the latter been the original reading. "God's fellow-worker" expresses a thoroughly Pauline idea (see 1 Cor. iii. 9; 2 Cor. vi. 1), and would serve to exalt Timothy in the eyes of the Church. It agrees with what the Apostle says of him in 1 Cor. xvi. 10: "Timothy worketh the work of the Lord, as I also do; let no one therefore despise him." The Received Text, as in many other instances, results from the combination of two earlier and briefer readings of the passage. Codex B, the best of the Greek MSS, reads simply, **our brother and fellow-worker in the gospel of Christ**.

to establish you, and to comfort you concerning your faith] Establish is **stablish** in ver. 13 and elsewhere; the same word is rendered "*strengthen* thy brethren" in Luke xxii. 32, also Rev. iii. 2; it signifies to *make stable, fix firmly*.

For *comfort* **exhort** or **encourage** is a preferable rendering. St Paul employed another and quite different verb for "comfort," in express distinction from that here used, in ch. ii. 11 (see note). The Greek verb has a wide range of meaning; but all its uses in these two Epp. may be brought, with that of the cognate noun, under the ideas of *appeal* (ch. ii. 3, 11, iv. 1, 10, v. 11, 14; 2 Ep. iii. 12), or *encouragement* (ch. iii. 2, 7; 2 Ep. ii. 16, 17). This latter was indeed an older sense of *comfort* in English (Latin *confortare*).

The Apostle sends Timothy to do what he wished to do himself, and continues to do by this letter—what, above all, he prays God to do for them; see ver. 13, 2 Ep. ii. 16, 17: "May He encourage your hearts, and stablish you." (Comp. *Introd.* p. 35.) They were afflicted, and needed "encouragement;" they were new to the Christian life, and needed "establishment."

Concerning is, more strictly, **on behalf of (in furtherance of) your faith**. In ch. i. 3 *faith, love,* and *hope;* in ver. 6 *faith* and *love ;* here *faith* alone stands for the whole religion of a Christian.

3. *that no* man *should be moved by these afflictions*] Better, **that no man be moved** (R.V.). "Objective sentence, explaining and specifying

these afflictions: for yourselves know that we are appointed
thereunto. For verily, when we were with you, we told you 4
before that we should suffer tribulation; even as it came to

the subject-matter of the exhortation" (Ellicott). "That" means "to
the effect that."

With "moved" comp. the fuller expression of 2 Ep. ii. 2, "Shaken
in mind or troubled"; also Col. i. 23, "moved away from the hope of
the gospel." But the Greek verb here used seems to imply "moved to
softness" (Jowett).

Not *by*, but literally **in**, or **amid these afflictions**; for these were not
so much the *cause by which* faith was likely to be shaken, as the *circumstances amid which* it was assailed and which lent force to every temptation. "Amid these afflictions" the reasonings of unbelief and the
enticements of idolatry and sin would have redoubled force. It was
Timothy's business to shew that such trials ought not to disturb, but
rather to confirm their faith.

for yourselves know that we are appointed thereunto] The R.V. gives
the verb its proper emphasis: **hereunto we are appointed**.

St Paul delicately associates himself with his persecuted friends,
passing from "you" of the last sentence to "we;" comp. the transition
in ch. v. 4, 5. Indeed "these afflictions" were directed in the first
instance against *the apostles* (see ch. ii. 2, 14, 15; iii. 7, &c.), and came
on the Thessalonians through association with them.

Appointed is identical with "*set* for defence of the gospel" (Phil. i.
16) and "*set* upon a hill" (Matt. v. 14), indicating the situation in
which one is placed. This was their *appointed post* and *station*. And
they well "knew" that such was their "calling of God:" "the fiery
trial" was no "strange thing" (comp. 1 Pet. ii. 20, 21; iv. 12).

4. *For verily, when we were with you, we told you before*] More
precisely, **used to tell you**; this was no single warning, but one repeated and familiar. For other references to the apostles' previous instruction, see ch. ii. 11, 12; iv. 1, 2; 2 Ep. ii. 5, 15; iii. 10.

that we should suffer tribulation] So rendered again in 2 Ep. i. 4, 6,
and elsewhere in the A.V.; but the word is the same as that used in
vv. 3, 7, and ch. i. 6—**affliction** (R.V.). The A.V. too often breaks
the connection of the sacred writer's thought by needless variations of
this sort.

should is made clearer by the Revised **are to suffer**: this was matter
of certainty in the future, being Divinely appointed (ver. 3),—a thing
one might count upon. And so the event proved: *even as it came to
pass, and ye know*.

All this is recalled to the minds of the readers and dwelt on with
iteration, not to justify the Apostle's foresight—for it needed no gift
of prophecy to anticipate persecution at Thessalonica—but to make
them realise how well they had been prepared for what they are now
experiencing, and so far to reconcile them to it; comp. John xiv. 29;
1 Pet. iv. 12, "Beloved, count it not strange." Dr Jowett gives an admirable analysis of the causes of persecution in the Apostolic times in his

5 pass, and ye know. For this cause, when I could no longer forbear, I sent to know your faith, lest by some means the

notes upon this Chapter (*The Epp. of St Paul to the Thessalonians*, &c., pp. 70—73, 2nd edition), from which we extract the following sentences:—"The fanatic priest, led on by every personal and religious motive; the man of the world, caring for none of these things, but not the less resenting the intrusion on the peace of his home; the craftsman, fearing for his gains; the accursed multitude, knowing not the law, but irritated at the very notion of this mysterious society of such real, though hidden strength, would all work together towards the overthrow of those who seemed to them to be turning upside down the political, religious, and social order of the world......The actual persecution of the Roman government was slight, but what may be termed social persecution and the illegal violence employed towards the first disciples unceasing."

5. *For this cause, when I could no longer forbear, I sent to know your faith*] Rather, **I also, no longer enduring it, sent**, &c. St Paul repeats what he said in ver. 1, but in a different manner, there stating the facts themselves, here indicating his own share in the trouble of his readers: "You were in affliction, and your faith endangered; and I too felt for you an unendurable anxiety." He has just spoken of Timothy as sent to comfort *them*, but he was sent at the same time to comfort *him* (the Apostle), to relieve his distressing fears about them (see *vv.* 5*b* and 6). His own troubles and despondency at Corinth helped to make him apprehensive for the Thessalonian Church (see ver. 7, and comp. Acts xviii. 5, 9, 10 and 1 Cor. ii. 3).

The Greek verb for "know" in this clause is different from that employed in the last; it means *to ascertain, get to know*—**that I might ascertain your faith**—"might learn its condition, and know whether or not you were still standing fast in the Lord."

lest by some means the tempter have tempted you] "Have" is here the English subjunctive perfect, modern "should have"; but the Greek verb is indicative, and implies a positive expectation: *lest by any means the tempter had tempted you* (R.V.)—a fact of which there was little doubt; the apprehension is revealed in the next clause (Greek subjunctive),—*and our labour should prove in vain*. This was the dark thought which crossed the Apostle's mind, that he could "no longer bear."

This "labour" (or "toil," same word as in ch. i. 3, see note, and ch. ii. 9) is that which St Paul described pathetically in ch. ii. 1—12, beginning with the "entrance" that certainly "was not vain." To think that all this labour might be lost, and a success at first so glorious end in blank failure!—The sentence might be rendered quite as grammatically, and more vividly, in the *interrogative*, expressing the apprehension as it actually arose in the Apostle's mind : **I sent that I might know about your faith: had the Tempter haply tempted you, and would our labour prove in vain?**

"The Tempter" is so styled once besides, in the account of Christ's

tempter have tempted you, and our labour be in vain. But now when Timotheus came from you unto us, and brought us good tidings of your faith and charity, and that ye have good remembrance of us always, desiring greatly to see us,

Temptation, Matt. iv. 3. Comp. note on *Satan*, ch. ii. 18. While "hindering" Paul from coming to their help, Satan would be "tempting" the Thessalonians to forsake their faith. This fear wrung the Apostle's heart.

In passing from ver. 5 to 6 there is a striking change from painful suspense to relief and joy—

6. *But now when Timotheus came from you unto us*] **But when Timothy came even now unto us from you** (R.V.): this rendering puts due emphasis on the words "from you" (it was Timothy's coming with news *from Thessalonica* that relieved the Apostle's mind); and it gives the proper meaning and connection to the introductory "now," which qualifies "came" and denotes *just now, at this juncture.* Timothy's return has been anxiously awaited; and no sooner has he arrived and told his story, than Paul sits down and writes out of a full heart this affectionate and grateful letter. For Timothy **brought us glad tidings of your faith and love** (R.V.).

"Brought-glad-tidings" forms a single word in the Greek, the same that everywhere else in the N.T. signifies "*the* glad tidings"—the news of God's salvation and of the coming of His kingdom. Hence the peculiar force of the word here. This was *gospel* news, witnessing to the truth and enduring power of God's message; for this reason it was glad tidings to the Apostle from the Thessalonians ("now we *live*," ver. 7)—a gospel sent to *him* in return for his gospel brought to them (ch. i. 5; ii. 2, &c.).

of your faith and charity] for these comprise the whole Christian life, and imply the "hope in our Lord Jesus Christ" added to them in ch. i. 3; comp. 2 Ep. i. 3; Eph. i. 15; Philem. 5—7; 1 John iii. 23: "that we should believe in the name of His Son Jesus Christ, and love one another." This is the sum of our religion. Read, **faith and love** (R.V.).

and that ye have good remembrance of us always] So that the Thessalonians reciprocate Paul's feelings towards them; he "remembers" them "without ceasing" (ch. i. 3), they equally remember him. *Good* is *kindly, well-disposed remembrance;* their sufferings and the slanders of his enemies might have alienated their minds from the missionaries, but it was otherwise.

"Remembrance" represents the same Greek noun as "mention" in ch. i. 2; following *make* it has a more active, following *have* a passive signification.

desiring greatly] R.V., in one word, **longing**,—which renders fitly a delicate Greek verb, rare except in St Paul, that denotes yearning regret for an absent beloved object (comp. ch. ii. 17, "*bereaved* of you"). He uses it in 2 Cor. v. 2 to express his desire for the new, spiritual body, "the house from heaven." **Longing to see us, even as we also to see**

7 as we also *to see* you: therefore, brethren, we were comforted
8 over you in all our affliction and distress, by your faith: for

you. The expression recurs in Rom. i. 11 and 2 Tim. i. 4. For the Apostle's "longing," see ch. ii. 17, 18.

7. *therefore, brethren, we were comforted over you*] for this cause (R.V.), the Greek phrase being identical with that of ver. 5. But while its reference there was to the *peril* of the tempted Thessalonians causing the Apostle intense anxiety, here it is to their *loyalty and affection* bringing him a corresponding joy. For a similar instance, comp. 2 Cor. vii. 6, 7: "He that comforteth the downcast, even God, comforted us by the coming of Titus...and in the comfort with which he was comforted over you," &c.

For the verb "comfort" see note on ver. 2.

in all our affliction and distress] distress and affliction (R.V.), or necessity and affliction. The first of these terms, as e.g. in 1 Cor. ix. 16 ("Necessity is laid upon me"), implies *outward constraint, stress of circumstances*, or sometimes *of duty;* while the second (see ch. i. 6; iii. 3, 4) commonly denotes *trouble from men.* For similar and more extended combinations, see 2 Cor. vi. 4; xii. 10.

The preposition is literally over (as in last clause), not *in.* It was not simply that Timothy's tidings brought comfort to the Apostle *amidst* his present trials; but this comfort *bore upon* those trials. The steadfastness of the Thessalonians heartened him to meet his troubles at Corinth. This effect of Silas and Timothy's arrival "from Macedonia" is hinted in Acts xviii. 5.

we were comforted...through your faith (R.V.). This conveyed the needed solace to the lonely Apostle. Their "faith" was the essential point, that about which Timothy was sent to enquire (ver. 5); if this remained, all would go well. So our Lord prayed for Peter, "That *thy faith* fail not" (Luke xxii. 32). "By faith ye stand" (2 Cor. i. 24; see next verse).

8. *for now we live, if ye stand fast in the Lord*] "if *ye* stand fast:" the pronoun bears the emphasis. St Paul felt as though his life was wrapped up in this Church. A load of apprehension was lifted from his mind, and he resumed his work at Corinth with the sense of renewed health and vigour, saying to himself, "Yes, now one really lives!" For in truth

"The incessant care and labour of his mind
Had wrought the mure, that should confine it in,
So thin, that life looked through and would break out."

His heaviest burden, weighing down body and mind alike, was "the care of the Churches" (2 Cor. xi. 28, 29).

This passage, like the Epistle to the Galatians and the Second to Corinth, shews St Paul as a man of high-strung and ardent nature, sensitive in his affections to an extreme degree. His whole soul was bound up with the Churches he had founded (comp. ch. ii. 8, and note). They were his "children," his "loved and longed for," his "joy and

now we live, if ye stand fast in the Lord. For what thanks 9 can we render to God again for you, for all the joy wherewith we joy for your sakes before our God; night and day 10 praying exceedingly that *we* might see your face, and might

glory, and crown of boasting." He lived for nothing else. Read in illustration of this 2 Cor. vii. 2—16.

9. *For what thanks can we render to God again for you*] "Again" belongs to the verb "render;" and "thanks" is strictly "thanksgiving." So we may translate, more freely: **what due return of thanksgiving can we make to God?** The Apostle puts this question in proof of the strong declaration he has made in ver. 8. He says: "The news that Timothy brings from you is new life to me, so much so that I can find no words sufficient to express my gratitude to God for the abounding joy which now fills my heart in thinking of you."

The same verb, *to render due return* (one word in Greek), is employed in a very different connection in 2 Ep. i. 6.

for all the joy wherewith we joy for your sakes] More exactly, **because of you**, or **on your account**. Observe the emphasis of delight with which the Apostle dwells on "you;" he repeats the pronoun eight times in the last four verses.

before our God] comp. ver. 13, and ch. i. 3. God was the witness of this exceeding joy, which strove in vain to find expression in fit words of praise.

The condition of alarm and depression which St Paul had previously experienced made this rebound of joy the more vivid. Only those who have suffered much know joy in its full capacity, "as dying, and behold we live! as sorrowing, but ever rejoicing" (2 Cor. vi. 9, 10).

10. *night and day praying exceedingly*] In this last adverb, peculiar to St Paul, he strains language to express the ardour of his feeling: **beyond measure exceedingly**; it recurs in ch. v. 13 and Eph. iii. 20. *Night and day* puts more vividly the "without ceasing" of ch. i. 3; comp. ch. ii. 9.

"Praying" is here, more strictly, **begging**, or **beseeching**, and points to the *want* of the suppliant (comp. 2 Cor. v. 20, "We *beg* you, on Christ's behalf, Be reconciled to God"); whereas the ordinary word for prayer (see e.g. ch. i. 2; 2 Ep. iii. 1) indicates *devotion towards the object of worship*. Prayer goes with thanksgiving, as in ch. i. 2, 3, and constantly in St Paul; comp. ch. v. 17, 18.

that we *might see your face*] *might* makes the realisation seem distant and doubtful; read **may** (R.V.). See notes on ch. ii. 17.

and might perfect that which is lacking in your faith] Or, **may make good the deficiencies of your faith**; not so much what was *lacking in* as *lacking to* their faith. Thessalonian faith was in itself steadfast and vigorous (ch. i. 3, 8; .ii. 13; iii. 6—8; 2 Ep. i. 3, "Your faith groweth exceedingly"); but it needed the supplement of added Christian light and moral wisdom. Hence the teaching and admonition the Apostle supplies in chaps. iv., v. and in the Second Epistle (see *Introd.* pp. 23— 25). Timothy's return from Thessalonica and the news he brought,

11 perfect that which is lacking in your faith? Now God himself and our Father, and our Lord Jesus Christ, direct our
12 way unto you. And the Lord make you to increase and abound in love one towards another, and towards all *men*,

while removing St Paul's great anxiety, made him still more sensible of the need this young and most promising Church had for the continued instruction which he alone could supply. This increased his eagerness to revisit the Thessalonians. For a similar wish—less warmly expressed, inasmuch as it concerned strangers—see Rom. i. 9—15, xv. 23.

The word rendered "perfect" means to *fit up, furnish, fully equip;* it is used of "*mending* nets" (Matt. iv. 21), of "*vessels fitted* for destruction" (Rom. ix. 22), and of "*perfecting* saints for work of ministration" (Eph. iv. 12).

11. *Now God himself and our Father*] **Now may our God and Father Himself** (comp. ch. i. 3), **and our Lord Jesus** (R.V.). For this title of Christ, see notes on ch. ii. 15 and 19. The copyists have added *Christ*.

Literally the verse begins, **But may our God**, &c. There is a transition, by way of contrast, from the thought of Paul's own (human) wish and longing, that has been so fervently uttered, to the thought of *God*, Who alone can fulfil His servant's desire. The prayers of ch. v. 23 and 2 Ep. ii. 16 begin in the same style.

direct our way unto you] Lit., **make straight**. This verb is rendered "*guide* our feet into the way of peace" in Luke i. 79; 2 Ep. iii. 5 gives the only remaining example of it in the N.T. It is frequent in the Septuagint; see, e.g., Ps. xxxvii. 23, "The steps of a good man are *ordered* (Greek, *directed*) by the Lord; and He delighteth in his way." Perhaps this verse of the Psalm was running in the Apostle's mind.

It is notable that the Greek verb of the prayer is *singular*, though following a double subject; similarly in 2 Ep. ii. 16, 17 (comp. the Salutation, ch. i. 1). For Christ is one with the Father in the prerogative of hearing and answering prayer. This belief was derived from our Lord's own teaching: see John v. 17, 19; x. 30, 38; xiv. 13, 14; Matt. xxviii. 18—"I and the Father are one...If ye shall ask Me (R. V.) anything in My name, I will do it," &c.

The prayer of ver. 11 has its goal in ver. 13. "Our Lord Jesus" is He whose "coming" Paul and his readers are looking for. And He, together with the Father, is desired to "direct" the Apostle's steps to Thessalonica, with the aim, ultimately, of furthering their preparation for His coming (comp. ch. v. 23; also i. 10).

12. *And the Lord make you to increase and abound in love one towards another*] In the Greek order, **But you may the Lord make to increase**, &c.—" whatever it may please Him to appoint in respect to *us* and our coming " (Ellicott). Ver. 12 is linked with 11, just as ver. 11 with 10, by contrast. The Apostle is thinking now of what the Thessalonians were to each other and might do for each other, in distinction from himself.

even as we *do* towards you: to the end *he* may stablish your 13

"The Lord" is still the "Lord Jesus" of the adjoining verses, the Pattern and Fountain of love. Comp. John xiii. 34; Eph. v. 2 ("Walk in love, as the Christ also loved you"). Christ is invoked as *the Lord*, in His Divine authority and power to grant this prayer (comp. 2 Ep. iii. 5).

Increased *love* would be the best supplement of their "defects of *faith*" (ver. 11), and the basis of the unblameable *holiness* in which they are to appear at Christ's coming (ver. 13). In "brotherly love" the Thessalonians already excelled (ch. iv. 9, 10; comp. i. 3 and 2 Ep. i. 3); but this is a grace of which there can never be too much. Its "increase" lies in its own growth and enlargement; its "abundance" is the affluence with which it overflows toward others. These synonyms are delicately varied in Rom. v. 20: "where Sin *increased* (or *multiplied*), Grace *superabounded*."

But this multiplied and overflowing love is not to be confined to the brotherhood: **toward one another, and**, he adds, **toward all**. Similarly in ch. v. 15. For the Thessalonian Church, cruelly persecuted, this wider love was peculiarly necessary, and difficult. It meant loving their enemies, according to Christ's command (Matt. v. 44).

The Apostle has shewn them by his example how to love each other in Christ (see ch. ii. 7—12, 19, 20); and remembering this he adds, **even as we also toward you**. Comp. the appeal of Christ in John xiii. 34 ("even as I loved you"). Paul's love too was not stationary, but living and growing. This verse has the same turn of expression as ver. 6, "even as we also (long to see) you."

Faith was the object of the Apostle's prayer in ver. 10; Love in ver. 12; and now ver. 13 crowns both, as it seeks for the Thessalonians, in view of Christ's coming, a well-assured *Hope* (comp. ch. i. 3):—

13. *to the end* he *may stablish your hearts*] On "stablish" see note to ver. 2; and on "hearts," ch. ii. 4; comp. also 2 Ep. ii. 17.

This is an O.T. phrase, found in Ps. civ. 15, "Bread that *strengtheneth* (Greek, *stablisheth*) man's *heart*"; and cxii. 8, "His *heart* is *established*, he shall not be afraid." The only N.T. parallel is in Jam. v. 8, "Be patient; *stablish your hearts*; for the coming of the Lord is at hand." In all these places it signifies the *imparting of conscious strength*; and denotes here, therefore, not so much a *making firm or steadfast in character*, but *giving a firm confidence, a steadfast and assured heart* (contrast the language of 2 Ep. ii. 2). This would be the effect of the abounding love prayed for in the last verse. The Apostle's thought runs in the same groove as St John's in 1 Ep. iii. 18—21 and iv. 16, 17, "Herein is love made perfect with us, that we may have boldness in the day of judgement....Perfect love casteth out fear." The Church was living in the expectation of Christ's speedy return to judgement, a prospect before which the heart naturally quails; in order to "assure their hearts before Him," the Thessalonian believers must increase and abound in love. "Love" is the one thing that "never faileth" (1 Cor. xiii. 8). Ch. iv. 13, 18, and v. 14 show that courage and joyous confidence in Christ were wanting in some members of this Church.

hearts unblameable in holiness before God, even our Father, at the coming of our Lord Jesus Christ with all his saints.

The words *unblameable in holiness* form, then, a secondary predicate of the sentence: "to the end He may establish your hearts, making them unblameable," or "so as to be unblameable in holiness before our God," &c. The clause appears to be *proleptic*, or anticipatory (comp. 1 Cor. i. 8; Ph. iii. 21). Similarly in ch. v. 23 the *keeping* of "spirit, soul and body" prayed for belongs to the present, but *unblameably* carries our thoughts at once to "the coming of our Lord Jesus Christ" (see note). We take the Apostle's thought, amplified, to be this: "May the Lord make you to abound in love...so that you may have the confidence and strength of heart in which abiding you will be found blameless in holiness before God at Christ's coming." This blamelessness will be manifest at the coming of the Judge; but it is imparted already, and belongs to those whose hearts are filled with love to their fellow-men, and so with confidence toward God (comp. again 1 John iv. 16, 17); in which confidence they anticipate the day when they shall be found "holy and without blemish before Him." This assurance of heart resembles St Paul's, expressed in 2 Cor. i. 12: "Our glorying is this, the testimony of our conscience that in holiness and sincerity of God we have behaved ourselves in the world." Such confidence must always be guarded by strict self-scrutiny and absolute dependence upon Christ. It was *encouragement*, however, rather than caution that St Paul's readers just now required (see ver. 2). This verse and the last set forth Christian perfection in its twofold aspect, as constituted at once by an unbounded love to men and a blameless consecration to God.

On "holiness" see notes to ch. iv. 3 and 7, also ii. 10.

This "blamelessness" of the Thessalonians will be approved **before our God and Father**, Who listens to the Apostle's prayers and thanksgivings and witnesses his joy on their account (ver. 9, ch. i. 3), and delights to see the good pleasure of His will accomplished in His children. He, the Trier of hearts (ch. ii. 4), permits them now through Christ, and will surely permit them hereafter to stand in His presence with hearts unafraid—**in the coming of our Lord Jesus with all His saints.**

This is the goal of the Apostle's prayers and labours for the Church (comp. ch. ii. 19; v. 23; 2 Ep. i. 11, 12); and the aim of the hopes and strivings of the Thessalonian believers (ch. i. 3, 10; iv. 13; v. 11; 2 Ep. i. 5, &c.). He prays that they may be able with good right to look forward confidently toward that Day, trusting not to be "ashamed before Him at His coming" (1 John ii. 28; iii. 3). On the title "Lord Jesus" see notes to ver. 11, and ch. ii. 15, 19; and on "coming" (*parousia*), ch. ii. 19.

Observe that "the Lord" (Christ) is the Agent of all that is set forth in *vv.* 12 and 13. Christ fills His people's hearts with love and sanctifies them by His Spirit, so that at the last He may present them to the Father as His joy and crown. Then He will be "glorified in His saints, and admired in all them that believed" (2 Ep. i. 10—12).

Furthermore then we beseech you, brethren, and exhort 4

His saints (or *holy ones*) are those, "unblameable in holiness," whom Christ will acknowledge and associate with Himself at His coming. These last words have been shaping the Apostle's prayer all along. To those who possess abundantly the spirit of love (ver. 12) the hope is given of being found amongst the "holy ones," approved by God, who will attend the Lord Jesus on His glorious return to earth. Christ will not then be solitary, but will have a vast retinue of "the saints," visible in forms of splendour like His own (Ph. iii. 20, 21) and "*with Him* in glory" (Col. iii. 4). For this association of the returning Saviour and His saints, see further ch. iv. 14, 17, and notes; v. 10; and 2 Ep. ii. 1, "The coming of our Lord Jesus Christ, and *our gathering together unto Him*."

CHAPTER IV.

SECTION V. A LESSON IN CHRISTIAN MORALS.
CH. IV. 1—12.

WE now pass from the first to the second of the two main divisions of the Epistle (see *Introd.* Chap. VII.), from *narrative* to *exhortation*. Chaps. i.—iii. are complete in themselves, and the letter might fitly have terminated with the prayer just concluded (ch. iii. 11—13). For the Apostle has accomplished the chief objects with which he began to write,—viz. to assure his readers of the intense interest he takes in their welfare, to express his sympathy with them under their persecutions, and to explain how it was that he had not himself returned to them. But he cannot let the occasion pass without adding counsel and exhortation on certain subjects in which the Thessalonian Church was specially in need of guidance. Chief amongst these were the misunderstandings that had arisen touching the *parousia*, or second advent of Christ (ch. iv. 13—v. 11). But before he deals with this topic, there are a few things he wishes to say to them about *morals* and matters of *conduct toward each other*, which we have before us in this Section. It is significant that the Apostle puts these things first in his exhortation, although the question of the Parousia was of such absorbing interest.

The topics embraced in this Section are (1) and chiefly, that of *chastity* and *the sanctification of the body, vv.* 3—8; (2) *brotherly love, vv.* 9, 10; (3) *diligence* in secular work, *vv.* 11, 12.

That chaps. iv., v. form an addendum, supplementing the primary intention of the Epistle, is shown by the introductory phrase :—

1. *Furthermore then*] R.V., *finally*; as the same Greek phrase is rendered by A.V. in Phil. iii. 1, iv. 8, &c. Lit., **for the rest therefore,** *for what remains.*

we beseech you, brethren, and exhort you *by the Lord Jesus*] More exactly, and in the Greek order : **brethren, we beseech you, and exhort in the Lord Jesus.**

you by the Lord Jesus, that as ye have received of us how ye ought to walk and to please God, *so* ye would abound 2 more *and more*. For ye know what commandments we

The first of these verbs, "beseech" (or "ask"), frequent with St John, is only found in St Paul besides in ch. v. 12; 2 Ep. ii. 1; and Phil. iv. 3. The Apostle *asks* as in a matter touching himself and his interest in his readers; he *exhorts*, as it concerns them and their own duty and relation to Christ; for it is on the basis and within the sphere of this relationship—in fact, *because they are Christians*—that such an appeal is addressed to them. Comp. note on "church in the Lord Jesus Christ," ch. i. 1; and for the title "Lord Jesus," on ch. ii. 15, 19.

St Paul's deep affection for the Thessalonians and his longing to see them prompted the prayer with which the last chapter concluded, that the Lord Himself would make them to be found *blameless in holiness* at His coming. And it is "therefore"—in accordance with this prayer and these desires—that he now urges them to a still more earnest pursuit of Christian virtue.

that as ye have received of us how ye ought to walk and to please God] "That" requires a comma after it, as in R.V.; for it looks forward to the final clause of the verse—" that ye abound more and more."

"Received" corresponds to the first of the two words so rendered in ch. ii. 13 (see note), and signifies the reception as matter of instruction. Beside the doctrine of the Gospel the apostles taught its practice—what men should do and what should be the "work" and effect of their faith (ch. i. 3), as well as what they should believe. In their earliest lessons the Thessalonians had received the moral along with the theological elements of Christianity,—"how you *ought to walk*." On this last word comp. note to ch. ii. 12.

"Ought to walk *and* please God" is not the same as "walk *so as to* please God," though this is implied; but rather "how you ought to walk, and ought to please God." The *duty of pleasing God* had been a subject of St Paul's admonitions, and he had set all other duties in this light. Similarly in ch. ii. 4 he spoke of himself and Silas as governed in their work by the thought of "pleasing God," while in ver. 15 the condemnation of the Jews was found in the fact that they were "not pleasing God." Our conduct is always, and in everything, pleasing or displeasing to Him; and the religious man finds in this the highest sanction of right-doing. The word Sanctification (ver. 3) expresses in another way the same religious necessity attaching to moral obligation.

The clause **even as ye do walk** is restored to the text by the Revisers, on the best authority. Comp. *vv.* 9, 10, "for indeed you do it;" also ch. v. 11. The Apostle would not appear to censure his readers. He is sure that they *are* walking in the true path, mindful of his instructions; he wishes to keep them in it, and to urge them forward. The sum of his entreaty is (resuming the "that" left incomplete in the earlier part of the sentence), **that ye abound more and more** (R.V.).

2. *For ye know what commandments we gave you by the Lord Jesus*] Lit., **charges...through the Lord Jesus**; similarly in ver. 11, "as we

gave you by the Lord Jesus. For this is the will of God, 3 *even* your sanctification, that ye should abstain from fornica-

charged you," and in 2 Ep. iii. 4, &c. The Greek word signifies an *announcement*, then a *command* or *advice publicly delivered*. In 1 Tim. i. 5 and 18 the whole practical teaching of Christianity is called a "charge." Here the Apostle is referring to particular items of conduct as matter of so many "charges." These charges were given "*through* the Lord Jesus," since His name and authority were used to support them (comp. 2 Ep. iii. 6, "in the name of our Lord Jesus Christ"); while they were given "*in* the Lord Jesus" (ver. 1), as they appealed to the Christian standing of the readers and their conscious relationship to Christ, Whose coming in glory they expected.

The Apostle is "writing no new commandment;" he recalls to his readers' remembrance what he had so often urged upon them (see note on ch. i. 5). It is on one prominent subject of those well-remembered charges that he has now to dwell:—

3. *For this is the will of God*, even *your sanctification*, &c.] The connection will be clearer if we render thus: **For this is God's will— it is your sanctification—that you abstain from fornication**, &c.

It was not some counsel or wish of his own that he pressed on the Thessalonians under the authority of Christ; it was nothing less than *God's holy will:* the primary ground of this charge. At the same time it was *their sanctification*. God's will and their consecration to Him are the double reason for their leading a chaste life; and these two reasons are one, the latter springing out of the former. God had chosen them to be His own (comp. ch. i. 4). And He willed that their sanctification should be realised and carried into effect in the important particular about to be stated. This will of God was proclaimed in His "call," by which the Thessalonians had been summoned to a pure and holy life (ch. v. 23, 24; comp. ii. 12). In all endeavours after purity it is our best support to know that God wishes and means us to be holy; that His almighty help is at the back of our weak resolves, Who both "puts into our minds good desires" and "brings the same to good effect."

"Sanctification" is *the act or process of making holy:* then, in the second instance, it comes to denote the result of this process, *the state of one who is made holy*,—as in Rom. vi. 22, "You have your fruit unto sanctification, and the end eternal life;" similarly in Heb. xii. 14, "Follow after sanctification." It is synonymous with *consecration*, i.e. *devotion to God*,—but to God as the Holy One.

Holy is the single word which by itself denotes *the Divine character*, as it is revealed to us in its moral transcendence, in the awfulness and glory of its absolute perfection, raised infinitely above all that is earthly and sinful (see 1 Sam. ii. 2, Ps. xcix., cxi. 9, Isai. lvii. 15, &c). Now it is the character of God—"thy Maker...and thy Redeemer, *the Holy One of Israel*"—that constitutes His right to the consecration of those to whom He is revealed. Our "sanctification" is the acknowledgement of God's claim upon us as the Holy One Who made us. This involves our assimilation to His nature. In Him, first the character, then the claim:

4 tion: that every one of you should know how to possess his

in us, first the claim admitted, then the character impressed. In short, Sanctification is fulfilment of the supreme command, "Be ye holy, for I am holy" (1 Pet. i. 15, 16; Lev. xi. 44; xix. 2; xx. 7).—See, further, notes on ver. 7, and ch. v. 23; also on ch. ii. 10, for the difference between the two Greek words for *holy* used in this Ep.

St Paul makes *chastity* a part of holiness. He finds a new motive and powerful safeguard for virtue in the fact of the redemption of the body. Our physical frame belongs to God; it is a sharer in Christ's resurrection, and in the new life received through Him. "Know you not," he asks, "that your bodies are limbs of Christ,—a temple of the Holy Ghost, which you have from God? Therefore glorify God in your body" (1 Cor. vi. 15—20). This is *bodily sanctification*. And faith in Christ effectually subdues impure and sensual passion.

The foul and heathenish vice of *fornication* was so prevalent in Greek cities and so little condemned by public opinion—it was even fostered by some forms of pagan religion—that abstinence from it on the part of the Thessalonians was a sign of devotion to a Holy God. But their purity was imperilled from the condition of society around them, and in many cases from former unchaste habits. The temptations to licentiousness assailing the first generation of Christians were fearfully strong; and all the Epistles contain urgent warnings upon this subject. The sense of purity had to be re-created in men gathered out of the midst of pagan corruption.

4. *that every one of you should know how to possess his vessel*] Rather, **that each one of you know how to possess himself of his own vessel** (R.V.); or, freely rendered, **that each be wise in the mastery of his bodily frame.**

This is the positive side of what has just been expressed negatively. The "vessel" we take to be *the body*, regarded as the vehicle and instrument of the inner self—"the vessel of himself." What the tool is to the hand, or vase to the essence it holds, that the body is to the man's self. Comp. 2 Cor. iv. 7, "this treasure in earthen vessels"; similarly in 2 Cor. v. 1—4 the body is "the earthly *house* of our tabernacle," the *clothing* without which we should be "found naked." The victim of sensual passion ceases to be master of his own person—he is *possessed;* and those who formerly lived in heathen uncleanness, had now as Christians to *possess themselves* of their bodies, to "win" the "vessel" of their spiritual life and make it truly their own, and a fit receptacle for the redeemed and sanctified self (comp. Luke xxi. 19, "In your patience ye shall *win* your souls," R.V.,—the same Greek verb). This they must "know how" (i.e. *have skill*) to do—a skill for which there was continual need. The Greek expression for Temperance— *enkrateia*, i.e. *continence, self-control*—expresses a similar thought; so the simile of 1 Cor. ix. 27, "I buffet my body, and make it my slave."

in sanctification] For it was under this idea, and within the sphere of the new, consecrated life that such mastery of the body was to be gained (see notes on *vv.* 3 and 7). And in *honour ;* for as lust dishonours and degrades the body (Rom. i. 24, 26; 1 Cor. vi. 15), so its devotion to

vessel in sanctification and honour; not in the lust of concu- 5
piscence, even as the Gentiles which know not God: that 6
no *man* go beyond and defraud his brother in *any* matter:
because that the Lord *is* the avenger of all such, as we also

God in a life of purity raises it to "honour." Self-respect and regard for the honour of one's own person, as well as reverence for God, forbid unchastity.

5. *not in the lust of concupiscence*] Far better, **not in the passion of lust** (R.V.). The sense of the last verb (*to possess*) is carried on, with a modified application, into this clause: not (to have it: i.e. your body) **in a state of lustful passion**. (For the altered meaning of the verb, comp. 1 Cor. iii. 2: "I gave you milk to drink, not meat"). This condition—the state of one immersed "in" wicked desire—is the opposite of "sanctification and honour."

The word "passion" signifies not so much a violent feeling, as an *overpowering* feeling, one to which the man so yields himself that he is borne along by evil as if he were its passive instrument; he has lost the dignity of self-rule, and is the slave of his lower appetites. Comp. Rom. vii. 5, "the passions of sins which wrought in our members;" and ver. 20, "It is no longer I that do it, but sin that dwelleth in me."

In such shameful bondage lived *the Gentiles which know not God* (an O. T. expression, Ps. lxxix. 6, Isai. xlv. 4, 5; recurring in 2 Ep. i. 8, see note). For impurity, often in most abandoned and revolting forms, was a prevailing feature of Pagan life at this time. In Rom. i. 24, &c., St Paul speaks of this as a punishment of the heathen world for its wilful ignorance of God: "He gave them up unto passions of dishonour." Man first denies his Maker; then degrades himself.

The God Whom these degraded "Gentiles knew not," is the "living and true God" of ch. i. 9, to Whom Thessalonian believers had "turned from their idols." Coming to know Him by His gospel, they had devoted themselves to Him; and so their bodies had been redeemed from vice and dishonour, and the soul had a clean house to live in, a clean vessel to use for holy service.

6. *that no man go beyond and defraud his brother in any matter*] More exactly, **that none overreach and take advantage of his brother in the matter**. "*The* matter" is obviously that which occupies the last two verses. Acts of impurity are *social* wrongs, as well as sins against the offender's person. The warning may include any injury done to another touching the affections and engagements that belong to marriage,—"the matter" concerned in the present charge—which is expressly violated by "fornication." The Apostle sets the wrong in the strongest light: it is to "cheat one's brother," and that in what touches most nearly the sanctities of life. Hence the stern warning that follows:—

because that the Lord is the avenger of all such] Rather, **an avenger; and concerning all these things**—in everything that concerns the honour of the human person and the sacredness of wedded life. Comp. Heb. xiii. 4, "Let marriage be had in honour...Fornicators and adul-

7 have forewarned you and testified. For God hath not called
8 us unto uncleanness, but unto holiness. He therefore that
despiseth, despiseth not man, but God, who hath also given
unto us his holy Spirit.

terers God will judge." It is written that "Vengeance belongs to God;" and in this matter He is peculiarly bound to exercise it.

as we also have forewarned you and testified] or, **solemnly attested**: the latter verb implies reference to God, as it is expressed in 2 Tim. iv. 1, "before God and Christ Jesus." On this subject it appears—as to the moral consequences of faith in Christ and the social purity that belongs to the sanctified life—the apostles at Thessalonica had spoken very plainly and solemnly from the first.

7. *For God hath not called us unto uncleanness, but unto holiness*] The two prepositions alike rendered "unto" in the A.V., are quite distinct in the Greek. St Paul writes, **God called us not for** (with a view to) **uncleanness, but in sanctification**; similarly in 2 Ep. ii. 13, "God chose you from the beginning unto salvation *in sanctification* of spirit." The call of God was from the first a sanctifying call for the Thessalonians, and was attended with holy influences that forbade all uncleanness. Certainly He never intended them to live impure lives, when He "called them to His own kingdom and glory" (ch. ii. 12); the understanding on which that call was received was the opposite of this. The entire purpose and tendency of God's message to them was "in sanctification." For this last word, see notes to *vv.* 3 and 4. True believers in Christ are necessarily "saints;" so the Apostle commonly addresses all Christians to whom he writes (see Rom. i. 7, &c.—"called saints," i.e. "saints in virtue of your calling"); and their sainthood excludes impurity and wrong-doing.

Observe that *God's call* is the starting-point of a Christian's life. All the motives and aims by which that life is governed are virtually contained in this. "Walk worthily of the calling wherewith you were called" is with St Paul an exhortation that includes all others (Eph. iv. 1). So he comes to his last word on this matter:—

8. *He therefore that despiseth, despiseth not man, but God*] *Therefore* should stand first, as in R.V.; it gathers up and re-affirms with emphasis the charge of *vv.* 2—7: **Wherefore then.**

For *despiseth* read **rejecteth** (A.V. *margin*, and R.V.), as this word is rendered in Luke x. 16; in Gal. ii. 21 we read it, "I do not *make void* the grace of God." It points to some authority set at nought, or engagement nullified. It was God's call which had summoned the Thessalonians to their new life; His voice, not man's, had reached them by the Gospel (see ch. ii. 12, 13). It will be *God's* authority therefore, not man's, that they defy, if this charge is disregarded; comp. ver. 1, "how you ought to please God;" and ver. 3, "This is God's will."

And the God Whom they would thus set at nought, is **He who gives His Holy Spirit unto you**. The Greek text of this clause is doubtful in several points. The Revisers are probably right in reading

But as touching brotherly love ye need not that *I* write 9 unto you: for ye yourselves are taught of God to love one

giveth in place of *hath also given* (A.V.); and *you* in place of *us* (A.V.), this word closing the sentence with emphasis.

The preposition is strictly **into you**, implying beyond the mere fact of the impartation of the Holy Spirit, His *entrance into* the soul. There is probably a reminiscence of Ezek. xxxvii 6, where the LXX represents the LORD as saying to the dry bones, "I will *give* (Hebrew, *put*) My Spirit into you, and you shall live, and shall know that I am the LORD." Similarly in Gal. iv. 6, "God sent forth the Spirit of His Son *into* your hearts;" and in Eph. iii. 16, "strengthened through His Spirit (entering) *into* the inward man." The gift of the Holy Spirit of God, bestowed to dwell within the soul of him who believes in Christ, is the peculiar distinction and the essential blessing of Christ's religion. "I will pray the Father," said Jesus, "and He will give you another Paraclete, that He may be with you for ever, even the Spirit of truth. He abideth with you, and shall be in you" (John xiv. 16, 17; comp. Luke xi. 13). The whole grace of the Gospel is summed up by St Paul in "the promise of the Spirit," received "through faith" (Gal. iii. 14). Through His indwelling we know the love of God, and are conscious of being sons of God and heirs of life eternal (Rom. v. 5; viii. 14—17; Gal. iv. 6, 7; Eph. i. 13, 14).

Now the unchaste act or thought is an affront to the Holy Ghost, Who dwells as Guest in the soul and body of the Christian. This final warning seals the Apostle's charge. He appeals to the presence of the Holy Spirit, of Whose continued visitations and influence his readers were sensible. To "reject the God Who gives" this gift would be for the Thessalonians to sin against the light that was in them. We are reminded again of 1 Cor. vi. 19, "Know you not that your body is a temple of the Holy Ghost Which is in you, Which you have from God?"

> "Gentle, awful, holy Guest,
> Make Thy temple in each breast,
> There supreme to reign and rest,
> Comforter Divine."

9. *But as touching brotherly love ye need not that I write unto you*] More exactly, **you have no need that one write to you.** "Have no need" recurs in ch. v. 1; comp. ch. i. 8 and 1 John ii. 27. There *was* need for the Apostle to write on the previous subject (*vv.* 3—8). But in this grace the Thessalonian Church excelled (comp. note on ch. i. 3, also 2 Ep. i. 3).

In this respect they were (literally, and in one word) **God-taught**—an expression found only here in the N.T.; comp. "God-breathed," 2 Tim. iii. 16. The separate elements of the compound appear in John vi. 45, where our Lord cites the words of Isai. liv. 13, "They shall be all taught of God." The former "charge" the Thessalonians had received through men from God (*vv.* 2, 8): the lesson of "brotherly love" they learnt so readily and with so little need of human instruction,

10 another. And indeed ye do it towards all the brethren which are in all Macedonia: but we beseech you, brethren, 11 that *ye* increase more *and more;* and that *ye* study to be quiet, and to do your own *business*, and to work with your

that they were evidently taught it *by God Himself.* It seemed to come to them "naturally" as we say—**ye are of yourselves God-taught**; or as we ought to say, more reverently, "by God's direct endowment."

taught of God to love one another] Lit., **to the end** (or **effect**) **that you love one another.** This was *the purport and issue*, rather than the mere content of the Divine teaching: God taught them many lessons; this was the aim of all.

10. *And indeed*] should be **For indeed**. Their practice of the Divine lesson, as described in this verse, showed that they were truly "taught of God" to this effect.

ye do it towards all the brethren which are in all Macedonia] Thessalonica was a prosperous commercial city and the capital of Macedonia (see *Introd.* Chap. I.). It was the natural centre of the Macedonian Churches—including Philippi and Beroea, with other communities which had probably sprung up around these principal towns. The Thessalonian Christians were using their position and influence for the good of their brethren around them, and thus giving proof that they had learnt the great lesson of Divine grace. Silas and Timothy, recently returned from Macedonia (Acts xviii. 5; see ch. iii. 6), had doubtless told the Apostle how well they did their duty towards the neighbour Churches (comp. ch. i. 7, 8, and notes).

but we beseech you, brethren] should be **exhort** (R.V.), as in ver. 1 (comp. note, also on "comfort," ch. iii. 2); same word in ver. 18, and ch. v. 11, 14.

that ye increase &c.] Better rendered, **that you abound still more;** the Apostle repeats the exact phrase employed in ver. 1, which takes up the verb of ch. iii. 12 (see notes).

In all Christian virtues growth is possible and desired, but "brotherly love" above others is susceptible of constant and unlimited increase. The Apostle reverts to this point once more, in ch. v. 16.

Philadelphia (brother-love) in common Greek did not go beyond its literal sense. In Christian speech it was at once applied to the "brothers" of the new life in Christ, those who are united in the acknowledgement of God as their Father (ch. i. 1, see note). Comp. 1 John iv. 21, and v. 1, "This commandment have we from Him, that he who loveth God love his brother also....Whosoever loveth Him that begat, loveth him also that is begotten of Him." The word recurs in Rom. xii. 10; Heb. xiii. 1; 1 Pet. i. 22; also in 2 Pet. i. 7, where in "brother-love" *charity* (or *love*) is directed to be "supplied," as its spiritual and universal principle.

From the second topic of his "charge," which the Apostle is happily able to dismiss in a few words, he proceeds to the third:—

11. *and that ye study to be quiet, and to do your own* business] Lit., **that you be ambitious to be quiet**—an example of St Paul's character-

own hands, as we commanded you; that ye may walk 12 honestly toward them that are without, and *that* ye may have lack of no*thing*.

istic irony; the contrast between *ambition* and *quiet* giving a sharper point to his exhortation, as though he said, "Make it your ambition to have no ambition!" The love of personal distinction was an active influence and potent for mischief in Greek city life; possibly the Thessalonians were touched with it, and betrayed symptoms of the restless and emulous spirit that afterwards gave the Apostle so much trouble at Corinth. Comp. 1 Tim. ii. 2, where he makes it an object of prayer, "that we may lead a tranquil and quiet life." Eager and active as his own nature was, St Paul much admired this kind of life, and deemed it ordinarily the fittest for the cultivation of Christian character, **and** (study), he continues, **to be occupied with your own affairs.** This, too, was to be their aim and ambition, in contrast with the busybody, gad-about habits to which some of them were inclined (see 2 Ep. iii. 11, and note).

Those who meddle with other people's business, commonly neglect their own; and idleness goes hand in hand with officiousness. Accordingly St Paul adds, **and to work with your hands.** Most of the Thessalonian Christians were probably handicraftsmen of one kind or other. Even for the few who possessed larger means the Apostle may have thought manual labour a good discipline; comp. note on ch. ii. 9, and 2 Ep. iii. 7—12. He perceived the danger, especially marked in this Church, arising from the unsettling effect which great spiritual excitement is apt to have upon the pursuance of the ordinary duties of life. Hence this had been a subject of his warnings from the beginning—**even as we charged you** (comp. ver. 2). The Apostle Paul combined in his teaching a lofty spirituality with a quick sense for practical necessities.

12. *that ye may walk honestly toward them that are without*] *Honestly* is rather **honourably**, *honestè* (Vulgate)—*in decent, comely fashion*, in such manner as to "adorn the doctrine of God our Saviour" (Tit. ii. 10), and to win for Christian faith respect even from those who did not embrace it. In 1 Tim. iii. 7 this is laid down as a condition specially important in the case of men appointed to office in the Church, that they should "have a good testimony from them that are without."

Those without—"outsiders," as we say—is an established phrase, used by contrast with "those within" the fold of Christ, or the walls of the city of God; see 1 Cor. v. 12, 13; Col. iv. 5, "Walk in wisdom toward those outside;" also Mark iv. 11. In a thriving commercial town like Thessalonica, indolence or unfitness for the common work of life would bring great discredit on the new society.

and that *ye may have lack of no*thing] Better, **need of nothing** (R.V.), **or of no one** (*no man*, A.V. margin). As much as to say: "That every one, inside or outside the Church, may respect you, and you may be no man's dependents."

The sense of honourable independence was strong in St Paul (see ch. ii. 6, 9, and again 2 Ep. iii. 8): he desires to see it in all his

13 But I would not have you to be ignorant, brethren, con-

people. The Church was already in danger of having its charities abused by the indolent, so as to foster a spirit of pauperism. In Eph. iv. 28 the Apostle enlists on the side of diligent secular work the spirit of charity, in addition to that of self-respect—"that he may have to give to him that needeth;" comp. Acts xx. 34, 35, "It is more blessed to give than to receive." And in 1 Tim. v. 8 he includes under the necessities to be met by honest labour those of the man's household, condemning the neglecter of these claims as "denying the faith" and "worse than an unbeliever."

SECTION VI. THE COMING OF THE LORD JESUS.
CH. IV. 13—V. 11.

This solemn topic, as we have already seen (note on ch. i. 10, and *Introd.*, pp. 18—21), is the principal theme of the Epistles to the Thessalonians. It is not treated by way of argument or indoctrination, but as a matter already familiar to the readers; on which, however, further explanation and admonition were needful. The Apostle's teaching about this event had been on some points misunderstood, while new and anxious questions had arisen respecting it. Death had visited the Christian flock at Thessalonica since St Paul left them; and this had aroused in the survivors a painful fear lest those who were thus snatched away should have lost their place and their share in the approaching advent of Christ. This apprehension the Apostle proceeds to remove; and we may entitle the remaining verses of the chapter: *Concerning them that fall asleep.*

St Paul (1) bids his readers be assured of *the safety of their departed fellow-believers, vv.* 13, 14; and he makes the revelation (2) that *these will have the first place* in the assembling of the saints *at Christ's return, vv.* 15—17. He goes on to remind them (3) of *the uncertainty of the time* of His coming, ch. v. 1—3; and (4) exhorts them to *be always ready* for the event, like soldiers on guard and fully armed, *vv.* 4—9.

13. *But I would not have you to be ignorant*] True reading, **we would not**,—consistently with the first person plural ("Paul and Silas and Timothy") in which the Epistle commenced (ch. i. 1). This impressive phrase ("would not—ignorant") the Apostle employs, as in Rom. xi. 25 and elsewhere, to call attention to a new topic on which he is especially anxious to have a clear understanding with his readers.

concerning them that fall asleep (R.V.), or **are falling asleep**: *are asleep* (A.V.) represents a different and faulty Greek reading. The Greek participle is *present*, and denotes what is now going on. The Apostle had not been long absent from Thessalonica, and apparently this question had now arisen for the first time. There were members of the Church who were evidently *dying;* in some instances death had already supervened (*vv.* 14, 15), in others it was impending. So vivid

cerning them which are asleep, that ye sorrow not, even as was the expectation of the Lord's return, that this contingency had not been thought of till it arose; and it seemed as though these dying men would miss the great hope that had been so precious to them, of seeing Christ return to reign in His glory. The "brotherly love" which St Paul has just commended in the Thessalonians, would make this apprehension intensely painful.

Death is "sleep" to the Christian. Occasionally it bears this title in pagan writers, but only by way of poetical figure. Jesus Christ made it the standing name for Death in the dialect of His Church (Luke viii. 52; John xi. 11, &c.). This expression indicates the *restful* (and perhaps *restorative*) effect of death to the child of God, and at the same time its *temporary nature*. The use of the word by our Lord in connection with the raising of Jairus' daughter and of Lazarus brings out strikingly this latter truth. So the early Christians called their place of burial (in Greek) *koimētērion* (cemetery),—i.e. *dormitory*, *sleeping-chamber*.

that ye sorrow not, even as others] More precisely, **in order that**: the Apostle corrects the ignorance of his readers "in order" to remove their sorrow; he would give them "words" with which they may "encourage one another" (ver. 18).

Lit., **as the rest**: synonymous with "those without" (ver. 12), and occurring in the same sense in Eph. ii. 3; the expression has a note of sadness, as of those who are *left* to sorrow and darkness.

Even before Christ came and "brought life and immortality to light" (2 Tim. i. 10), the Church had attained hope in view of death. See the noble passage in the Apocryphal Book of Wisdom (c. 100 B.C.), ch. iii. 1—4: "The souls of the righteous are in the hand of God, and there shall no torment touch them.... Their hope is full of immortality." But of "the rest"—the unconverted Gentiles—it is sorrowfully added, *which have no hope*. Comp. Eph. ii. 12, "having no hope, and without God in the world." Hopelessness was a prevalent feature of the world's life at this time. The more enlightened and thoughtful a Greek or Roman citizen might be, the less belief he commonly had in any existence beyond death. See, e.g., the speeches of Cato and of Cæsar given in the *Catiline* of Sallust. The loss of Christian faith in modern times brings back the old Pagan despair, and throws over us again "the shadow of a starless night." Amongst many sorrowful examples, the *Journal of Marie Bashkirtseff*, recently published, supplies one of the most touching. Dying at 24, with her splendid gifts wasted and hungry ambition unappeased, this Russian girl writes: "O to think that *we live but once*, and that life is so short! When I think of it I am like one possessed, and my brain seethes with despair!" Against this great sorrow of the world the word *sleep*, four times in this context applied to Christian death, is an abiding protest.

The specific hope which the Thessalonian Christians had embraced and which those they had left behind in heathenism were without, was "hope in our Lord Jesus Christ," centring in the prospect of His glorious return from heaven (ch. i. 3, 10). This hope, the Apostle

14 others which have no hope. For if we believe that Jesus died and rose again, *even* so them also which sleep in Jesus will show, belongs to all who are "in Him;" and the circumstance of their having fallen asleep before His coming makes no difference in this relationship. "Whether we live or die, we are the Lord's" (Rom. xiv. 8; comp. ch. v. 10): to be "the Lord's" is the essential thing.

We gather that it was not their personal resurrection, but *their share in the Parousia* about which the Thessalonians were anxious on behalf of their departed friends. Probably they had sent enquiries to St Paul, through Timothy, upon the subject.

14. *For if we believe that Jesus died and rose again*] The faith of a Christian man in its briefest and simplest form. So in Rom. x. 9 the Apostle declares the faith that "saves" to be the belief of the heart that "God raised Jesus from the dead." This involves everything else; it carries with it the conviction that Christ is Divine (Rom. i. 4), and that His death brings "justification of life" for men (Rom. iv. 25). Such faith St Paul assumes, for himself and his readers, as a fundamental fact. He speaks of "Jesus," thinking of Him in His human Person and in the analogy of His experience to our own. He is "Firstborn of many brethren, Firstborn out of the dead" (Rom. viii. 29; Col. i. 18); and what we believe of *Jesus*, we may expect to see fulfilled in His brethren.

even *so them also which sleep in Jesus*] Rather, **which fell asleep.** The verb is *past* (historical) in tense. The Apostle is looking back with his readers to the sorrowful event of their friends' decease, that he may give them comfort; comp. ver. 15.

in Jesus is in the Greek **through Jesus**,—or more strictly, **that fell asleep** (possibly, **were laid to sleep**) **through the Jesus** just spoken of,—Him "Who died and rose again." For the force of the preposition, comp. ver. 2 and note. The departed Thessalonian Christians had "fallen asleep;" for them Death was robbed of his terrors and transformed to Sleep. "Through Jesus" this came to pass—*the* Jesus of their faith, the dying, risen Saviour! Trusting in His Name, remembering and realising what it meant, they had met the last enemy, and conquering their fears they "laid them down and slept." Such is the power of this *Name* in the last conflict:

"Jesus! my only hope Thou art,
Strength of my failing flesh and heart!"
(Chas. Wesley's Dying Hymn.)

them that fell asleep through Jesus, God will bring with Him. *God* (expressed with emphasis) is the Agent in their restoration, as in ch. i. 10 in the "raising" of "His Son from the dead." He "Who raised up the Lord Jesus, will raise up us also with Jesus" (2 Cor. iv. 14; comp. Eph. i. 19, 20). But the Apostle does not say here "will *raise* them with Jesus," it is not the *resurrection* of the dead that is in question, but their relation to the Parousia, their place in Christ's approaching kingdom. Therefore he says: "God will *bring* them with

will God bring with him. *For this we say unto you by the* 15 *word of the Lord, that we which are alive* and *remain unto Him*,"—they will not be forgotten or left behind when Jesus comes in triumph.

The argument of this verse is condensed and somewhat subtle. When the Apostle begins, "If we believe" &c., we expect him to continue, "so we believe that those who died will, by the power of Christ's resurrection, be raised to life, and will return to share His glory." But in the eagerness of his inference St Paul passes from the certainty of *conviction* in the first member of the sentence ("If we *believe*") to the certainty of the fact itself ("*God will bring* them") in the second. In the same eagerness of anticipation he blends the final with the intermediate stage of restoration, making the resurrection of Jesus the pledge not of the believer's resurrection simply (as in 2 Cor. iv. 14), but of his *participation in Christ's glorious advent*, of which His resurrection is the prelude (comp. ch. i. 10, "to wait for His Son from the heavens, Whom He raised from the dead," and note). The union between Christ and the Christian, as St Paul conceives it, is such that in whatever Christ the Head does or experiences, He carries the members of His body with Him. The Christian dead are "the dead *in Christ*" (ver. 16); they will therefore be in due course the risen and the glorified in Christ (2 Ep. i. 12); comp. 2 Tim. ii. 11, "If we died with Him, we shall also live with Him." The point of the Apostle's reasoning lies in the connection of the words "*died and rose* again." Jesus has made a pathway through the grave, and by this passage His faithful, fallen asleep, still one with the dying, risen Jesus, will be conducted, to appear with Him at His return.

15. *For this we say unto you by the word of the Lord*] Lit., **in a word of the Lord,**—in the character of a message coming from "the mouth of the Lord;" comp. 1 Cor. vii. 10, "I give charge,—not I, but the Lord;" and ch. ii. 13 above, "not men's word, but God's." The "word" that follows (*vv.* 15—17) can hardly be explained as a traditional saying of Christ, unrecorded in the Gospels, like Acts xx. 35; nor as an inference from the teaching of Jesus on the subject of His return. St Paul claims to have received this communication directly from Christ, "the Lord" of His Church, as a revelation to himself (comp. Gal. ii. 2, Eph. iii. 3 for similar instances), given to him expressly in order to allay the fears of his readers. The *Lord* is manifestly Christ, as it is four times in the immediate sequel. St Paul applies to Christ's word the same august phrase that in the O. T. denotes "the word of God" Himself; comp. note on ch. i. 8.

that we which are alive and *remain unto the coming of the Lord*] This should be: **we that are alive, that remain** (or **survive**) **unto the coming of the Lord.** The second designation qualifies the first,—"those (I mean) who survive till the Lord comes." St Paul did not count on any very near approach of the second Advent: comp. 2 Ep. ii. 1, 2. At the same time, his language implies the *possibility* of the great event taking place within his lifetime, or that of the present generation.

the coming of the Lord shall not prevent them which are
16 asleep. For the Lord himself shall descend from heaven
with a shout, with the voice of the archangel, and with the

This remained an open question, or rather a matter on which questioning was forbidden (see Acts i. 7; Matt. xxiv. 36). "Concerning the times and seasons" nothing was definitely known (ch. v. 1, see note). The Apostles "knew in part" and "prophesied in part" (1 Cor. xiii. 12); and until further light came, it was natural for the Church, ever sighing "Come Lord Jesus, come quickly!" to speak as St Paul does here. The same "we" occurs in this connection in 1 Cor. xv. 51, 52. But from the time of the dangerous illness recorded in 2 Cor. i. 8, 9, the prospect of death occupied the foreground in the Apostle's thoughts of his own future, and he never afterwards writes "*we* that remain."

shall not prevent] "Prevent" is obsolete in this sense: comp. the Collect, "*Prevent* us in all our doings with Thy most gracious favour." Better, **shall in no wise precede** (or *anticipate*) **those that fell asleep**. The shadow which the event of their premature death had cast over the fate of the sleeping Thessalonian believers was wholly imaginary, and should be dismissed at once from the minds of their sorrowing friends. Instead of their having no place, they will have, as Christ now reveals to His Apostle, the *foremost* place in His triumphant return. Though dead, they are "dead in Christ" (ver. 16),—departed to "be with Christ"—"absent from the body" but "at home with the Lord," as St Paul subsequently teaches (2 Cor. v. 6—8; Phil. i. 23). So it cannot be that those who are found in the flesh when He comes again, will be beforehand with them in this reunion. "God will bring them with Him," for they are with Him already.

The Apostle proceeds to support this assurance by a description of Christ's coming, derived from the revelation, or "word of the Lord," to which he has just appealed. This was one of the most remarkable of the many "visions and revelations" which St Paul experienced (comp. 2 Cor. xii. 1—5).

16. *For the Lord Himself*] "In His personal august presence" (Ellicott). Comp. 2 Ep. ii. 16, iii. 16, for this kind of emphasis; also ch. iii. 11, v. 23, "God Himself:" in each case we feel the majesty with which God (or "the Lord") rises above all human doings and desires.

with a shout] Strictly, **word of command**, or *signal*,—the shout with which the general gives the order to his troops, or the captain to his crew. Such "command" might be given either by voice,—his own or another's; or through a trumpet: both are added here, to complete the impressive picture,—**with the voice of an archangel, and with the trumpet of God.**

We must not look for literal exactness where things are depicted beyond the reach of sense. These three may form but one idea, that of "the voice of the Son of God," by which the dead will be called forth (John v. 28), Christ's "command" being expressed by an "archangel's voice," and that again constituting the "trumpet of God." Christ predicted His return attended by *angels* (Matt. xxiv. 31; xxv.

trump of God: and the dead in Christ shall rise first: then 17
we which are alive *and* remain shall be caught up together

31; comp. 2 Ep. i. 7); and the Divine voice of the Book of Revelation is constantly uttered by an "angel," or "mighty angel" (Rev. v. 2; vii. 2; &c.). In the same Book *voice* and *trumpet* are identified, where St John describing the glorified Son of Man says, "I heard behind me a great voice, as of a trumpet talking with me" (Rev. i. 10, 12; iv. 1). This verse, like the above passages of the Apocalypse, echoes the words of Christ in Matt. xxiv. 31: "He shall send forth His angels with a trumpet of great voice." In 1 Cor. xv. 52 the whole is described in one word: "The-*trumpet*-shall-sound, and the dead shall be raised."

This is the *military* trumpet, like "word of command" above, by which the Lord of Hosts musters and marshals His array. Comp. ch. v. 8, with its "breastplate" and "helmet;" see note. "As a Commander rouses his sleeping soldiers, so the Lord calls up His dead, and bids them shake off the fetters of the grave and rise anew to waking life" (Hofmann).

St Paul does not write "*the* Archangel," as though pointing to some known Angelic Chief who is to blow this trumpet; his words are, **with an archangel's voice**, indicating the majesty and power of the heavenly summons. This is the earliest example of the title *archangel*. In Jude 9 we read of "*Michael* the archangel"—an expression probably based on Dan. xii. 1, "Michael the great prince" (LXX: "the great angel;" comp. Rev. xii. 7, where "Michael and his angels" are arrayed against "the Dragon and his angels"). Of equal rank with Michael is *Gabriel*, the angel of comfort and good tidings in Dan. viii. 16, ix. 21, and Luke i. 19, 26. The military style of this passage suits rather the character of Michael. Amongst the seven chief angels recognised at this time in Jewish teaching, *Raphael* stood nearest to the two that appear in the New Testament (Tobit xii. 15). St Paul probably ranged the Archangels amongst the Principalities (Greek *Archai*) to which he refers in Rom. viii. 38 (*angels and principalities*), Eph. i. 21, iii. 10, Col. i. 6, ii. 10, 15. See the Article on *Angels* in Smith's *Dictionary of Christian Antiquities*.

the Lord Himself, &c....**will descend from heaven.** See note on ch. i. 10. These words close the sentence, the accompaniments of the descent being first described, and then *the descent itself*, with solemn brevity and an effect of peculiar grandeur.

and the dead in Christ] This gives us the key to the Apostle's meaning throughout. Being "in Christ," having died as they lived *in Him*, nothing can part them from Him, "neither death nor life" (Rom. viii. 38). And when He returns in bodily presence, their bodies must rise to meet Him and do Him homage.

shall rise first] Not *before the other dead*, as though theirs were a select and separate resurrection (comp. John v. 28, 29); the antithesis is plainly given in the next verse,—"first," i.e. *before the living saints*: "we shall not take precedence of them, but rather they of us."

17. *then we which are alive* and *remain*] Better, **we that are alive,**

with them in the clouds, to meet the Lord in the air: and
that remain (or **survive**). The phrase of ver. 15 repeated; see note. The Apostle distinguishes, as in 1 Cor. xv. 51, 52, between those "living" and those "dead in Christ" at the time of His advent, marking the different position in which these two divisions of the saints will then be found.

shall be caught up together with them in the clouds] In the Greek order: **together with them will be caught up in the clouds**, emphasis being thrown on the precedence of *the dead*: "we the living shall join their company, who are already with the Lord." *Together with* implies full association.

"Caught" in the original implies a sudden, irresistible force,—**seized**, *snatched up!* In Matt. xi. 12 it is rendered, "The violent *take it by force;*" in 2 Cor. xii. 2, 4 St Paul applies it to his *rapture* into the third heaven.

"In" signifies not *into*, but *"amid* clouds,"—surrounding and up-bearing us "like a triumphal chariot" (Grotius). So Christ Himself, and the angels at His Ascension, promised He should come (Matt. xxvi. 68; Acts i. 9—11); comp. the "bright overshadowing cloud" at the Transfiguration, and the "voice out of the cloud" (Matt. xvii. 5). There is something wonderful and mystical about the clouds, half of heaven and half of earth, that fits them to be the medium of such events. They lend their ethereal drapery to form the curtain and canopy of this glorious meeting. "What belongs to cloudland is no less real than if set down on the solid ground."

Such a raising of the living bodies of the saints, along with the risen dead, implies the physical transformation of the former to which the Apostle afterwards alludes in 1 Cor. xv. 51: "we shall not all sleep, but we shall all be changed" (comp. 2 Cor. v. 1—4; Phil. iii. 21). Some change had taken place in the sacred body of Jesus after His resurrection, for it was emancipated from the ordinary laws of matter. And this transformation the Apostle conceived to be possible without dissolution.

to meet the Lord in the air] Lit., *into* (raised into) **the air**. "The air," like the "clouds," belongs to the interspace between the heaven from which Christ comes and the earth to which He returns. Here He will meet His Church. She will not need to wait until He sets foot on earth; but those who are ready, "looking for their Lord when He shall return" (Luke xii. 35—40), will hear His trumpet call and "go forth *to meet* the Bridegroom" (Matt. xxv. 1, 6). St Paul employs the same, somewhat rare Hebraistic idiom which is found in this passage of St Matthew, as though the words of Christ lingered in his ear.

and so shall we ever be with the Lord] *Where* the Apostle does not say; whether still on earth for some longer space, or in heaven. The one and all-sufficing comfort is in the thought of being **always with the Lord**. This, too, was the promise of Christ, "Where I am, there shall also My servant be" (John xii. 26; xiv. 3). Those living in the flesh cannot be so in any complete sense; "at home in the body," we are "absent from the Lord" (2 Cor. v. 6).

so shall we ever be with the Lord. Wherefore comfort one 18
another with these words.

But of the times and the seasons, brethren, ye have no 5

18. *Wherefore comfort one another with these words*] Lit., **in these words,**—in the revelation just communicated the readers are to find comfort for each other under their recent bereavement, and in all such seasons. Observe how wishful the Apostle is that his flock should minister *to each other.* Comp. ch. v. 12, 14, and notes.

Comfort—or **encourage**: same as the "exhort" of *vv.* 1, 10; it denotes any kind of animating and cheering address. See notes on "exhortation," ch. ii. 3, iii. 2.

> "Listen! it is no dream: the Apostles' trump
> Gives earnest of the Archangel's;—calmly now,
> Our hearts yet beating high
> To that victorious lay,
> (Most like a warrior's, to the martial dirge
> Of a true comrade,) in the grave we trust
> Our treasure for a while."

CHAPTER V.

SECTION VI. (continued): *vv.* 1—11.

THE first part of this Chapter stands in close connection with the last six verses of ch. iv. Together they form the most distinctive and the weightiest section of the Epistle. The two paragraphs of the section touch upon two different aspects of our Lord's Coming, viewed first *as it concerns departed Christians,* and then *in its relation to men living on the earth.* The former passage supplies comfort respecting the dead in Christ, the latter enjoins watchfulness and preparedness upon the living. See note introductory to ch. iv. 13.

From *vv.* 1 and 2 it appears likely that the Thessalonians had been enquiring from St Paul "about the times and the seasons" of Christ's return and the Day of Judgement.

1. *But of the times and the seasons*] Better, **concerning the times and the seasons.** The Greek word for "times" denotes *stretches of time,* that for seasons *particular times:* the question as to the former was, "How long before the Lord comes? what periods will elapse before the final establishment of His kingdom?" as to the second, "What events will transpire meanwhile? how will the course of history shape itself?" These enquiries our Lord put aside. "It is not for you," said He, "to know times or seasons, which the Father has put within His own province" (Acts i. 7); and previously Jesus had declared respecting the end of the world, "Of that day and hour knoweth no man, not even the angels in heaven, neither the Son,—only the Father" (Mark xiii. 32). Such knowledge, it appears, is outside the province of human thought. Speculations of this nature have been

² need that *I* write unto you. For yourselves know perfectly that the day of the Lord so cometh as a thief in the night.

repeatedly ventured on since the Apostle's day; they have proved invariably worthless, and afford so many confirmations of the Lord's warning. Chrysostom remarks on this passage somewhat severely: "Our nature is officious and greedy for the knowledge of things invisible and hidden from us. This comes of our conceit, and from having nothing to do. Often therefore is the mind in haste to learn and understand these things before the time."

ye have no need that I write unto you] Lit., **that aught be written to you** (R. V.). The phrase is a repetition of that of ch. iv. 9, except that there the emphasis lies on *you* as persons not needing this instruction, here upon the *writing* as a thing in itself needless. On the topic of the last paragraph, viz. the position of Christians dying before the Lord's return, it *was* needful that something should be written; as to the "times and seasons" nothing need be *written*, for the readers already *knew* so much as could be known (ver. 2).

2. *For yourselves know perfectly*] "For yourselves know:" a turn of expression characteristic of these Epistles; ch. i. 5 (see note), ii. 1 (identical with this), 2, 5, 11; iii. 4; iv. 2; 2 Ep. ii. 6; iii. 7 (identical).

"Perfectly" is a somewhat vague rendering of an adverb that with verbs of *knowing* signifies **precisely**, or *accurately;* in Mat. ii. 8, &c., it is rendered *carefully* (R.V.). Possibly the Thessalonians in sending their query had used this very word: "We should like to know more precisely," they may have said, "about the times and seasons, and when the Day of the Lord will be." 2 Ep. ii. 1—3 shows that the Church was full of eagerness about the Second Advent, and even after this caution many of its members continued to listen to those who professed to answer their irrepressible questions. The Apostle replies, with a touch of gentle irony (comp. note on ch. iv. 11): "You already know precisely that nothing precise on the subject can be known,—that the Great Day will steal upon the world like a thief in the night!"

the day of the Lord so cometh as a thief in the night] More exactly, **as a thief in the night, so there is coming a day of the Lord**; the definite article is absent in the Greek. Such a Day of the Lord as the Church expected *is coming;* it is on the way (comp. note on ch. i. 10). The event is certain: *when* it will arrive, no man can tell. Even in the act of going away Jesus said repeatedly, "I come," "I am coming to you" (John xiv. 3, 18, 28; &c.).

The figure of the *night-thief* points, as the next verse shows, to the effect of the Day upon the unprepared. The simile is taken from the lips of Jesus in His discourse of the Judgement (Matt. xxiv. 43; also Luke xii. 39, 40, where it is applied in warning to Christ's servants): it is employed by other Apostles, in 2 Pet. iii. 10; Rev. iii. 3, &c. It signifies, beside the *unexpectedness* of the event, its *bereaving effect:* it brings "sudden destruction" (ver. 3); the house of the worldling is "broken through."

"The day of the LORD" was a standing designation in the O.T., occurring first in Joel (ch. i. 15; ii. 1, 2, 11, 31; iii. 14; comp. Amos

For when they shall say, Peace and safety; then sudden 3
destruction cometh upon them, as travail upon a *woman*

v. 18) amongst the written prophets and handed down to Isaiah and Ezekiel, denoting the great epoch of judgement which in their age impended over Israel and the surrounding nations, and closed the prophetical horizon. In the O.T. therefore, the Day of the LORD has chiefly, if not exclusively, a judicial aspect. This meaning the expression carries over into the N.T.; and "the day of the LORD" is synonymous with "the day of Judgement" (Matt. xi. 22, &c.)—often called simply "that day" (Matt. vii. 22; Luke xvii. 31; &c.), also "the last day" (John vi. 39, &c.). Moreover Christ ascribes to Himself, "the Son of Man" (Luke xvii. 24, 26, 30), what the O. T. in this connection predicts of "the LORD" (Jehovah). Hence St Paul describes the same Day of the Lord as "the day of Jesus Christ" (Phil. i. 6, &c.). But our Apostle loves to regard the Day on its brighter side, as the time when Christ's glory will be revealed in His people (2 Ep. i. 10; Phil. ii. 16; &c.), "when He comes to be glorified in His saints and wondered at in all that believed." Now the world is having its day; "this is your hour," said Jesus to those who seized Him, "and the reign of darkness" (Luke xxii. 53). But that will be *the Lord's* day, when the Lord and His Christ will be manifested, and vindicated whether in salvation or judgement,—when "the glory of the LORD shall be revealed, and all flesh shall see it together" (Isai. xl. 5). Afterwards the weekly day of Christ's resurrection came to be called "the Lord's Day," as we call it now (Rev. i. 10)—this also a day of Divine vindication, and a pledge and foretaste of the final and perfect Day of the Lord: comp. the connection of the resurrection of Jesus with the Last Judgement in ch. i. 10 and Acts xvii. 31.

We have already observed a tacit reference under the words "as a thief in the night" to our Lord's discourse on the Judgement; and we shall find others in the sequel. These allusions make one think that the Apostle in his preaching at Thessalonica had surely quoted from Christ's words on this solemn theme. Otherwise, how would the Thessalonians "precisely know" that "the Day comes as a thief in the night"? While in regard to the state of the sainted dead a new revelation was needed (ch. iv. 15), on the question of the time of His coming His own well-remembered words were sufficiently explicit.

3. *For when they shall say*] Rather, **when they are saying** (R. V.). In the very act of their saying "Peace and safety"—just when men of the world pronounce everything secure and quiet—then the thief comes, who steals from them the possessions they imagined safe from all attack. A reminiscence of Ezek. xiii. 10, "Saying Peace, and there was no peace!" Such times of security are pregnant with judgement to the wicked, and premonitory of some "day of the Lord."

then sudden destruction cometh upon them] Or, in the vivid order of St Paul's Greek, **then suddenly over them stands destruction.** Without a moment's warning ruin comes,—not seen approaching, but first visible *hanging over* the doomed transgressors! We hear again Christ's warning of Luke xxi. 34, "lest that day come upon you

4 with child; and they shall not escape. But ye, brethren, are not in darkness, that *that* day should overtake you as a 5 thief. Ye are all the children of light, and the children of

suddenly (a Greek word found only in these two places in the N. T.), as a snare; for so will it come on all them that dwell on the face of all the earth." Christ compares His advent to the coming of the Flood "in the days of Noah" (Matt. xxiv. 36—39).

The Apostle describes the calamity under another figure, frequently applied in the O. T. to Divine inflictions: **as the birth-pang upon her that is with child.** This image signifies, beside the *suddenness* of the disaster, its *intense pain*, and its *inevitableness*. Accordingly he continues: **and they shall in no wise escape.** See 2 Ep. i. 9, and note; and comp. the terrible picture of the Judgement in Rev. vi. 15—17.

4. *But ye, brethren, are not in darkness, that* that *day should overtake you as a thief*] Properly, **the day**—the great Day, the "day of the Lord" (ver. 2); comp. the other elliptical phrase, "the wrath," of ch. i. 10, ii. 16. At the same time, this word, while it looks back to *vv.* 2 and 3, suggests the wider, figurative sense of *day* that comes out in ver. 5. Since the Thessalonians are "not in darkness," the coming of day will be no terror or surprise to them. The Day of the Lord will not "overtake them as a thief," stealing on them suddenly and despoiling them of their treasures unawares, but it will come to them as the welcome daybreak, full of light and joy. To the wicked and careless, by a sad contradiction, the Day of the Lord will be *night!* it is to them "darkness and not light,—yea, very dark, and no brightness in it" (Amos v. 20). But for "the sons of light" (ver. 5) it is day indeed, and wears its true character.

The *margin* of the R. V. contains the interesting reading, found "in some ancient authorities," preferred also by Westcott and Hort: *overtake you as thieves!* This gives a striking sense. It depicts the guilty as themselves "thieves," surprised by daylight. But it involves an abrupt change of metaphor, not sustained by the following context; it transforms the "thief" from the *cause* of the surprise (ver. 2) into its *object*.

5. *Ye are all the children of light, and the children of the day*] More correctly, **For you are all sons of light and sons of day.** This confirms positively what was stated by way of denial in ver. 4. Those cannot be "in darkness" who are "sons of light." Light is their native element and abode.

By a common Hebrew idiom, a man is said to be a *son* of any influence that determines or dominates his character. So there are "sons of Belial" (worthlessness) in the O. T.; and Christ speaks of "sons of thunder," "sons of the Resurrection," &c.

Light is a favourite figure with St Paul: see Rom. xiii. 11—14; Eph. v. 8—14; Col. i. 12. St John employs it still more frequently; in his Gospel, Christ applies it with emphasis to His Person as well as to His doctrine: "*I* am the light of the world" (John i. 49, viii. 12), &c. Both conceptions meet in the words of Ps. xxxvi. 9, addressed to God: "In Thy light shall we see light." This natural and

the day: we are not of the night, nor of darkness. There- 6
fore let us not sleep, as *do* others; but let us watch and be

beautiful metaphor describes the truth revealed by God to men (1) in its *moral purity*, as opposed to the darkness of sin (see *vv.* 7, 8; comp. Rom. xiii. 12, 13, John iii. 19, 1 John i. 5—7); but especially (2) in its *saving effect*, as the bringer of life, deliverance and joy (Ps. xxvii. 1, "The LORD is my light and my salvation;" Isai. lx. 1—3; John viii. 12; 2 Cor. iv. 6; &c.). These two meanings are united in St Paul's conception. (3) The thought of *mental enlightenment* also accompanies the figure (see e.g. Eph. i. 17, 18).

"Day" is here not a mere synonym for "light" in general; it takes up again the "day of the Lord" of *vv.* 2, 4. Now receiving the light of Christ's truth and assimilated to it, the sons of light will be ready for "that day." Christ's advent will be to them like sunrise after long twilight. It is their birthday, the time of their full redemption and revelation. "The day of the Lord" claims them for its own,—"sons of day," being "sons of God" and "the resurrection" (Luke xx. 34—36). See 2 Ep. i. 7; Rom. viii. 18—24; Col. iii. 4.

This the Apostle assumes of "all" his readers; for he counts upon them all maintaining the watchful hope that befits the sons of light.

we are not of the night, nor of darkness] The Apostle passes from the *second* person to the *first* (comp. ch. iii. 3, 4); he associates himself with his readers in this repudiation of night and darkness.

Night, as the opposite of "day," is the period, or the state, of ignorance and estrangement from God, which for believers in Christ has passed away. And yet in contrast with the full light which will burst forth on "the day of the Lord," the present hour is even for them one of comparative darkness and obscuration: see Rom. xiii. 12; Col. iii. 1—4; 1 John iii. 2. *Darkness* is the element and empire of night; the condition in which "the rest" (ver. 6) live and have their being. Such darkness involves, along with ignorance of God, moral debasement (see ver. 7, and ch. iv. 5) and insensibility (2 Ep. ii. 11, 12; Rom. i. 30; Matt. xxiv. 38—40); hence exposure to surprise and ruin (*vv.* 2, 3).

6. *Therefore*] More exactly, **Accordingly then**. The double conjunction here employed is an idiom peculiar to St Paul, which appears once in 2 Thess. (ch. ii. 15), eight times in Romans, and twice besides in his Epistles. It combines the *logical* and *practical* inference,—that which both reason and duty require.

let us not sleep, as do *others*] **the rest** (R. V.); as in ch. iv. 13, see note. "Sleep" is natural to those who are "of the night" (comp. Eph. v. 11-14); it is symbolic of the insensibility and helplessness that sin produces. Comp. Rom. xiii. 11, 12: "It is high time to awake out of sleep...Let us put off the works of darkness, and put on the armour of light." In this sense we may well pray the prayer of Ps. xiii. 3, "Lighten Thou mine eyes, lest I sleep the sleep of death."

but let us watch and be sober] Lit., **let us keep awake**. It is our Lord's word of warning and entreaty in the Garden, Mark xiv. 34, 37,

7 sober. For they that sleep sleep in the night; and they
8 that be drunken are drunken in the night. But let us, who
are of the day, be sober, putting on the breastplate of faith

38; comp. Luke xii. 36, 37, "Be ye like unto men looking out for their lord, when he shall return from the wedding...Blessed are those servants whom the Lord when He cometh shall find *watching.*" It indicates the *wakeful activity* of a mind devoted to Christ's service and busy with thoughts of His coming. Of such "watching" *prayer* is a necessary accompaniment (Mark xiv. 38; Col. iv. 2).

"Be sober" gives the moral, as "watch" the mental side of the attitude enjoined in view of the coming Day; comp. ver. 8; also 1 Pet. v. 8. *Soberness,* in its narrower sense the opposite of drunkenness (ver. 7), includes habits of moderation and self-control generally. It excludes, for one thing, morbid excitement and unreasoning credulity about the Parousia (2 Ep. ii. 1—3).

7. *For they that sleep sleep in the night; and they that be drunken are drunken in the night*] The "sons of day" must be wakeful and sober, for the opposite conditions belong to *night* and are proper to its children. To be drunken *by day* was a monstrous and almost unheard-of thing (comp. Acts ii. 15). Negligence and wantonness have no place in those who belong to "the day."

These words look beyond their literal sense, as "sober" in ver. 6. Drunkenness signifies the condition of a soul besotted and enslaved by evil. We catch here another echo of our Lord's warnings: "Lest haply your hearts be overcharged with surfeiting and drunkenness and cares of this life, and that day come upon you suddenly as a snare" (Luke xxi. 34; comp. ver. 3 above; also Luke xii. 45, 46; and Rom. xiii. 13). Thus dawn surprises guilty revellers.

8. *But let us, who are of the day, be sober*] Better, **since we are of the day** (R. V.); comp. notes on "sober" (ver. 6), and "day" (ver. 5).

Watchfulness has been sufficiently urged already. The Apostle now reiterates the other half of the appeal made in ver. 6: "let us be *sober.*"

putting on the breastplate of faith and love; and for a helmet, the hope of salvation] The daylight rouses the soldier to action. If he has slept, with the dawn he is awake and alert; if he has spent the night in carousals, he is instantly sobered. The things of darkness are dismissed and forgotten. At the bugle-call he starts up, he dons his armour and is ready for the field. In Rom. xiii. 12, 13 the same figure is still more graphically applied: "Let us put off the works of darkness—revellings, drunkenness, and the like"—loose and shameful garments of the night— "and let us put on the armour of light...Let us walk in the day, becomingly." Comp., for the *military* style of the passage, ch. iv. 16, and notes.

In the later passage parallel to this, Eph. vi. 13—17, the Christian armour, "the panoply of God," is set forth in greater detail and somewhat differently. "Breastplate" and "helmet" make up this picture, being the two chief pieces of defensive armour, that protect

and love; and for a helmet, the hope of salvation. For God 9 hath not appointed us to wrath, but to obtain salvation by

the two most vital parts of the body. "The breastplate of faith and love" guards the *heart*, the centre of life and spring of the body's forces; and to this quarter "faith and love" are naturally assigned. What belongs to "breastplate" here, is virtually divided between "shield" and "breastplate" in Ephesians.—The "helmet" is the same in both Epistles: there consisting of "salvation," here "the hope of salvation," in accordance with the fact that Hope is the dominant key-note of this Epistle (see ch. i. 3, and note). The fitness of this metaphor lies in the place of the helmet as the crown of the soldier's armour, its brightest and most conspicuous feature, covering the *head*, the part of his person that most invites attack. The simile, in both Epistles, is based on Isaiah lix. 17, where the LORD appears "putting on righteousness as a breastplate" and "an helmet of salvation upon His head," as He goes forth to fight for His people.

Observe again the Apostle's favourite combination, *Faith, Love, Hope*, in the same order as in ch. i. 3 (see notes); also in 2 Ep. i. 3, 4. As we might expect, "hope the helmet" is that on which he is here most disposed to dwell. Accordingly he continues—

9. *For God hath not appointed us to wrath*] In the strict order of the words, **appointed us not unto wrath, but** (to something very different) **unto the obtaining of salvation through our Lord Jesus Christ.**

"Obtaining" is *securing, making a thing absolutely one's own*,—as in 2 Ep. ii. 14 (see note), "the obtaining of the glory of our Lord Jesus Christ." In Heb. x. 39 the same word is rendered "*saving* of the soul;" in Eph. i. 14 it signifies, passively used, a *sure possession*. In all these instances it points beyond the present attainment of salvation, still subject to trial and hazard, to the full realisation thereof, which is the object of the Christian's hope (ver. 8), as it is the end of God's designs for him.

"Salvation," in St Paul and in the N. T. generally, includes the whole of the benefits and blessings of the Gospel, the entire new life and well-being that it brings, both to the individual man and to the world; but it is referred more specifically to two essential elements, or moments, in the great process of renewal—(1) that spoken of in Luke i. 77 as "knowledge of salvation...in *remission of sins*," and (2) to man's *deliverance from the grave* and entrance on the risen life of the future world,—"salvation that is in Christ Jesus with eternal glory" (2 Tim. ii. 10). In the word *redemption* this double reference is even more conspicuous: see, e.g., Eph. i. 7 and 14. To this ultimate "salvation" the Apostle directs his readers' thoughts and hopes.

"Appointed" reminds us of "election" (ch. i. 4, see note); it implies the *authority* with which God called the Thessalonians to salvation (comp. ch. ii. 12), as well as the fact of His gracious *intention* respecting them. Comp. 1 Tim. i. 12, "appointing me to service," and ch. iii. 3 above. In 2 Ep. ii. 13, 14 (see notes) this Divine *appointment* of grace is more fully set forth.

10 our Lord Jesus Christ, who died for us, that, whether we

For the negative side of God's purpose—**not unto anger**—see notes on *wrath* in ch. i. 10; ii. 16; 2 Ep. i. 8, 9. With the thought of Christ's second coming, so constantly present to St Paul's mind at this time (see *Introd.* pp. 18—21), there were present also the issues of the Last Judgement and its solemn contrast—the glorious "salvation" then to be attained by the sons of God, and the final and awful manifestation of His "anger" against the wicked. Similarly "the day of the Lord" is seen in Rom. ii. 5 as a "day of wrath and revelation of the righteous judgement of God;" and in this light, wrath and future salvation are contrasted in Rom. v. 9, 10, just as they are here. There also, as in this passage, Christ's *death* (see ver. 10) is set forth as our ground of hope in this prospect; through "His blood" we are brought from the sense and fear of God's anger into His favour, and entitled to expect that eternal redemption will be ours.

It was the conviction that such is God's *purpose and will* respecting those who believe in Christ that made St Paul's "helmet of salvation" so strong, and gave it all its splendour. Read Rom. viii. 31—39 as a commentary on this saying.

On the full title "our Lord Jesus Christ" see note to ch. i. 3.

10. (through our Lord Jesus Christ,) *who died for us*] It has been said that the gospel which Paul preached at Thessalonica was "not the gospel of the Cross of Christ, but of the Coming of Christ." But these two are not exclusive or conflicting doctrines; they are complementary parts of one and the same Gospel. This clause is enough to show how far the apostles were from ignoring the Cross of Christ in their ministry at Thessalonica. When St Paul writes, "Christ died for us... that we should live together with Him," his words involve the entire doctrine of Redemption by the death and resurrection of Jesus, as it is set forth at length in the next group of Epistles—in Rom. iii. 21—26; iv. 25—v. 2; vi. 1—11; viii. 1—4; Gal. ii. 10—21; iii. 9—14; 2 Cor. v. 14—vi. 2; &c. They imply the Atonement and Salvation by Faith, the receiving of Christ's Spirit of sonship, and abiding union with Him in His risen and heavenly life. The whole theology of the Cross is in this sentence,—which indeed could only be interpreted and understood by the Thessalonians in the light of such teaching as we find in the later Epistles. The message of salvation through the death of Christ had been the staple and centre of the Apostle's testimony all along. In writing to the Corinthians, and referring to his preaching in Corinth at the very time when he wrote the letters before us, he calls his message simply "the word of the cross" (1 Cor. i. 17, 18, 23; ii. 2); comp., for an earlier period, Acts xiii. 38, 39; Gal. iii. 1, also vi. 14. See *Introd.* pp. 16, 17.

that, whether we wake or sleep] More exactly, **whether we be awake or asleep**, i.e. *living or dead*—with allusion to the use of the same terms to denote spiritual wakefulness or slumber in *vv.* 6, 7 (see notes).

At the same time these words carry us back, with a sudden change of metaphor, to ch. iv. 13—18. There it was shewn that believers living at the Lord's return, and those who "fall asleep" before He

wake or sleep, we should live together with him. Wherefore **11** comfort yourselves together, and edify one another, even as also ye do.

comes, alike belong to Him, and will share alike in the glory of His advent. And now it appears that this deep and sure relationship of the saints to Christ, unbroken by the sleep of bodily death, is grounded upon *His death for them.* That death He underwent for the very purpose of giving them a deathless life: **in order that...together with Him we should live** (comp. Rom. xiv. 8, 9: "Whether we live or die, we are the Lord's....Christ died and came to life, that He might be Lord of both dead and living"). The stress lies upon the last word: Christ *died* for us, that we might *live* with Him—a life consisting in spiritual union with Him, and continuing undestroyed whether the man wakes or sleeps to this world. "I came," said Jesus, "that men might have life...I am the living bread, which came down from heaven. If any one eat of this bread, he shall live for ever. Yea, and the bread which I will give is My flesh, for the life of the world" (John x. 10; vi. 51). Risen from the grave, our Saviour "lives" evermore "to God; death no longer lords it over Him" (Rom. vi. 9, 10). And those who are Christ's, "joined to the Lord" as "one spirit" with Him (1 Cor. vi. 17), share His life, which flows from the heavenly Head to all the earthly members of His Body. This is the life "that is life indeed" (1 Tim. vi. 19); it is superior to the accidents of time, since in its spring and essence "hid with Christ in God" (Col. iii. 1—4). Such is St Paul's conception of the nature of the Christian's life.

The "with Him" of ch. iv. 14, 17 is echoed and unfolded in the "together with Him" of this verse, as it formed the basis of the "together with *them*" of ch. iv. 17. All joy and strength for the present life and hope for that to come, for ourselves and for those dear to us, are centred in the words "together with Him." So the Apostle resumes the strain of consolation, from which he had turned aside in ver. 1 to utter words of caution; and he concludes, almost in the language of ch. iv. 18—

11. *Wherefore comfort yourselves together*] **exhort** (or **encourage**) **one another**—same verb as in ch. iv. 18 (see note, and on ch. iii. 2).

While "encouragement" would be drawn especially from *vv.* 9, 10, as from the closing *vv.* of ch. iv., the appeal to the Thessalonians to *edify*, i.e. **build up each other**, rests on the whole content of the paragraph, from the beginning of the chapter. The warnings of *vv.* 3—8 tend to *edification*, promoting as they do seriousness and solidity of Christian life.

The word "edify"—a favourite word of St Paul's—points to the Church as *a house*, the "habitation of God in the Spirit" (Eph. ii. 22), each part contributing to the welfare of every other and furthering the life and strength of the whole. In this word lies the germ of the Apostle's conception of the Church, which he unfolded at a later time, in 1 Cor. xii. 12—27, and still further in the Epistle to the Ephesians.

even as also ye do] Comp. ch. iv. 1, 9, 10, and notes. These re-

12 And we beseech you, brethren, to know them which labour among you, and are over you in the Lord, and ad-

peated acknowledgements attest the high quality and spirit of this Church. It excelled especially in mutual kindness and helpfulness.

St Paul ascribes the functions of "edification" to the whole body of the Church, and does not regard them as confined to the official ministry, of which he has immediately to speak (*vv*. 12, 13). This collective office of edification is powerfully set forth in Eph. iv. 16: "All the Body, jointed together and compacted...each single part operating in its measure, makes its growth, to the end it may build up itself in love."

SECTION VII. RULES FOR THE SANCTIFIED LIFE.
CH. V. 12—24.

In Section v. (ch. iv. 1—12) the *saintship* of his readers supplied the basis and the nerve of the Apostle's charge. He there enforced on the Thessalonian believers the virtues which they needed to cultivate, in the light of their *consecration to God*. The indwelling of the Holy Spirit served as the sovereign motive for the leading of a pure life (ch. iv. 3, 7, 8). The same thought runs through this Section. The string of sententious exhortations it contains, find their goal and their uniting principle in the prayer, "May the God of peace Himself sanctify you fully" (ver. 23). Hence the title we prefix to the paragraph.

Vv. 12—15 relate to *social* duties, spreading out in widening circles from "those who preside over you in the Lord" (ver. 12) to "all men" (ver. 15). Then we pass to *religious* duties, *vv*. 16—22: to those (1) of the most general character, *vv*. 16—18; and (2) to the more specific injunctions arising from the special gifts of the Spirit then bestowed upon the Church, *vv*. 19—22. These directions lead up to the great prayer of the Apostle for entire sanctification, *vv*. 23, 24.

12. *And we beseech you, brethren*] For "beseech" (or "ask") see note to ch. iv. 1. The Apostle resumes the line of exhortation which he there commenced, and which was interrupted by the consolations and warnings he had to give on the subject of the Second Coming.

The "But" with which this entreaty begins, points back to ver. 11. The Apostle has been directing his readers generally to "encourage and edify each other:" *but* at the same time they must not ignore the services of their official ministry or deem their oversight and teaching needless.

to know them which labour among you, and are over you in the Lord, and admonish you] A clear testimony, from this earliest writing of the N.T., to the existence in the Church at the beginning of a ministerial order—a *clergy* (to use the language of a later age) as distinguished from the *laity*—charged with specific duties and authority. But there is nothing in the grammar of the sentence, nor in the nature of the duties specified, which would warrant us in distributing these functions

monish you; and to esteem them very highly in love for ¹³ their work's sake. *And* be at peace among yourselves. Now ¹⁴ amongst *distinct orders* of Church office. "Labouring," "presiding," and "admonishing" form the threefold calling of the local Christian ministry. Doubtless St Paul had organized this Church before leaving it, as he and Barnabas did the Churches of Lycaonia at an earlier time, "ordaining elders in every city" (Acts xiv. 23). It is not likely that it had advanced beyond the incipient stage of Church government. The Epistle to the Philippians, in which "bishops and deacons" are addressed (Ph. i. 1), was written nearly ten years later.

"Labour"—or **toil**, as in ch. i. 3 (see note)—implies *difficulty* in the work; the Apostle uses it of his own spiritual work in 1 Cor. xv. 10; Gal. iv. 11; Ph. ii. 16; Col. i. 29. The chief instrument and method of this "labour" are pointed out in 1 Tim. v. 17: "who labour in word and doctrine."

Lit., **and preside over you in the Lord.** The Pastoral Epistles, describing Church office in its more advanced development, represent this as the chief duty of *the elders:* "Let the elders who preside (*rule*, A.V. and R.V.) well, be counted worthy of double honour"; comp. also 1 Tim. iii. 5 and 12. There, however, as here, "labouring" is honoured even more than "ruling." The presidency of the elders in the Church assemblies naturally carried with it, as in Jewish communities, the right of exercising discipline over the moral life of the community. Hence "preside" comes to signify "rule," as also in Rom. xii. 8. In Heb. xiii. 7, 17 the ministers are called "your leaders."—To "preside *in the Lord*" is to preside over a Christian assembly in Christ's name and authority.

The duty of *admonition* devolved chiefly on the officers of the Church; but not exclusively, as *vv.* 11, 14 and 2 Ep. iii. 15 show.

To "*know* those who labour and preside and admonish" is to understand them and the nature of their duties—to *know their character and labours*, to *have* due *acquaintance with them*. Ministers are often told that they must *know* their people: the Apostle points out the duty that exists on the other side. Such knowledge, wanting apparently in some of the Thessalonians, would result in high esteem:—

13. *and to esteem them very highly in love for their work's sake*] **exceeding highly** (R.V.)—the same Greek adverb as in ch. iii. 10, the strongest intensive possible to the language. So deep and warm should be the affection uniting pastors and their flocks. Their appreciation is not to be a cold esteem; it has mutual "love" for its pervading element, a grace in which the Thessalonians were already "taught of God" (ch. iv. 9). Their "work," described in ver. 12, is the reason for this devoted esteem. In *work* this Church excelled (ch. i. 3); and this it knew how to appreciate.

And *be at peace among yourselves*] *And* is wanting in the Greek. But this appeal is closely connected with the last. Looking, moreover, at the exhortation to "admonish the unruly" that follows, and at the command "study to be quiet" of ch. iv. 11, and the measures pre-

we exhort you, brethren, warn *them that are* unruly, comfort the feebleminded, support the weak, be patient toward all men. See that none render evil for evil unto any *man;* but

scribed against the idle and disorderly in 2 Ep. iii. 6—15, we can read between the lines sufficiently to see that the tendencies adverse to peace in this community were interfering with its discipline, and set the Church authorities at variance with a certain section of its membership.

14. *Now we exhort you, brethren, warn* them that are *unruly*] More strictly, **But we exhort,** &c. The Apostle is not passing to a new topic. His exhortation to "peace" needs to be qualified. "The unruly" must not for the sake of peace be left unreproved. It is a false and cowardly peace that leaves disorder to range unchecked.

Read **admonish** for *warn*—same verb as in ver. 12. The Church at large must second its presiding elders in such admonishing. In every well-ordered community, whether church or school or nation, needful discipline claims the support of public opinion. The disorder that required this general censure was doubtless that hinted at in ch. iv. 11 (see note), and which had grown more pronounced when St Paul wrote 2 Ep. iii. 6—15; it was a common injury and discredit.

The unruly: better, **the disorderly** (R.V.), as in 2 Ep. iii. 11.

comfort the feebleminded, support the weak] Rather, **the fainthearted** (R. V.). The former verb was used in ch. ii. 11 (see note), where the Apostle reminds his readers how he had "exhorted, and *comforted* (or *consoled*)" them, "as a father his own children." The second of these directions also St Paul enforces by his example, in Acts xx. 35: "In all things I have shown you how that so labouring you ought to *help the weak.*" Comp. Eph. iv. 28, for the same sentiment.

"The weak" and "fainthearted" stand in contrast with "the disorderly." The latter are overbold, and need to be checked: the former are despondent, and need stimulus and help. Fainthearted men think themselves weak, but perhaps are not so; and encouragement may make them bold. The mourners whom St Paul consoled in ch. iv. 13—18, would be amongst "the fainthearted" at Thessalonica.

be patient toward all men] **longsuffering toward all** (R.V.)—"whether weak or strong, whether they try you by their presumption or timidity, by rude aggressiveness or by feebleness and incapacity." *Longsuffering* is one of the special marks of Christian grace: "Charity suffereth long" (1 Cor. xiii. 4); it was a chief quality of Jesus Christ, and is an attribute of God Himself (1 Pet. iii. 20; 1 Tim. i. 16; &c.).

15. *See that none render evil for evil unto any* man] The stress lies not on the personal object, as in the former clause (*all, any*), but on the quality of the act: better, **See that none render unto any one evil in return for evil.** The Thessalonian Christians were receiving much evil from the world; possibly some of its members were wronging others: there must be no retaliation. "Blows may fall on you; you must never return them." This command is linked closely with the last; for while that bids each man restrain his own anger, this requires him to

ever follow *that which is* good, both among yourselves, and to all *men*. Rejoice evermore. Pray without ceasing. In 16 17 18

check the resentful spirit wherever it appears. It is a reproach to all, a discredit to the common faith, when a Christian gives back wrong for wrong. Comp. Rom. xii. 19—21, "Be not overcome of evil, but overcome evil with good;" also 1 Pet. ii. 18—25; and especially the teaching of Christ in Matt. v. 38—48. On *evil*, see note to ver. 22.

but ever follow that which is *good*] This is to "follow" not by way of imitation, as in ch. i. 6, ii. 14, but *by way of aim and pursuit*: hence, **follow after** (R.V.). And "the good" is here "the beneficial." As much as to say: "Make the good of your fellow-men your constant pursuit, and let no injury or unworthiness on their part turn you aside from it."

This line of conduct is to be pursued both within and without the Church: **one toward another, and toward all.** Amongst Christians such seeking of the good of others is mutual, and there its best results will appear. But its exercise is to be unlimited. No follower of Christ will do wilful harm to any man. The distinction made "by them of old time, Thou shalt love thy neighbour, and hate thine enemy," Christ, our Lawgiver, has abolished (Matt. v. 43—48).

From *social* duties the Apostle's homily now rises to matters of *religion*, from the claims of Christians on each other to "the will of God" concerning them. See note introductory to ver. 12.

16. *Rejoice evermore*] **alway** (R.V.)—same as in ch. i. 2, ii. 16, &c. This seems a strange injunction for men afflicted like the Thessalonians (see ch. i. 6, ii. 14, iii. 2—4; 2 Ep. i. 4). But the Apostle had learnt, and taught the secret, that in sorrow endured for Christ's sake there is hidden a new spring of joy. See Rom. v. 3—5, "Let us glory in our tribulations;" 2 Cor. xii. 10; and the Beatitude of Christ in Matt. v. 10—12; also 1 Pet. iv. 12—14.

This phrase supplied the key-note of St Paul's subsequent letter, written from prison, to the Philippians (ch. iv. 4, 5).

17. *Pray without ceasing*] Twice the Apostle has used this adverb (ch. i. 3, ii. 13), referring to his own constant grateful remembrance of his readers before God. Numberless other objects occupied his mind during the busy hours of each day; and the Thessalonians could not be distinctly present to his mind in every act of devotion; still he felt that they were never out of remembrance, and thankfulness on their account mingled with and coloured all his thoughts and feelings at this time. In like manner Prayer is to be the accompaniment of our whole life—a stream ever flowing, now within sight and hearing, now disappearing from view, forming the under-current of all our thoughts and giving to them its own character and tone.

18. *In every* thing *give thanks*] This again the Apostle taught by example as well as precept; see ch. i. 2; iii. 9, 10; and comp. Ph. iv. 6; Col. iv. 2. "In *everything*," even in persecution and shame, suffered for Christ's sake; comp. Phil. i. 29, 2 Cor. xii. 9, 10.

Prayer and Thanksgiving are the two wings of the soul by which it rises upward to God.

every *thing* give thanks: for this *is* the will of God in Christ Jesus concerning you. Quench not the Spirit. Despise

for this is the will of God in Christ Jesus concerning you] Rather, **to you-ward** (R.V.):—"You Thessalonian believers—so greatly afflicted and tempted to murmuring and despondency—are the special objects of this Divine purpose, whose attainment is made possible for you in Christ Jesus. God intends that your life should be one of constant prayer, constant joy and thanksgiving." In ch. iii. 3 it was said that the Thessalonians were "appointed" to their extraordinary sufferings (comp. ch. iv. 3). Now the reason of this appointment is shown; it is that they may grow perfect in thankfulness, grateful for the bitter as well as for the sweet in their experiences,—for

"each rebuff
That turns earth's smoothness rough,
Each sting that bids nor sit nor stand, but go."

Such cheerfulness of soul needs strong faith, and is won through hard trial. Rom. v. 3—5 supplies the reasoning by which tribulation is made matter of thanksgiving and the sorrows of the Christian are turned to songs of joy.—On *Christ Jesus*, see note to ch. ii. 14.

From *joy, prayer and thanksgiving* the Apostle passes by a natural transition to *the Spirit and prophesying*. For Christian joy and Christian prayer are inspired by the Holy Spirit. See ch. i. 6, "with joy of the Holy Spirit"; also Rom. viii. 26, Eph. vi. 18, and Jude 20, "praying in the Holy Spirit." "Praying" and "prophesying" are kindred, spiritual exercises (see 1 Cor. xi. 4, 5).

19, 20. *Quench not the Spirit. Despise not prophesyings*] The R.V. properly reduces to a semi-colon the full stop between these sentences.

What is *revelation* on God's part, is *prophecy* in its human instrument. "Prophecy" bears to "revelation" the same relation as "teaching" to "knowledge" (1 Cor. xii. 6), the former being the utterance and outcome of the latter. *Prediction*, to which we limit the term in common speech, is but a part—and not an essential part—of Prophecy, in its Biblical sense. It is, etymologically, the *forth-speaking* of what was otherwise unknown and hidden in the mind of God.

This power of declaring by direct inspiration the mind of God was widely diffused amongst the first Christians; see 1 Cor. xii. 10, xiv. 1—5, Rom. xii. 6, where it is spoken of as an ordinary and familiar thing. This gift manifested in the highest and most effective way the power of God's Spirit in man; but it was liable to be abused (see 1 Cor. xiv. 26—31), and to be simulated (1 John iv. 1). The expression "through Spirit" in 2 Ep. ii. 2 probably refers to some spurious prophetic manifestation. A fanatical element appears to have mingled with the prophesyings of the Thessalonian Church; and this had doubtless given offence to sober minds, and created distrust in regard to prophecy itself. Hence the double caution. Contempt for this great gift of His must of necessity grieve the Holy Spirit, and limit His action in the Church. Nothing is more chilling to religious life than a cold rationalism which suspects the supernatural beforehand,

not prophesyings. Prove all *things;* hold fast *that which is* good. Abstain from all appearance of evil. And the very

and is ready to confound the manifestations of the Spirit of God with morbid excitement or insincere pretension.

But the command, "Quench not the Spirit," is universal. Whatever obstructs or disparages His work in the souls of men—whether in others, or in ourselves—is thus forbidden. It is a strange and awful, but very real power that we have to "resist the Holy Spirit." (Acts vii. 51).

Since He may be "quenched," He is a *fire*, as appeared on the Day of Pentecost (Acts ii. 3). This emblem sets forth the sudden and vehement activities of the Holy Spirit, with His gifts of warmth for the heart and light for the mind and His power to kindle the human spirit. Prophecy exhibited His presence under this aspect, in its intensity and ardour. On the other hand, He appears in gentler form under the emblem of *the dove*, in whose guise the Spirit descended on Jesus at His baptism.

21. *Prove all* things; *hold fast* that which is *good*] Some of the best ancient authorities read, **But prove all things**. In any case, this exhortation, while capable of the widest application, arises out of the subject of the last. "Instead of accepting or rejecting wholesale what is addressed to you as prophecy, use your judgement; learn to discriminate; sift the wheat from the chaff." So needful was it to distinguish between true and false revelations, that a special endowment was bestowed on some persons for this end—the "discernment of spirits" (1 Cor. xii. 10). And St Paul gives a criterion for the purpose in 1 Cor. xii. 3. Comp. 1 John iv. 1—3, "Beloved, believe not every spirit; but try the spirits, whether they are of God."

"The good" represents a different word from that of ver. 15 (see note); it signifies what is *good* or *fine in quality*, as in 2 Ep. iii. 13.

22. *Abstain from all appearance of evil*] **from every form of evil** (R.V.). The Apostle does not advise the Thessalonians to avoid what *looks like* evil; the command thus understood encourages the studying of appearances, and tends to the "doing of our works to be seen of men" which our Lord condemns (Matt. xxiii. 5). But in completing on the negative side the previous command, "hold fast the good (in prophesyings)," he gives to it the widest possible extension: "Keep yourselves not only from this, but *from every sort of evil.*" It is difficult, however, for the Greek scholar to justify the reading of *evil* in this sentence as a substantive, and the rendering of the governing noun by *kind* instead of *appearance* (rendered *form, fashion, shape,* in Luke iii. 22, ix. 29, John v. 37). This noun St Paul uses once besides, in 2 Cor. v. 7: "We walk by faith, not by *sight*"—i.e. with no visible form, or appearance, to walk by. His meaning here may be similar: **Abstain from every evil sight** (or **show**)—from all that is evil in the outward show of things about you: *ab omni specie mala* (Vulgate).

There are two words for "evil" in Greek—that used here, signifying *harmful, mischievous* (so designating "the Evil One," see note on

God of peace sanctify you wholly; and *I pray God* your

2 Ep. iii. 3); and that employed in ver. 15, denoting *bad, base, malicious*.

With this emphatic word, **keep yourselves**, the Apostle concludes his directions to the Thessalonians, extending from ver. 12—22, as to *what they must do* in order to preserve and sustain the life of grace in themselves. The prayer of the next verse invokes *the power of God* to accomplish for them that which mere human effort can never attain. Comp. the transition of ch. iii. 11, expressed in similar language (see note), and of 2 Ep. ii. 16 and iii. 3. All that the Christian can do for his own safe-keeping, or for the service of his fellows, is merged in the greatness and completeness of that which God will do for them.

23. *And the very God of peace*] **the God of peace Himself** (R.V.)—so "God Himself" in ch. iii. 11, and "our Lord Jesus Christ Himself" in 2 Ep. ii. 16, where the like contrast is implied between human wish or endeavour and Divine power. With this contrast in his mind, St Paul begins, **But**, not *and:* "I bid you keep yourselves from evil; *but may God*, Who only can, cleanse and preserve you." Comp. Ph. ii. 12, 13, "Work out your own salvation; for God is He that worketh in you."

"The God of peace" is a favourite designation with St Paul (found also in Heb. xiii. 20), in wishes and blessings: see 2 Ep. iii. 16; Rom. xvi. 20, &c. For *peace*, see note on ch. i. 1. This is God's distinguishing gift in the Gospel, that by which He makes Himself and His grace known in the hearts of men. In like fashion He is named from other gifts, "The God of patience and consolation" (Rom. xv. 5), "of hope" (ver. 13), "of love and peace" (2 Cor. xiii. 11), "of all grace" (1 Pet. v. 10). While He is "the God of peace," true peace is "the peace of God" (see Phil. iv. 7 and 9). And His peace bears fruit in our *sanctification*.

sanctify you wholly] Rather, **unto completeness**, or **full perfection**. The readers are already sanctified in Christ Jesus (see ch. iv. 7, 8, "in sanctification"; 2 Ep. ii. 13; comp. 1 Cor. i. 2); the Apostle prays that they may be sanctified to the fullest extent,—or rather, that God may so sanctify them as to bring them to the full perfection of their nature, that as sanctified men they may realise the end of their being in all its length and breadth. See Trench's *Synonyms of the N.T.*, § xxii., on the relation of this expression to *entire* in next clause.

On *sanctification*, see notes to ch. iv. 3 and 7; also 2 Ep. ii. 13.

and I pray God your whole spirit and soul and body be preserved blameless] "I pray God" is needlessly supplied in the A.V. More precisely, and in the Greek order: **entire** (or **in full integrity**) **may your spirit and soul and body, without blame at the coming of our Lord Jesus Christ, be preserved**. The word "entire" takes up the thread of the last sentence, to the prayer of which the Apostle seeks to give more comprehensive expression. But the completeness of blessing desired now assumes a new aspect. From the degree of holiness desired we pass to its range, from its *intension* (as the logicians would say) to its *extension*. St Paul prays that *in the integrity of their human person*

whole spirit and soul and body be preserved blameless unto

and nature they may be preserved,—"spirit, soul, and body" alike finding their safety, with their oneness, in the holy service of God.

St Paul has already treated, in ch. iv. 3—8, of one chief branch of *bodily* sanctification. Now he thinks of this sanctity as penetrating the whole being of the man. It is not necessary to regard *spirit* and *soul* and *body* as three distinct logical divisions of man's nature[1]. The Apostle aims at making his wish exhaustive in its completeness. He begins with the innermost—"your spirit," nearest to God "Who is spirit," and with which the Holy Spirit directly unites Himself, "witnessing to our spirit" (Rom. viii. 16); and he ends with "body," the vessel (ch. iv. 4) and envelope of our nature, through which it belongs to the external world and holds intercourse with it. The "soul," poised between them, is the individual self, the living personality, in which spirit and flesh, common to each man with his fellows, meet and are actualised in *him*. When St Paul bids the Corinthians to "cleanse" themselves "from all defilement of flesh and spirit" (2 Cor. vii. 1: contrast 1 Pet. i. 22, "having purified your *souls*"— your individual selves), that phrase covers the same ground as this, but it treats the matter as one of contrast between man's outer and inner relations; whereas the stress here lies on *the integrity of the man himself*, with his balanced and developed nature, and all his faculties in exercise. Hence the verb (*be preserved*) is singular: spirit, soul, and body forming one whole man. The "spirit" is "kept," when no evil reaches the inner depths of the man's nature, or disturbs his relations to God and eternity; his "soul," when the world of self is guarded, when all his feelings and thoughts are sinless; his "body," when his outward life and relations to the material world are innocent.

The connection between *sanctity* and *safety* ("be preserved") lies in the fact that what is sanctified is given over to God. "No one is able to pluck them out of My Father's hand," said Jesus (John x. 29). See the next verse, and comp. 2 Tim. i. 12; also Ps. cxxi.; Isai. xxvii. 3. The word "preserved" stands with emphasis at the end of the sentence. In the intercession of John xvii., our Lord prays first, "Holy Father, *keep* them" (*vv.* 11, 15), then "*sanctify* them" (ver. 17). But He is thinking there of the situation of His disciples, in the midst of the world; the Apostle leads up to their future manifestation, at His coming.

St Paul writes **blamelessly**—not *blameless* (A.V.); and **in**—not *unto*—**the coming** &c. This adverbial adjunct must belong, despite its position, to the foregoing adjective (*entire*), not to the verb (*be preserved*); for *God* is the keeper in this context, and no blame can conceivably attach to the manner of His keeping: "In full integrity may your spirit and soul and body be preserved,—blamelessly entire in the coming of our Lord Jesus Christ."

---

[1] Those who maintain a threefold analysis of human nature in Scripture are called *Trichotomists*; and the advocates of a twofold division, *Dichotomists*. Amongst the chief expositions of the former view is that given in Delitzsch's *System of Biblical Psychology*, and in Heard's *Tripartite Nature of Man*; on the other side, consult Beck's *Biblical Psychology*, or Laidlaw's *Bible Doctrine of Man*.

24 the coming of our Lord Jesus Christ. Faithful *is* he that calleth you, who also will do *it*.

25 26 Brethren, pray for us. Greet all the brethren with a holy

"The coming of our Lord Jesus Christ" is the end of the Apostle's thoughts in this letter, the goal of his readers' hopes. It will supply the final *test* of the worth of character, and of the completeness of the sanctification effected in believers. Then the whole work of Christ's servants will be brought to its issue and determination. "The Day will declare it" (1 Cor. iii. 13).

On "the coming" (*parousia*), and "our Lord Jesus Christ," see notes to ch. i. 1, 3; ii. 19; iii. 13; iv. 14—17; on "blamelessly," iii. 13.

24. *Faithful* is *he that calleth you, who also will do* it] **who will also do it** (R.V.). The Apostle often appeals to the faithfulness of God, as of One pledged to carry out what He promises in the Gospel; see 1 Cor. i. 9; 2 Tim. ii. 13, &c. The Thessalonians were conscious that God was calling them (ch. ii. 12, see note) to a life of consecration to Himself, a consecration that claimed every power of their nature. This call was itself a proof of the possibility of their entire sanctification, which probably appeared to some of them a thing out of the question.

will do (the object is unexpressed),—as well as *call*. God will carry out His own purpose. His "calling" declared His intention toward the Thessalonians, which the Apostle declares He "will execute." In the like emphatic sense "do" is frequently used of God in the O.T.: "Hath He *said*, and shall He not *do?*" (Numb. xxiii. 19; comp. Ps. xxii. 31, Isai. xliv. 23; &c.). God is the great *Doer* in the work of man's salvation, in deed true to His word; "no word from God shall be powerless" (Luke i. 37; comp. Phil. ii. 13).

The Conclusion.

vv. 25—28.

The conclusion of the Epistle is very brief. It contains no reference to the autograph signature, which St Paul in 2 Ep. iii. 17 and in subsequent letters is careful to notify. The urgent request "that the Epistle be read to all the brethren," is its notable feature.

25. *Brethren, pray for us*] St Paul has just prayed for his readers (ver. 23; comp. ch. i. 2; iii. 10—13); he desires that they in turn should pray for him. "Some ancient authorities," very suitably, "read *also*" (R.V. *margin*): **pray also for us**,—i.e. *as we do for you*.

In 2 Ep. iii. 1, 2 he repeats this request, in more definite form. Comp. Eph. vi. 19; Col. iv. 3, 4; Phil. i. 19; Rom. xv. 30, "that you strive together with me in your prayers to God for me." St Paul, in all the strength of his gifts and his office, yet felt his dependence on the prayers of the Church, and realised through this means his fellowship with brethren in Christ however distant.

26. *Greet all the brethren with a holy kiss*] Better, **Salute** (R.V.). The *kiss*, as the common sign of affection amongst kindred and near

kiss. I charge you by the Lord that *this* epistle be read 27
unto all the holy brethren. The grace of our Lord Jesus 28
Christ *be* with you. Amen.

friends in meeting or parting, was universal in the primitive Christian assemblies, and is still a usage of the Greek and Oriental Churches, especially at Holy Communion. In the West the ceremony gradually died out during the Middle Ages. It was unsuitable to the reserved manners of the Germanic races. The custom was naturally liable to abuse and suspicion, when the simplicity of primitive Christian feeling declined; and it became the subject of numerous regulations in early Councils. The Apostle desires "a holy kiss" to be exchanged by those who heard the Epistle read, as an expression through the Church of his love to each of its members. So in Rom. xvi. 16, after bidding the Church "salute" by name a number of his personal acquaintances, he includes all present at the reading of the letter by saying, "Salute one another with a holy kiss." The same thing is said in 1 Cor. xvi. 20, followed by the words, "My love be with you all in Christ Jesus;" also in 2 Cor. xiii. 12. In 1 Pet. v. 14 the salutation is called "a kiss of love."

27. *I charge you by the Lord that* this *epistle be read unto all the holy brethren*] *Holy* is probably an erroneous insertion of the copyists, due to Ph. iv. 21, or Heb. iii. 1.

Charge should be the much stronger **adjure** (A.V. *margin*, and R.V.). It is as much as to say, "I put you on your oath before the Lord to do this:" an extraordinary expression, and one difficult to account for. There is no appearance of such jealousy or party spirit existing in this Church as could lead to the letter being intentionally *withheld* from any of its members. Two circumstances, however, occur to one's mind which might occasion in some cases *neglect* of the Epistle,—(1) the extreme desire that was felt for St Paul's presence at Thessalonica (ch. iii. 6), and the disappointment caused by his failure to return, to which he addressed himself so fully in chaps. ii. and iii. This feeling might lead some to say, "O, it is only a *letter* from him! We do not want that. Why does he not come himself?" (2) Further, amongst the bereaved members of the Church, some in consequence of their recent and deep sorrow (ch. iv. 13) might be absent from the Church meetings, so that unless the Epistle were carried to them and read in their hearing, they would miss the consolation designed especially for them. It must be remembered, too, that this is the first Apostolic letter extant, and that the custom of reading such letters officially to the whole Church had yet to be established.

Observe the repetition of "*all* the brethren" in *vv.* 26, 27. The same love which dictates the salutation to "all" without distinction, even though some had incurred censure (ver. 14), prompts the anxiety that "all" should hear this letter read, which contains so much of the Apostle's mind and heart.

28. *The grace of our Lord Jesus Christ be with you*] This is St Paul's usual form of final benediction. He expands it later into the full

¶ The first *epistle* unto the Thessalonians was written from Athens.

Trinitarian blessing of 2 Cor. xiii. 14, or shortens it into the brief "Grace be with you" of Col. iv. 18. It contains all spiritual good that one Christian can wish another. Such grace is *with* us, when it constantly attends us, when it forms the atmosphere we breathe, the light by which we see, the guiding and sustaining influence of our whole lives. Comp. note on ch. i. 1; and on *grace*, 2 Ep. i. 12.

The liturgical AMEN is added by the Apostle in some of his letters, and was very naturally supplied by devout copyists in others. Here it is not authentic.

¶ *The first* epistle *unto the Thessalonians was written from Athens*] This, like the other "subscriptions" to St Paul's Epistles, is a note of the Greek editors, which may be perhaps as old as the second century. It is almost certainly erroneous in point of fact; see *Introd.* pp. 22, 27. In the oldest MSS the words "To the Thessalonians I" are placed at the end, repeated from the beginning of the Epistle. See note on the title, p. 45.

THE SECOND EPISTLE OF PAUL THE APOSTLE
TO THE
THESSALONIANS.

PAUL, and Silvanus, and Timotheus, unto the church 1 of the Thessalonians in God our Father and the Lord Jesus Christ: grace unto you, and peace, from God our 2 Father and the Lord Jesus Christ.

OLDER TITLE, TO THE THESSALONIANS II.
(See note on title of 1 Epistle.)

SECTION I. SALUTATION AND THANKSGIVING. CH. I. 1—4.

1, 2. THIS *salutation* is nearly identical with that of Ep. I., see note. Only the Apostle writes here **church of Thessalonians in God our Father** (Father *of us*, whom He loves and calls to be His own: comp. ch. ii. 16, Rom. i. 7, Luke xii. 32, &c.), instead of "the Father" (1 Ep.); and the wish of **grace and peace** is followed by the words **from God the Father and the Lord Jesus Christ**, wanting in the true text of the former Epistle, but which became from this time a regular part of St Paul's epistolary greeting. So these great blessings are traced to their source,—twofold yet one: "God the Father" the ultimate spring, "the Lord Jesus Christ" the mediating cause of "grace and peace" to men.

He associates **Silas and Timothy** with himself, just as before.

The *Thanksgiving*, *vv.* 3 ff., while resembling that of the First Epistle, has a special character and fitness of its own. The Apostle dwells (1) on *the signal growth* of the Thessalonian Church *in faith and love*, ver. 3; (2) on *his own boasting over their faith and patience* to other Churches, ver. 4; and (3) on the token he sees in this of *God's righteous judgement* as between them and their oppressors, which is to take effect at the approaching advent of Christ, *vv.* 5—10. This third ground of thanksgiving assumes so much prominence in the Epistle, that it will be convenient to make it the subject of a distinct Section.

3 We are bound to thank God always for you, brethren, as it is meet, because that your faith groweth exceedingly, and the charity of every one of you all towards each other
4 aboundeth; so that we ourselves glory in you in the

3. *We are bound to thank God always for you, brethren*] The case is put in the same way in ch. ii. 13 ("we are bound to give thanks"), and nowhere else in St Paul. The Apostle feels himself under a special *debt* of gratitude to God for that which His grace had wrought in the Thessalonians. This is explained by 1 Ep. iii. 6—9 (see notes), where it appears that the faithfulness of this Church had cheered and sustained the Apostle in a season of peculiar trial, perhaps even of discouragement to himself; comp. Acts xviii. 9, 10; 1 Cor. ii. 3: "Now we live, if you stand fast in the Lord!"

even as it is meet] For this thanksgiving is matter of intrinsic fitness, not due from personal feeling only. "Your growth in grace *deserves* such acknowledgement to God." Comp. Phil. i. 7, "even as it is right for me to think this of you all;" and the pleonasm of the Liturgy, "It is very meet, right, and our bounden duty."

because that your faith groweth exceedingly] This was the essential point, about which St Paul was anxious when he sent Timothy "to establish you and exhort you *about your faith*," and on which Timothy had brought back reassuring news (see notes on 1 Ep. iii. 2 and 6); subsequent tidings confirmed Timothy's report, and testified to an extraordinary growth in Thessalonian faith. This was due to two causes: (1) to the practical and energetic character of their faith from the beginning (see note on "work of faith," 1 Ep. i. 3); and (2) to the persecution they had undergone. Great trials, if they do not destroy faith, strengthen it, as storms make the oak take deeper root.

"So fed by each strife won, each strenuous hour,
The strong soul grows, its patience ends in power."

We are not surprised that the Apostle adds: **and the love of each one of you all toward one another aboundeth** (R.V.). This is at once a consequence and cause of growth in faith. Faith and Love are the chief, sister graces of St Paul's theology; and Hope appears in the next verse, under the guise of "patience," to complete the trio; comp. notes on 1 Ep. i. 3, v. 8; also 1 Cor. xiii. 13, and Gal. v. 5, 6.

In this fundamental quality of Love the Thessalonian Church excelled; see 1 Ep. iv. 9, 10,—where the Apostle, acknowledging their excellence, had exhorted them to "abound yet more *in love*." This they are doing, and he is "bound to thank God" for it. He dwells on the universal prevalence of mutual love in this admirable Church—"the love of each one of you all!"

4. *so that we ourselves glory in you in the churches of God*] The triumph of the Gospel at Thessalonica had given peculiar gratification to the Apostle (1 Ep. i. 8; iii. 7—9; ii. 20, "You are our glory and joy"). For the advantageous position of this Church and its great activity caused its testimony for Christ to spread throughout the neigh-

churches of God for your patience and faith in all your persecutions and tribulations that ye endure: *which is* a 5

bouring provinces. He is thinking now, however, of more distant Churches—those of Judæa, for example (which he calls "churches of God" in 1 Ep. ii. 14), and of Syria, with whom Silas and himself would be in correspondence. To them he had sent this cheering news, expressing his joy over the faith and devotion of the new converts in language of exultation. Similarly in 2 Cor. ix. 2 he speaks of "boasting to the Macedonians" of the liberality of Corinth. He delighted to praise one Church before another.

But why does he write "we *ourselves*," laying stress on the fact that *he and his companions* were thus boasting? Because, surely, they were slow to boast of anything that redounded to their own credit (see Gal. vi. 14; 2 Cor. xii. 1—6, "It is not expedient for me, doubtless, to glory"), as the Thessalonians well knew (1 Ep. ii. 6, 7); and yet they could not refrain from "boasting" over them. This unwonted and irrepressible *glorying before men* shows how deep and fervent was St Paul's *thanksgiving to God*.

for your patience and faith] On "patience" see note to 1 Ep. i. 3. There we find *endurance of hope*, here *endurance and faith* are linked together. For it was the persistence of the Thessalonians' faith, the way in which it endured the severest strain, that was so wonderful and made the Apostle point them out with pride to the older Churches.

in all your persecutions and the afflictions which you are enduring: so the last clause of the verse literally reads. "Persecutions" formed the chief element in their sufferings (1 Ep. ii. 14; Acts xvii. 5—9); but they had to endure afflictions of many kinds. Comp. Heb. x. 32, 33, "Ye endured a great conflict of sufferings,—being made a gazing-stock by reproaches and afflictions,...and partakers with those so used."

Afflictions: same word as in 1 Ep. i. 6; iii. 3, 4, 7 (see notes on the last two *vv.*).

SECTION II. THE APPROACHING RETRIBUTION. CH. I. 5—12.

These *vv.* contain further reasons for *thanksgiving* on the writer's part, concluding with a *prayer* that his readers may receive the entire fruition of the blessedness to which their sufferings are designed to lead. At the same time, the thoughts here expressed travel far from those which formed the immediate ground of the Thanksgiving, and present a distinct topic of their own. We therefore treat them under a separate heading.

The Retribution the Apostle foresees is twofold,—consisting of *rest and glory* for Christ's persecuted saints, *vv.* 5, 7, 10, 12; and of *punishment* for their godless persecutors, *vv.* 6, 8, 9. In the view presented to us of this judgement we must carefully observe—(1) its essential *righteousness*, *vv.* 5, 6; (2) that it attends on *Christ's advent*, *vv.* 7, 9,

manifest token of the righteous judgement of God, that ye may be counted worthy of the kingdom of God, for which

10; (3) that the chief purpose of the Saviour's coming is *the glorification of His people*, to which the vengeance falling on their oppressors appears to be incidental, *vv.* 8, 10.

5. which is *a manifest token of the righteous judgement of God*] Better, without the connecting words of the English version,— **a token of the righteous judgement of God.**

The heroic faith of the Thessalonians showed that God was on their side. By the courage He inspired in them the Righteous Judge already showed what His judgement was in their case, and gave token of His final recompense. Comp. 1 Ep. i. 6; Phil. i. 27, 28, "Stand fast—in nothing terrified by your adversaries, which is to them an evident token of perdition, but to you of salvation, and that from God." So the joy of Stephen, when before the Council his face shone "as it had been the face of an angel" (Acts vi. 15); so the triumph of Paul and Silas singing psalms in prison ; so the rapture of Christian martyrs at the stake, were signs of God's presence with them and omens of retribution to their enemies.

that ye may be counted worthy of the kingdom of God] More precisely, **to the end that** (R.V.): "a token of God's righteous judgement, given with the purpose that you may be counted worthy of His kingdom."

God's judgement in this controversy is already manifest to those who have eyes to see, in the brave endurance and growing faith of the persecuted Christian flock. But this sign looks onward and points to the final award, when "the blessed of My Father," said Jesus, shall "inherit the kingdom prepared for them" (Matt. xxv. 34). God *designs* this blessedness for them—"chosen from the beginning unto salvation" (ch. ii. 13);—He "calls them unto His own kingdom and glory" (1 Ep. ii. 12). And this "manifestation" of His approval helps to prepare them for it.

That kingdom will be "given to those for whom it has been prepared" (Matt. xx. 23); but at the same time, only to those who are "counted worthy" (see ver. 11; 1 Ep. ii. 12, iii. 13 and notes; also Luke xx. 35; Matt. xxii. 8, "The wedding-feast is ready; but those who were called were not worthy"). There must be manifest in the final judgement a personal fitness of character, corresponding to God's purpose, in those admitted to His heavenly Kingdom. Read the solemn words of Rev. xxii. 10—15.

The sufferings of the Thessalonians were endured for the Kingdom's sake: **for the sake of which you are also suffering.** Their strong hope of the coming of Christ and the triumph of God's Kingdom sustained them in their distress. "If we endure, we shall also reign with Him" (2 Tim. ii. 12): so sang the early Christians. But yet it was not so much their own share in it, as the prospect of the glory of the Kingdom itself, that made them "exult in tribulations." Comp. Heb. x. 34; Rom. viii. 16, 19; Phil. i. 20.

ye also suffer: seeing *it is* a righteous *thing* with God to recompense tribulation to them that trouble you; and to you who are troubled rest with us, when the Lord Jesus

6. *seeing* it is *a righteous* thing *with God*] Lit., **if verily** (if, as all will admit) **it is righteous with God.**

The Apostle has just spoken (ver. 5) of "God's righteous judgement" as manifest in the unshaken faith and courage of His servants. That visible token points to their future and unrevealed reward—*on the admitted assumption*, on which he now dilates, that the retribution awaiting the persecutors and the persecuted from His hand is in truth *a righteous thing*.

Now the justice of the award is self-evident; since it is **affliction to them that afflict you, and to you the afflicted ease.** Once besides St Paul speaks of the future suffering of the wicked as "affliction," in Rom. ii. 9—"affliction and distress upon every soul of man that doeth evil." The term represents this suffering as of the nature of *a personal infliction*. It indicates the reversal that will take place in the other world between the position of the sufferers and inflicters of wrong; comp. our Lord's picture of Dives and Lazarus in Hades: "Now he (Lazarus) is comforted, and thou (Dives) art tormented," Luke xvi. 25. Similarly in Col. iii. 25, "He that doeth wrong shall receive back the wrong that he did." In Rev. xiii. 10, Matt. xxvi. 52, the same principle of *retribution in kind* is illustrated. This is "just with God:" He must count it so; for it is a common rule of justice, and of all true justice He is the Fountain.

If this law demands that the inflicters of wrongful suffering shall suffer and smart for it, so it requires that faithful endurance shall win "relief." The Greek word denotes *relaxation, abatement,*—as of a tightly strung bow, or the paroxysms of fever. So the Apostle designates his own "relief" from anxiety in 2 Cor. ii. 13, vii. 5; it is contrasted with "affliction" again in 2 Cor. viii. 13.

> "Sleep after toil, port after stormy seas,
> Ease after war, death after life does greatly please."

Job iii. 17 is a striking parallel to the phrase *to you the afflicted rest:* "There the wicked cease from troubling; and there the weary be at rest." But the rendering of the LXX in this passage is so different, that it is scarcely likely that these words were in the Apostle's mind. Nor is he thinking, like Job and Edmund Spenser, of rest in death.

7. *rest with us*] St Paul's was a life full of harassment and fatigue, and the hope of *rest* was sweet to him (note the outburst of Gal. vi. 17). Men of an easy untroubled life miss the delight of the thought of Heaven.

But in his visions of future joy his children in Christ always shared. Comp. 2 Cor. iv. 14, "God will raise us up with Jesus, and will present us *with you;*" again in 2 Tim. iv. 8, "the crown of righteousness, which the Lord, the righteous Judge (comp. ver. 5 above), shall give me at that day—and not to me only, but *also to all who love His appearing*."

8 shall be revealed from heaven with his mighty angels, in
flaming fire, taking vengeance on them that know not God,

when the Lord Jesus shall be revealed from heaven] Lit., **in the
revelation of the Lord Jesus from heaven.** His advent is His people's
deliverance; it guarantees, and virtually contains in itself the relief for
which they sigh.

Note, once again, the prevalence of the title *Lord Jesus* in these
letters—the designation of the returning, triumphant Saviour. Compare
notes on 1 Ep. ii. 15, 19.

Here and in 1 Cor. i. 7 (so in 1 Pet. i. 7, 13, iv. 13) Christ's second
coming is called His *revelation;* for it will exhibit Him in aspects of
majesty unknown and inconceivable before. In like manner there will
be a "revelation of the sons of God," and "of the righteous judgement
of God" upon the wicked (Rom. viii. 19, ii. 5); those events, along with
this, certified beforehand, but in their form and nature beyond our
present conception. The "coming" of Antichrist is also foretold as a
"revelation" (ch. ii. 3, 6, 8, see notes). So this revelation comes—

from heaven] comp. 1 Ep. i. 10 (see note); iv. 16; Phil. iii. 20, "from
whence we wait for a Saviour, the Lord Jesus Christ;" and the very
definite promise of Acts i. 11. It will be the unveiling of Christ in His
glory (*descending*) *from heaven;* whereas His previous coming was in
the form of a lowly man on earth.

with his mighty angels] Lit., **with angels of His power**: i.e. "attended by angels as signs and instruments of His power." Comp.
1 Ep. iv. 16 (and note) for the office of the angels in Christ's advent;
and for their relation to Divine Power, Ps. ciii. 20, "Ye angels,
mighty in strength, that fulfil His word." Their presence suits the
majesty in which He comes as the Judge of mankind, "in his Father's
glory, with the holy angels" (Mark viii. 38); and they are, perhaps, the
agents of those changes in material nature by which it will be accompanied. Comp. Deut. xxxiii. 2, Ps. lxviii. 17, for older theophanies.

New and severe features are added to the picture of the Advent in
the next verse:

8. *in flaming fire*] Lit., **fire of flame**; or, in other copies, **flame
of fire**. "Fire" is a symbol of Divine anger and majesty, in Scripture;
and "flame" is fire in motion, leaping and blazing out. According to
2 Pet. iii. 7, 10, fire will be the means of destruction for the visible
world at the Day of the Lord; while in Heb. i. 7, quoted from Ps. civ.,
this element is represented as a form of angelic manifestation (see last
note). In 1 Cor. iii. 13—15 *fire* is itself made the means of judgement.

The comma parting this clause from ver. 7 in the A.V. must be
struck out. The "flaming fire" is the element "in" which the Lord
Jesus is "revealed," not the means by which He "takes vengeance" on
the wicked. It is His awful robe of glory. The words which follow
show why He must appear in majesty so dreadful:

*taking vengeance on them that know not God, and that obey not
the gospel of our Lord Jesus Christ*] Better, **rendering vengeance
to them** (R. V.). We must dissociate from "vengeance" all notions of

and that obey not the gospel of our Lord Jesus Christ: who 9
vindictiveness and passion; it is the inflicting of *full justice* on the criminal—nothing more, nothing less. In this sense it is written, "Vengeance belongeth unto Me; I will repay, saith the LORD"(Deut. xxxii. 35; Rom. xii. 19; Heb. x. 30). The wronged are forbidden to avenge themselves, just because this is God's prerogative. Now "the Father hath committed all judgement to the Son" (John v. 22)—this, therefore, with the rest.

The R.V. properly distinguishes the two classes here marked out for retribution. **Those who know not God** belong to the heathen; on this expression comp. note to 1 Ep. iv. 5. In Rom. i. 18—25, speaking of the heathenism of his own day and of the course and working of Gentile idolatry, the Apostle declares that this ignorance of God was wilful, that idolatry was the outcome of ungodliness, and that its wickedness was shown by the horrible depravity of morals it produced. It was therefore culpable in the highest degree and merited vengeance, being the ignorance of men who "did not think God worth having in their knowledge" (Rom. i. 28). Such is the sentence that St Paul pronounces on the Paganism of his time, in view of its general character and fruits. By no means does he suppose that this "vengeance" will fall on all idolaters at the Last Day, and for the mere fact of "not knowing God" as Christians do. He speaks otherwise in Rom. ii. 14. Countless millions of heathen have had no such knowledge of God brought to them. Each will be judged according to his personal responsibility and share in the common offence. God "leaves Himself not without witness to any" (Acts xiv. 17; John i. 9); and by the measure of light and opportunity vouchsafed to him will the conduct of every man be weighed and estimated. The Apostle is thinking of the Gentile persecutors at Thessalonica (ver. 6), who refused the knowledge of God and showed their hatred to Him by their hatred toward His children (comp. John xv. 24; 1 John iii. 13).

Those who obey not the gospel are all, whether Jews or Gentiles, to whose knowledge God's good news of Christ is brought, and who reject the message. *Obedience* is practical faith, the submission of heart and life to the demands of Christ. This is what such men refuse; they will not say, "Jesus is Lord" (1 Cor. xii. 3; Phil. ii. 10). And the wilful rejecters of Christ became furious persecutors.

St Paul's warning echoes that of Christ concerning all who are brought face to face with His Gospel: "He that disbelieveth shall be condemned" (Mark xvi. 16). This condemnation takes effect at once, and operates in the present life; it has the certainty of a moral law: "He that believeth not is condemned already. And this is the condemnation, that light is come into the world, and men loved darkness rather than light" (John iii. 18, 19). This sentence the Lord Jesus pronounces now on those who, with His light shining upon them, refuse Him the obedience of faith. The Judgement of the Last Day will be the consummation of this present, actual judgement.

Read **our Lord Jesus**, for *our Lord Jesus Christ*.

9. *who shall be punished* with *everlasting destruction*] Rather,

shall be punished *with* everlasting destruction from the presence of the Lord, and from the glory of his power;

men who will pay the penalty of eternal destruction. In these awful words the Apostle describes the retribution designed for godless men and rejecters of the Gospel. His word for "penalty" (*diké*, the root of the words *righteous* and *righteousness* in Greek) brings to a climax the idea of *justice* developed in *vv*. 5—8; see note on "vengeance." But the clause while defining, qualifies the foregoing; for "who" is equal to *such as, who with all like them*. The threatening applies to the impious and malignant opposers who were seeking to crush the infant Church. Their sin corresponded to that which our Lord denounced as the sin against the Holy Spirit, the "eternal sin," the "blasphemy against the Spirit which shall not be forgiven" (Matt. xii. 31, 32; Mark iii. 28, 29, R.V.).

"Destruction," as applied to man and his destiny in the N.T., signifies *perdition, ruin*, the utter loss of blessedness. It is opposed to "salvation" in Heb. x. 39; 2 Cor. ii. 15, &c.; and "eternal destruction" is the antithesis of "eternal life." There is no sufficient reason for interpreting the destruction of the reprobate as signifying their *annihilation*, or extinction of being; they will be *lost* for ever—lost to God and goodness. Nor can we limit the range of the word *eternal* in its relation to this fearful doom; it removes all limits of time, and is the express opposite of *temporary* (2 Cor. iv. 18). Seventy-two times the Greek original of the adjective is found in the N.T.: forty-four of these examples are repetitions of the phrase "eternal life;" it is arbitrary to suppose that in the opposite combination "eternal" bears a restricted sense. Christ's judicial words in Matt. xxv. 46 bar all attempts to minimize the penal effect of the sentence of the Last Day; "eternal punishment," He says, and "eternal life." Comp. Phil. iii. 19, "whose *end* is destruction."

from the presence of the Lord, and from the glory of his power] Better, as in R.V., and without the comma, **from the face of the Lord and from the glory of His might.** Language borrowed from Isai. ii., where it occurs thrice repeated, all but identically (*vv*. 10, 19, 21), in the prophet's picture of Jehovah's coming in judgement: "Enter into the rocks and hide yourselves in the earth *from the face of the fear of the Lord and from the glory of His might*, when He ariseth to shake the earth." The words of Rev. vi. 15, 16 are based on the same original: "They say to the mountains and rocks, Fall on us and hide us *from the face of Him that sitteth on the throne*, and from the wrath of the Lamb." The preposition here seems, however, after the word "destruction," to signify *coming from*, rather than *shrinking from* the face of the Lord. The sight of their Judge and His Almightiness, robed in fire and attended by His host of angels, will drive these wretched men, terror-stricken, into ruin. Their destruction proceeds "from the face of the Lord;" in His look the evildoers read their fate. So we can imagine it will be with the murderers of Jesus, and with malicious persecutors of His people. Comp. Ps. xxxiv. 16,

when he shall come to be glorified in his saints, and to be 10
admired in all them that believe (because our testimony

lxxvi. 7, "The face of the Lord is against them that do evil:" "Who may stand in Thy sight, when once Thou art angry?"

While the destruction of the persecutors and the deliverance of the persecuted are contrasted in themselves (*vv.* 6, 7), they are identified *in point of time.* For justice will overtake the former—

10. *when he shall come to be glorified in his saints, and to be admired in all them that believe*] Better, without the comma: **when He hath come to be glorified in His holy ones and wondered at in all those who believed.** The last verb, in the true reading, is *past* in tense. We are transported to the time of the Parousia. With astonishment all beholders look back on the faith of these now perfected saints, and view its glorious outcome; they think of the "mustard seed" which has grown into so mighty "a tree" (Matt. xiii. 31, 32). And they give the praise of all to Christ. Comp. ver. 12, and note; for *holy ones,* see note on 1 Ep. iii. 13.

At His coming "the glory of His might" brings ruin to the wicked (ver. 9). But there is another glory dearer to Him, that "of His grace" (Eph. i. 4—6), which will be now exhibited in its full splendour, *in His holy ones.* "I am glorified in them," said Jesus (John xvii. 10; comp. 2 Cor. viii. 23). Himself "the Holy One of God" and "Firstborn among many brethren," His triumph is realised in the multitude of those who through believing in Him have become holy like Himself. So the Thessalonian believers "in that day" will be Christ's high glory, as they are already the "glory and joy" of their Apostle (1 Ep. ii. 20).

With *glory* like that rendered to God, a tribute of *wonder* will then be paid to Christ—by the angels surely (see Eph. iii. 10, and 1 Pet. i. 12, for the interest they take in Christ's work on earth), and by the saints themselves, wondering at themselves and at each other, and at the undreamed-of results of their faith. It will be said then, in the fullest sense, "This is the LORD's doing; it is marvellous in our eyes" (Ps. cxviii. 23). The praise that will be rendered to Christ at His advent is anticipated in such words as those of Rev. i. 5, 6: "Unto Him that loveth us, and loosed us from our sins in His blood; and He made us His kingdom, made us priests unto His God and Father — to Him be the glory and the might for ever and ever."

because our testimony among you was believed] Rather, un:o you (R.V.)—"our testimony addressed to you," or "in its application to you." This parenthesis, characteristic of St Paul's style (see *Introd.* p. 33), emphasizes the fact of the Thessalonians' *faith,* the primary condition in all His holy ones of the glory He will reap from them. "Glorified, I say, *in you that believed.* Yes, for the testimony we addressed to you won your faith; and in that faith of yours we see the pledge of Christ's glorification." Similarly in 1 Ep. i. 3, 4 the Apostle found in the vigorous faith of his readers an evidence of their "election" to eternal life (see note).

in that day] Added with solemn emphasis to signalize the *time* of

11 among you was believed) in that day. Wherefore also we pray always for you, that our God would count you worthy of *this* calling, and fulfil all the good pleasure of *his* good-

the revelation of Christ, when He will win honour and admiration from His saints, and inflict ruin on their enemies and His. The clause looks beyond the foregoing parenthesis to "the revelation of the Lord Jesus" described in *vv.* 1—10. Comp. the position and emphasis of the similar adjunct in Rom. ii. 16. For "that day," see notes on 1 Ep. v. 2, 4.

The Apostle's Thanksgiving, as in other instances (1 Ep. iii. 9—13; Eph. i. 3—19; Ph. i. 3—11; &c.), ends in *prayer*, that the marvellous results which he anticipates from his readers' faith may be fully realised.

11. *Wherefore also we pray always for you*] Rather, **To which end also we pray always for you** (comp. 1 Ep. i. 2; iii. 10), **that our God may count you worthy of His calling.** God was "calling" the Thessalonians "to His own kingdom and glory," and calling them accordingly to the sanctification of their whole nature, such as would enable them to be presented faultless at the coming of Christ. All this we have learnt from the First Epistle (ii. 12; iv. 3—8; v. 23, 24). Now a third aspect of this calling is presented, which combines and completes the other two. The Thessalonian believers in Christ are called by the fruit and effect of their faith *to crown their Saviour with glory*. For that this is, in St Paul's mind, the end of their calling is manifest both from *vv.* 10 and 12. To exhibit in oneself the honour and worth of the Lord Jesus so as to make others think more highly of Him, to add something to the splendour of His heavenly crown, is a privilege of which we may well pray "that God may count us worthy."

For St Paul's idea of Christian *worthiness*, comp. ver. 5; 1 Ep. ii. 12; iii. 13, and notes; also Luke xx. 35; Rev. iii. 4, "They shall walk with Me in white; for they are worthy."

and fulfil all the good pleasure of his *goodness, and the work of faith with power*] Lit., **every good pleasure of goodness and work of faith in power.** As much as to say, "May God mightily accomplish in you all that goodness would desire and that faith can effect."

The "goodness," like the "faith," must be in the readers, since the two clauses are parallel—not "*His* (God's) goodness," therefore, as in the A. V. The Apostle afterwards tells the Romans how he is persuaded of them that they are "full of all goodness" (Rom. xv. 14). He thinks quite as highly of the Thessalonians, and believes that their desires are bent in the direction of Christ's glory. Still he is not thinking of *their* goodness so much as of what *goodness in itself*, *goodness as being goodness* must approve and desire. His prayer resembles the Collect for the days of Easter Week: "That as by Thy special grace preventing us Thou dost put into our minds good desires, so by Thy continual help we may bring the same to good effect."

For "work of faith" comp. 1 Ep. i. 3 (note). *Goodness* holds

ness, and the work of faith with power: that the name of our
Lord Jesus Christ may be glorified in you, and ye in him,

to Faith a relation similar to that of Love; it is *bonitas* and *benignitas*, an active excellence of disposition. "Goodness," the first "fruit of the Light" in Eph. v. 9 (R. V.), accompanies Love, the first "fruit of the Spirit" in Gal. v. 22.

"In power" belongs to the verb "fulfil," denoting the manner and style of God's working in believing men. See 1 Ep. i. 5; also Col. i. 29; Eph. iii. 20, for similar expressions.

The verb "fulfil" applies to *will* (*good pleasure*) and *work* in not quite the same sense. To fulfil the former is to carry it into practice and effect; to fulfil the latter is to perfect what is already commenced.

12. *that the name of our Lord Jesus Christ may be glorified in you*] Once more read **Lord Jesus** (R. V.), not *Lord Jesus Christ*.

For this end, "to be glorified in His saints," we were told in ver. 10, Christ is coming; the call by which God summoned the Thessalonians in the Gospel has this in view; with the same purpose, therefore, the Apostle prays for the fulfilment of the work of grace in them. There is nothing he desires in his own case so much as "that Christ may be magnified" (Phil. i. 20); nor anything that he covets more eagerly for his friends.

But now it is the Saviour's *name* that is to be glorified; for their salvation, when complete, will set forth with astonishing lustre the Divine-human name of *our Lord Jesus*. This "name" is "glorified," when its full import is recognized, and the worship which it requires is paid to Him who bears it. So in Phil. ii. 9, 10, we read how the work and sufferings of Christ will have their consummation when "in *the name of Jesus* every knee shall bow, and every tongue confess that Jesus Christ is *Lord!*"

and ye in him] This glorification will be mutual. It will be the honour of the Head to have such members, and of the members to have such a Head; of the "Firstborn" to have such and so many younger brethren (Rom. viii. 29), and theirs to have such an Elder Brother. This is the perfection of love, that each should see its own joy and pride in the other. Comp. 2 Cor. i. 14, "we are your glorying, as you are ours, in the day of our Lord Jesus." For *the glorification of the saints in Christ*, its nature and conditions, see further, Rom. viii. 17—23, 28—30; Col. iii. 1—4; Phil. iii. 20, 21; 2 Tim. ii. 10—13.

And this joyous and triumphant issue of the faith of the persecuted Thessalonians is **according to the grace of our God and the Lord Jesus Christ.** "Our God" is the fountain, "the Lord Jesus Christ" the channel of this grace.

The "grace of God and of Christ"—now named from one, now from another of its Divine Bestowers, seldom, as here, from *both*—had from the first this issue of its working in view. And the glorious result is only what we might expect from such grace. It is "the grace of *our* God," as it shows Him to be ours and makes Him ours in experience. *Our God* is a rare expression with St Paul, occurring twice here

according to the grace of our God and the Lord Jesus Christ.

(*vv.* 11, 12), twice in 1 Ep. (ii. 2; iii. 9), and only once elsewhere, 1 Cor. vi. 11; more frequent is *God our Father*, or occasionally *our God and Father*. It is found often in St John's Apocalypse.

For the meaning of *Grace*, and its place in St Paul's vocabulary, see note on 1 Ep. i. 1, adding the following observations.—There is no word in the N.T. more original and characteristic than this. Its usage springs from the nature of the Gospel of Christ, as that expresses the character of God and His relationship towards men. (1) The radical sense of Grace (*charis*) in common Greek is *pleasingness*. From the artistic feeling of the Greek mind, this came to be synonymous with *loveliness* (*gracefulness*), which was idolized in the three Graces (*Charites*), embodiments of all that is charming in person and in social life. Such was the connection of this word with religion in classical Greek. (2) It further signified *pleasingness of disposition, favour*—both in the active sense (*a*) of *obligingness, graciousness;* and in the passive sense (*b*) of *acceptableness*. In the Greek of the O.T., Ps. xlv. 2, "Grace is poured into thy lips," supplies an example of (*a*), similarly Col. iv. 6; while (*b*) is exemplified in the familiar phrase, to "find grace in the eyes of" so and so (comp. Luke ii. 52). On 2*a* is based the specific N.T. signification of Grace, so conspicuous in St Paul. It denotes, therefore, (3) *the favour of God towards mankind, revealed in Jesus Christ*. Hence, on the one hand, it stands in contrast with *human sin and ill-desert* ("where sin multiplied, grace superabounded," Rom. v. 20); and is the moving cause of man's salvation, embodied and acting in Jesus Christ, above all in His death upon the Cross (John i. 17; Tit. ii. 11; Gal. ii. 21; &c.): God's grace is His redeeming love to sinners. On the other hand, it is the attribute of *God's Fatherhood:* "Grace to you...from God the Father" (ver. 2, &c.; comp. ch. ii. 16; John i. 14). The revelation of the Grace and the Fatherhood of God go together. Grace acts in the way of *forgiveness* (St Paul's "forgive" in Eph. iv. 32; Col. ii. 13, iii. 13, is derived from *charis*, and signifies to "show grace"), and in the *free gift* of the blessings of salvation (Rom. iii. 24, v. 17, &c.). Hence, in the Apostle's teaching, Grace is opposed not only to *sin* which it conquers and destroys, but to human *merit* which it sets aside—to "works of law" regarded as means of our salvation, and to everything that would make God's benefits conferred on us in Christ matters of "debt" on His part: see Rom. iii. 19—21; iv. 4—15; Gal. ii. 15—21; Eph. ii. 1—10, for the establishment of this leading principle of St Paul's doctrine. It is the idea of *mercy* (not *grace*) that in the O.T. brings us nearest to this N.T. conception. But while the former expresses God's pitiful disposition as the Almighty toward man who is weak and wretched, this denotes His loving, forgiving disposition as our Father in Christ toward sinful and lost men.—Two further uses of the word, arising out of this principal use, should be noted. Grace signifies (4) sometimes *an act*, or *bestowment of God's grace*—this or that manifestation of grace (Rom. i. 5; Eph. iii. 8). (5) Sometimes, again, it denotes *a state of grace* in man,—God's grace realized and operative in the Christian: "this grace in which we stand," Rom. v. 2 (comp. 2 Tim. ii. 1; 2 Pet. iii. 18; &c.).—(6) Lastly, *charis* bears in the N.T. and in common Greek the sense of *thanks, gratefulness*.

The course of the Apostle's Thanksgiving has carried his readers far away from their present troubles into a region of heavenly rest and triumph; while for a moment, by the way, it lifts the curtain to reveal the judgement hanging over their tormentors. The "vengeance" that awaits the latter, and the "relief" that awaits the former, are in each case a just and inevitable recompense.

CHAPTER II.

Section III. The Revelation of the Lawless One.
Ch. II. 1—12.

In this Epistle, as in the former, the specific object of the letter comes into view at the beginning of the second chapter, so soon as the introductory prayer and thanksgiving have been offered. The Thessalonians were too eager and positive in their expectation of the Parousia, and the Apostle begs them "for its sake" to be cautious (ver. 1). Some of their teachers declared that "the day of the Lord was already come;" and it was reported that Paul himself had written to this effect (ver. 2). The Church was in danger of falling into mischievous deception (ver. 3). That they may "prove the prophesyings" addressed to them on this subject (1 Ep. v. 20, 21), the Apostle gives them a token or omen of the Second Coming, which indeed he had already supplied in his previous ministry (ver. 5). He foresees that before Christ's return in judgement there must be *a supreme manifestation of evil* (*vv.* 3—12). This development, as he indicates, will be twofold—producing (1) within the Church "the apostasy;" and (2) the "revelation" of "the Man of Lawlessness" (or "Sin"), a personage in whom the sin of humanity will be consummated, reaching its furthest possibilities and taking on an absolutely Satanic character (*vv.* 3, 4, 9, 10). This gigantic impersonation of evil is exhibited as the personal antagonist and antithesis of Christ, in such a way that though the Apostle does not himself give to his conception the name of *Antichrist*, yet it is probable that the designation, afterwards made familiar by St John's use of it in his great Epistle, was derived in the first instance from the passage before us. Meanwhile, we are told, there exists a "withholding" influence, that delays the appearance of Antichrist, although the lawlessness which in him will reach its climax "is already actively at work" (*vv.* 6, 7). When the revelation of the "mystery" at last takes place, while on the one hand it will herald the return of the Lord Jesus (ver. 8), on the other it will prove to be for His rejecters a signal means of judgement, captivating by its magical delusions all who are not armed against them by "love of the truth" (*vv.* 10—12).

This paragraph is the most obscure to us in St Paul's Epistle. It is

Lord Jesus Christ, and *by* our gathering together unto him,
2 that ye be not soon shaken in mind, or be troubled, neither

written in a reserved and elliptical fashion, and bears reference throughout to the Apostle's oral communications, without which, in fact, he did not expect what he wrote to be fully understood. In their recollection of the writer's words the Thessalonian Church had a key to his meaning not transmitted to our hands. We must grope for it as best we can. We find, however, considerable light thrown on this dark passage by its relation to other prophetical teachings of Scripture, and to the history of the Apostle's own time. Yet this added light casts its shadows over the field. We shall return to the subject in the *Appendix* attached to these Notes, on "The Man of Lawlessness."

1. *Now we beseech you, brethren, by the coming of our Lord Jesus Christ*] Lit., **But we beseech you, brethren, on behalf of the coming.** The prospect of this Coming has been held out in language of ardent hope (ch. i. 7, 10, &c.); "but" the readers must not entertain wild and unreasonable notions respecting it. The preposition (*touching*, R. V.) signifies "in the interest of," and not merely "with reference to;" for the confusion of mind and the alarm existing at Thessalonica upon this matter tended to discredit the Second Advent; they obscured the features of "the blessed hope" which the Apostle has just delineated (ch. i. 10—12).

He adds **and our gathering together unto Him**, remembering what he has written in 1 Ep. iv. 17 and v. 10 concerning the reunion of the living with departed saints at Christ's coming. The corresponding verb appears in the promise of Jesus (Matt. xxiv. 31; Mark xiii. 27): "He shall *gather together* His elect from the four winds;" comp. the echoes of our Lord's sayings on the Last Things noted in 1 Ep. iv. 13—v. 11. The intense sorrow of the Apostle at his separation from the Thessalonians (1 Ep. ii. 17, iii. 6, 11) may also have prompted this thought; comp. note on "rest with us," ch. i. 7.

On *beseech* (or *ask*) see note to 1 Ep. iv. 1.

2. *that ye be not soon shaken in mind, or be troubled*] Lit., **to the end that ye be not quickly shaken from your mind** (R. V.):—more freely rendered: **we beseech you...not to lose your balance of mind under any sudden shock**; or keeping nearer to the Greek, **not to be shaken out of your wits.**

"Quickly" points, as probably in Gal. i. 6, to the *speedy effect* of the disturbing cause. Startling declarations were made about the Second Advent; the Thessalonians must take care that they are not carried away by them. Let them resist the first impression of these sensational announcements, and put them to the test of cool judgement and enquiry, as men who "prove all things" (1 Ep. v. 21); they will find out how baseless they really are.

nor yet, he continues, **be kept in alarm**. The former clause describes the overthrow of one's mental equilibrium; this deprecates a continued agitation, a nervous, fluttered condition of mind. The word occurs in the like connection in Matt. xxiv. 6; Mark xiii. 7: "When ye shall hear

by spirit, nor by word, nor by letter as from us, as that the of wars, &c., *be not troubled*"—i.e. *alarmed, discomposed*. From the words that follow it is evident that various attempts were made to disturb the Church upon this subject; and while some would be startled at once out of their self-possession, others, less excitable, would still by the recurrence of the rumours be kept in perturbation.

neither by spirit, nor by word, nor by letter as from us] There is a contrast in the Greek between the two states of mind just referred to (*shaken, nor yet troubled*), but not between the various means by which they were produced; for the latter were used not as alternatives, but in combination. Hence the R.V. renders: **either by spirit, or by word, or by epistle as from us.**

The import of the phrase "by spirit" is apparent from 1 Ep. v. 19, 21 (see notes). Gifts of *prophecy* were possessed by various members of the Church, and men professing to speak "through Spirit"—i.e. under the inspiration of the Holy Spirit and by a supernatural influence— were declaring, "The Day of the Lord is come!"

"Word" stands in contrast with "spirit," just as "word of wisdom" and "of knowledge" with "prophecy," and "doctrine" with "revelation," in 1 Cor. xii. 8—11 and xiv. 26. It denotes the ordinary expression of rational thought and judgement, in distinction from the ecstatic or prophetic utterances of supernaturally inspired persons.

"As from us"—strictly, **as through (or by) us**; the preposition is the same that has been used thrice already in the clause. But this phrase appears to qualify *epistle* alone, not *spirit* or *word*; for these latter modes of communication belonged to others besides the Apostle. It was *by letter* that his authorisation was claimed for the rumour in question. "As through us" signifies **as though on our authority;** comp. "through the Lord Jesus," 1 Ep. iv. 2.—Was this opinion ascribed to the Apostle from misinterpretation of his previous letter, or of some other letter to the Thessalonians not preserved for us? or on the authority of a pretended, or even forged Epistle? It is impossible to answer with certainty. His reference is vague, perhaps intentionally so. He surmised that his authority was being abused in this way, but possibly had no precise information on the point. If some members of the Church had not had the former Epistle communicated to them, as when writing 1 Ep. v. 27 he feared might happen, it may easily have been misrepresented, or misquoted, to the effect indicated. On the other hand, the fact that at the close of this Epistle (ch. iii. 17) he guards his readers against *imposture*, suggests to us that actual deceit was attempted; comp. the words of the next verse, "Let no one *cheat* you." The authors of the false announcement must at least have hinted at the existence of another letter in their favour, if they wished to persuade those well acquainted with our First Epistle; for 1 Thessalonians lends no countenance to their views. A hint of this kind, brought to the Apostle's knowledge, would put him at once upon his guard.

as that the day of Christ is at hand] Both reading and rendering are at fault here. *As that* is equal to **supposing that**: the agitation which the Apostle deprecates being such as this belief would naturally create.

3 day of Christ is at hand. Let no *man* deceive you by any means: for *that day shall not come*, except there come a

Day of Christ should be **day of the Lord**, as in 1 Ep. v. 2 (see note), and elsewhere (*of Christ*, however, in Phil. i. 10; ii. 16). And the verb means more than *is at hand*,—rather, *is now present* (R.V.), **is upon us**; under the same verb (in its participle) "things *present*" are contrasted with "things to come" in Rom. viii. 38, and 1 Cor. iii. 22.

This enthusiastic Church, full of the thought of Christ's heavenly kingdom, was ready to believe what it wished, and lent too credulous an ear to those who in such a time of spiritual tension and exaltation were sure to be found crying out, "Lo here!" or "Lo there!" Against this class of agitators the Lord warned His people. When He does return, He will have no need of heralds or forerunners; "For as the lightning shines out, flashing from the one side of heaven unto the other, so will the Son of Man be in His day" (Matt. xxiv. 27; Luke xvii. 24).

3. *Let no* man *deceive you by any means*] **beguile you**,—as the Revisers commonly render this Greek verb, and the A. V. in 2 Cor. xi. 3; 1 Tim. ii. 14, and Rom. vii. 11 (comp. Gen. iii. 13, "the serpent *beguiled* Eve"). It implies a thorough, commonly a wicked deception; comp. also Rom. xvi. 18. The kindred noun (*deceit*) appears in ver. 10.

in any wise (R. V.) points to the variety of ways ("by spirit, word," &c., ver. 2) in which the readers were being plied with this delusion.

for that day shall not come, *except there come a falling away first*] The R. V. supplies the ellipsis more simply: **for it will not be**. The Apostle's mind becomes absorbed in his description of "the Man of Lawlessness" (ver. 4), and he forgets to complete the sentence; but his meaning is clear enough. For a similar dropped, or broken sentence comp. 1 Ep. ii. 11 (see note, and *Introd.* Chap. VI., on the *Style of St Paul*). His manner is that of a speaker rather than a studied writer, and such lapses are natural in the freedom of conversation.

"A falling away" is a mistranslation. The Apostle uses the definite article; he refers to **the apostasy** of which he had spoken distinctly to his readers (ver. 5). This word in common Greek denotes a military or political revolt, a *defection;* then in the LXX it is applied to *revolting from God*—e.g. in Jer. xxix. 32 ("rebellion against the Lord"), 1 Macc. ii. 15 ("revolt," consisting in sacrificing to idols): so the corresponding verb in Heb. iii. 12; comp. Acts xxi. 21 ("thou teachest apostasy from Moses"), 1 Tim. iv. 1. Here this ominous expression appears for the first time within the Christian Church, as signifying *revolt from Christ*, the faithless defection of men "denying the Lord that bought them" (2 Pet. ii. 1). It is sad to find such a prediction in the earliest writings of the N. T. It originated, doubtless, in the words of Christ, Matt. xxiv. 10—13: "Then shall many stumble...Many false prophets shall arise, and shall lead many astray. And because iniquity shall abound, the love of the many shall wax cold." Comp. the mournful prophecy of Moses concerning the future of his people (Deut. xxxi. 28, 29, &c.). This presentiment of St Paul grew in distinctness and was expressed with increasing emphasis, as time went on; comp. Rom. xvi. 17—20; Acts xx. 29, 30; Eph. iv. 14; 1 Tim. iv. 1, &c. Such words

falling away first, and *that* man of sin be revealed, the son

as those of 1 Cor. xvi. 22 ("If any man love not the Lord, let him be anathema"), and Col. ii. 19 ("not holding fast the Head"), shew that in his view personal loyalty to Christ was the safeguard of Christianity.

As to the particular form and direction of *the apostasy*, nothing is said, nor as to the time of its rise or duration. Disloyalty to Christ confronted St Paul in his later years in many forms; and ever since the Church has had to struggle with inward corruption, as well as with outward foes. The Apostle anticipates this conflict; he foresees that tares will spring up along with the wheat, and "both" must "grow together until the harvest" (Matt. xiii. 24—30). Such development of internal evil had not yet taken place, and by this the Thessalonians might be sure that the Day of the Lord had not dawned.

and that *man of sin be revealed*] Lit., *and there be revealed the man of sin;* or, according to the reading of the Greek preferred by Tischendorf, Westcott and Hort, in agreement with the two oldest MSS, **the man of lawlessness**. In ver. 7 the writer speaks of "the mystery *of lawlessness*," as of something present to his readers' minds; and in ver. 8 this same "man" is styled "the *lawless* one." Throughout St Paul lays the utmost stress upon this attribute of the system of evil, with which he apprehends that the Kingdom of Christ must have a final and conclusive struggle. Lawlessness is the essence of that system, and "the man of lawlessness" its complete impersonation (comp. 1 John iii. 4).

Now "lawlessness" is in the Apostle's eyes a characteristic of *the Gentile world*, which "knew not God" (ch. i. 8; 1 Ep. iv. 5) and had cast off moral restraint. But he looked beneath the formal and outward possession of God's law in the letter, and recognized in the Jewish people the like lawlessness of spirit (Rom. ii. 1, 17—19); while "Gentiles not having law," sometimes "shewed the work of the law written in their hearts" (Rom. ii. 14, 15). "The man of lawlessness" is therefore one in whom St Paul sees the lawlessness of a godless world culminating—the *ne plus ultra* of "the carnal mind" that is "enmity against the law of God," which "is neither subject to His law nor can be" (Rom. viii. 7). And he is emphatically "the *man* of lawlessness" (with no distinction of Jew or Gentile: comp. Rom. iii. 19, 23), being the person in whom human nature, in so far as it is separated from and opposed to God (see next ver.), finds its ultimate realisation.

We must distinguish, then, between "the apostasy" and "the man of lawlessness," in that the former is the corruption of *the Church*, while the latter is the culmination of the evil of *the world*. (Comp. "the wild beast" of Rev. xiii. 1, "rising out of the" murmuring and restless "sea" of the nations, the "many waters" of ch. xvii. 1, 15.) But the two influences, though not identical, are in combination. The former naturally contributes to the latter, an apostate Church paving the way for the advent of an atheistic world-power. We shall find in the next verse an echo of the prophecies of Daniel, so clear as to justify us in regarding these two evil powers as analogous to those of Dan. viii. 23: "When the transgressors are come to the full, a king of fierce countenance shall arise;" where, as it proved in the Maccabean

⁴ of perdition; who opposeth and exalteth himself above all that is called God, or that is worshipped; so that he as God

times, the apostasy within Israel gives the signal for the rise of the heathen despot.

"The man of lawlessness" is "the son of perdition," being the one to whom this doom peculiarly belongs, who like Judas Iscariot (John xvii. 12) in going to "perdition" will "go to his own place" (Acts i. 25). For the Hebraistic phrase "son of" comp. 1 Ep. v. 4, and note.

Perdition is synonymous with *destruction*, ch. i. 9; there it falls on the godless, here on the Lawless One—lawlessness being the moral counterpart of godlessness, and both fatal to man's true life.

4. *who opposeth and exalteth himself above all that is called God, or that is worshipped*] Better, as in R.V. **he that opposeth**, &c.; for this is a third and distinct designation of the personality in question. Also **against**, in place of *above*. And the comma after "God" in A.V. should be cancelled; the phrase **object-of-worship** (a single word in the Greek, found also in Acts xvii. 23) extends the idea of God to include everything religious: comp. 1 Cor. viii. 5, "There are that are *called gods*...gods many and lords many." The Man of Lawlessness embodies not merely an Anti-christian, but an Anti-theistic revolt. His aim will be to abolish religion in every existing form. This is made still clearer by the next clause.

"He that opposeth" renders the Greek word elsewhere translated **the adversary**, and is the equivalent of the Hebrew *Satan* (1 Ep. ii. 18, see note); so that the Lawless One bears the name of him "after" whose "working" he will come (ver. 9). He will be, therefore, in the most absolute sense, *the enemy of God*, concentrating in himself all that in human life and history is hostile and repugnant to the Divine nature.

For *exalteth himself* comp. 2 Cor. xii. 7, where the same compound verb is twice used, and is rendered "exalted-above-measure." The above description recalls the language of Dan. viii. 25 and xi. 36, 37, concerning the great enemy and persecutor of the Church delineated in that prophecy: "He shall magnify himself in his heart;...he shall also stand up against the Prince of princes...He shall exalt himself, and magnify himself above every god, and shall speak marvellous things against the God of gods...Neither shall he regard the god of his fathers, ...nor any god; for he shall magnify himself above all." (Comp. the similar language of Ezek. xxviii. 2, respecting the worldly pride of Tyre.) St Paul takes up and carries forward this O.T. prediction; and as the figure sketched in the Book of Daniel found its proximate realisation in the heathen tyrant Antiochus Epiphanes, who defiled the Temple at Jerusalem and attempted to crush the Jewish religion, it is along the same line that we must look for the accomplishment of this prophecy. In the words that follow we are carried, however, beyond the horizon of the Book of Daniel.

so that he as God sitteth, &c.] Omit *as God* (R.V.) More lit., in the Greek order, **so that he in the temple of God takes his seat, showing off himself**, to the effect **that he is God**.

sitteth in the temple of God, shewing himself that he is God.

So that the Man of Lawlessness will not only seek to abolish Divine worship, but will substitute for it the worship of *himself* (see the passages quoted from Daniel, p. 144), declaring his rule the supreme power and exhibiting his person to receive in place of Almighty God the reverence of mankind. Such atheism is, after all, but *egotism full-blown*, the kind of egotism to which men are tempted who have great power over the minds of their fellows.

The deification of the Roman Emperors suggested this trait of the description. Never has the world witnessed so blasphemous a usurpation, and so abject a prostration of the human spirit as the Cæsar-worship of St Paul's time—the only real religion now left to Rome. This passage reflects the horror inspired by it in the mind of the Apostle. So far-reaching was the impression produced by the Emperor-worship, that Tacitus represents the German barbarians as speaking in ridicule of *ille inter numina dicatus Augustus*—"Augustus, forsooth, enrolled amongst the gods!" (*Annals*, I. 59). The destructive effect which this cultus had on what remained of natural religion in the rites of Paganism is indicated by the pregnant words of Tacitus (*Annals*, I. 10): *Nihil deorum honoribus relictum, cum se templis et effigie numinum per flamines et sacerdotes coli vellet*—"The gods were stripped of their honours, when he (Augustus) consented to be worshipped with temples and statues as a deity, with flamens and with priests." Compare the words of Suetonius referring to Julius Cæsar, with whom the deification of the dead Cæsars began: "Omnia simul ei divina atque humana decreverat (senatus)...Periit sexto et quinquagesimo aetatis anno atque in deorum numerum relatus est, non ore modo decernentium, sed et persuasione volgi" (*De vita Caesarum*, I. 84, 88). The unconscious irony of the last sentence is finely pointed by the exclamation ascribed to the dying Emperor Vespasian (VIII. 23): *Vae, puto deus fio!*—"Woe's me! I think I am turning god!" The shout of the Greek populace at Cæsarea, hailing "the voice" of Herod Agrippa as that "of a god and not of a man," indicates the lengths to which a corrupt and servile heathenism was prepared to go in this direction (Acts xii. 20—24). Deep and wide-spread was the execration caused by the attempt of the mad Emperor Caius (Caligula), in the year 40, to place his statue in the Jewish Temple, an attempt only frustrated by the perpetrator's death. This was a typical event, showing of what the intoxication of supreme power might make a man capable. It was but the last of many similar outrages on "every so-called god." Amongst other monstrous profanities of Caligula, Suetonius relates (IV. 22) that he transported the statue of Olympian Jupiter to Rome, and put his own head upon it in place of the god's! Also, that he built his palace up to the Temple of the ancient Roman gods, Castor and Pollux, making of it a kind of vestibule, where he exhibited himself standing between their twin godships for the adoration of those who entered. Even this, as Olshausen remarks, was "modesty" compared to what the Apostle ascribes to Antichrist. The very name *Sebastos*, the Greek rendering of the Imperial title *Augustus*—to which *Divus* was added

5 Remember ye not, that, when I was yet with you, I told
6 you these *things?* And now ye know what withholdeth

at death—signifying "the one to be worshipped" (comp. *sebasma*, "object-of-worship," in the previous clause), was an offence to the religious mind. In later times the offering of incense to the deity of the Emperor became the crucial test of fidelity to Christ. *Cæsar or Christ* was the martyr's alternative.

When he speaks of "the temple of God," without other qualification, St Paul appears to refer to the existing Temple of Jerusalem (comp. Dan. xi. 31; xii. 11, cited by our Lord in Matt. xxiv. 15; Mark xiii. 14). Attempts have been made to show that the Apostle's words were literally fulfilled by certain outrages committed by Nero or Vespasian upon the sacred building. This does not seem to us clearly made out; and it will be evident from what has been said, that even the worst of the Roman Emperors was only a type, or adumbration of the Antichrist. The Jewish Temple being still, while it stood, God's holy place, St Paul naturally associates with it this crowning act of profanation. But we have learnt from 1 Ep. ii. 16 that he believed national Judaism to be immediately coming to an end; and its Temple was the type and representative of all places consecrated to the worship of the true God. The great Usurper who claims for himself that he "is God," appropriates consequently the sanctuaries of religion and prostitutes them to his own worship. "*Within the temple of God*—not in Jerusalem alone," says Chrysostom, "but in every church."

5. *Remember ye not, that, when I was yet with you, I told you these* things?] More precisely, **I used to tell you**; comp. 1 Ep. iii. 4, for the *tense*.

This reminder serves two purposes:—(1) It is a gentle reproof to the readers, who ought not to have been so easily unsettled by the alarmists, after what the Apostle had told them. (2) It obviates the necessity of explanation by letter. Any more explicit statement would probably have raised political suspicion, exposing the Apostle to a renewal of the charges which led to his expulsion from Thessalonica (see Acts xvii. 6, 7; *Introd.* pp. 15, 20, 21). St Paul had watchful enemies, who would be quick to seize on anything that might compromise him with the Roman Government.

6. *And now ye know*] After this allusion: "now that you call to mind what I used to say about the final struggle with the powers of evil, that will precede Christ's coming."

(ye know) *what withholdeth*] Better, **that which restraineth**—rendered "letteth" in ver. 7; only it is masculine there, denoting personal agency; here neuter, indicating a principle or power. The Thessalonians not only knew *what* the restraining influence was, *they were acquainted with it;* it lay within the range of their experience. We have not therefore to look far a-field for this "restraint." A hint was sufficient, *verbum sapientibus;* more than a hint would have been dangerous.

that he might be revealed in his time] The R.V. is more exact: **to the end that he may be revealed in his own season.** The unnamed

that he might be revealed in his time. For the mystery of 7 subject is the dread personality whose form looms through this paragraph in ever-growing proportions.

With this ver. comp. 1 Tim. vi. 14, 15; where we read of "the appearing of the Lord Jesus, which *in its own times* He shall show, Who is the blessed and only Potentate" (comp. Acts i. 7). As Christ's advent has its proper season reserved for it, so has that of Antichrist. To this end the restraining power operates, holding back and setting bounds to human lawlessness, until the set time has come for its final outbreak and *revelation*.

This order of things belongs to God's purposes. If He allows moral evil to exist in His creatures (and its possibility seems to be inseparable from moral freedom), yet He knows how to control its activity, till the time shall come when its full manifestation will best subserve its overthrow and judgement. This "season" of the Man of Lawlessness, in whom the bad element in human nature gets at length full play, will be the last and worst of many such crises; chiefest of which was that of Luke xxii. 53: "This is your hour," said Jesus to His enemies, "and the power of darkness."

7. *For the mystery of iniquity doth already work*] Better, **of lawlessness** (R.V.)—same word as that we adopted from the marginal Revised reading of ver. 3; comp. "the lawless one," ver. 8.

"Doth work," i.e. *is operative*, or *in operation*. See note on "working," ver. 9.

Lawlessness has indeed been "at work" ever since man fell from God by sin. But this "*mystery* of lawlessness" is surely some embodiment of the universal principle of sin which it has assumed in times recent to St Paul ("doth *already* work"), and which contained, in his belief, the germ and potency of the supreme revelation of evil reserved for the eve of Christ's advent.

A *mystery* is not some secret knowledge or practice reserved to a select few, like the Mysteries of Greek Paganism; it is, in St Paul's dialect, the counterpart of *revelation*, and the word here takes up again the "revealed" of ver. 6: "until he be *revealed*, I say; for the *mystery* (the thing to be revealed) doth already work." It denotes something by its nature above man's knowledge, which can only be understood when and so far as God reveals it. Comp. note on "revelation," ch. i. 7; also the various "mysteries" of Col. ii. 2, 3; Eph. iii. 4—6; Rom. xi. 25, &c. So monstrous and enormous are the possibilities of sin in humanity, that with all we know of its present and past effects, the character of the Man of Lawlessness must remain beyond comprehension,—till he be "revealed in his season."

only he who now letteth will let, *until he be taken out of the way*] Again, as in ver. 3, there is a hiatus in the Greek, due perhaps to the excitement raised by the apparition of this awful personality in the writer's mind. The R.V. completes the sense more simply and naturally: **only there is one that restraineth now**,—or, **there is at present the Restrainer**. "Let" has this sense in the Collect for the Fourth

iniquity doth already work: only he who now letteth *will*
Sunday in Advent, as often in old writers: "We are sore let and hindered in running the race set before us."

On "the Restrainer" see note, ver. 6. It passes from neuter to masculine; while *the thing restrained* makes an opposite transition, and appears predominantly in a personal form (comp. *vv.* 3, 4 with 7, and again with *vv.* 8, 9). For the Apostle contemplates the power of Lawlessness in its ultimate manifestation, as embodied in some one human antagonist of Christ; whereas the restraint that delays his appearance is thought of rather as a general influence, or principle, which at the same time has its personal representatives. We prefer, therefore, to render St Paul's phrase **he that restraineth** rather than *one that restraineth;* for it signifies not an individual, but a class.

Where then are we to look, amongst the influences prevalent in the Apostle's time and known to his Thessalonian readers, for the check and bridle of Lawlessness? Where but *to law itself* (*Staat und Gesetz,* Dorner)? The fabric of civil law and the authority of the magistrate formed a bulwark and breakwater against the excesses both of autocratic tyranny and of popular violence. For this power St Paul had a profound respect (see Rom. xiii. 1—7). He was himself a citizen of Rome, and had reason to value the protection of her laws. (See Acts xvi. 35—39; xxii. 23—29; xxv. 10—12.) About this very time he found in the upright Proconsul, Gallio (brother of Seneca, the tutor and ill-fated "restrainer" of Nero), a shield from the lawlessness of the Jewish mob at Corinth; the Thessalonian "politarchs" at least tried to do him justice (Acts xvii. 5—9). We must distinguish between the laws of the Roman State and the personal power of the Emperor, whose despotism habitually trampled on the laws and yet was checked by them. Within a year of the writing of this letter Nero assumed the purple, who pushed the principle of lawless autocracy, the idolatry of a wicked human will, to lengths unimagined before. In Nero's reign it seemed as though St Paul's vision of the Man of Lawlessness were already realised. This monster of depravity, "the lion" of 2 Tim. iv. 17, stood for the portrait of "the wild beast" of St John's Apocalypse, which carries forward Paul's image of the Lawless One, as the latter takes up Daniel's conception of the godless king, impersonated in Antiochus Epiphanes. The absolutism of the bad Cæsars found, after all, its limit in the strong framework of civil legalism and the sense of public justice, native to the Latin race. Nero fell, and did not drag down Rome with him, nor bring about the final ruin. Wiser rulers and better times remained for the Empire. In the crisis of the 8th Century, "the laws of Rome saved Christianity from Saracen domination more than the armies...The torrent of Mohammedan invasion was arrested"—for 700 years. "As long as Roman law was cultivated in the Empire, and administered under proper control, the invaders of the Byzantine territory were everywhere unsuccessful" (Finlay, *Hist. of Byzantine Empire*, pp. 27, 28). Nor did Roman Law fall with the Empire itself, any more than it rose from it. It has been in spirit, and to a large extent in substance, the parent of the legal systems of Christendom. Mean-

let, until he be taken out of the way. And then shall *that* °
Wicked be revealed, whom the Lord shall consume with the
spirit of his mouth, and shall destroy with the brightness of

while *Cæsarism* survives, a legacy from Rome and a word of evil
omen,—the title and model of illegal sovereignty.

The lawlessness of the world holds this "mystery" of St Paul in
solution, ready to precipitate itself. It betrays itself in many partial and
transitional manifestations, until "in its season" it shall crystallize into
its complete expression. Let reverence for law disappear in public life,
along with religious faith, and there is nothing to prevent a new Cæsar
becoming master and god of the civilized world, armed with infinitely
greater power.

8. *And then shall* that *Wicked be revealed*] *Then*, "in his own
season" (ver. 6), in contrast with the *now* of the last clause, the time of
his restraint: **then shall be revealed the lawless one** (R.V.).

It is essential that we keep in mind the identity of the figure depicted from ver. 3 onwards. The variety of synonyms employed by the
A.V. is distracting. This "revealing of the Lawless One" is the
unveiling of "the mystery of lawlessness already at work;" he is no
other than "the man of lawlessness, the son of perdition" announced in
ver. 3. Three times, with persistent emphasis, the word *revealed* is
repeated (*vv.* 3, 6, 8), as of some unearthly and portentous object, that
holds the gazer spell-bound. Comp. note on "mystery," ver. 7.

"The lawless" (*anomos*) is a term frequently occurring in the LXX,
both in the singular and plural; it denotes the typical "sinner," or
"wicked person" of the O.T.

whom the Lord shall consume with the spirit of his mouth] According to the true reading, and better rendering, **whom the Lord Jesus
shall slay with the breath of his mouth** (R.V.).

On the title "Lord Jesus" and its relation to the Second Advent, see
note to 1 Ep. ii. 19. *Jesus*, the human Name, could not be wanting
here, where the overthrow of "the *man* of lawlessness" is in question.

The words that follow come from the prophecy of the judgement of
the Rod of Jesse, Isai. xi. 4: "He shall smite the earth with the rod of
His mouth, and with the breath of His lips shall He slay the wicked."
Such predictions had not been accomplished in the humble, suffering
Messiah,—or but in foretaste, by the denunciations of Jesus (Matt. xxiii.
&c.); they remain to be verified in His triumph. The Lawless One,
being the ultimate embodiment of the world's wickedness and defiance
of God, must suffer the conclusive fulfilment of the prophet's words.

Just as *the sight* of the Lord Jesus will suffice to bring ruin on cruel
persecutors (ch. i. 9), so it will need but *the breath of His mouth* to lay
low the haughty and Titanic Antichrist: "A word shall quickly slay
him!"

and shall destroy with the brightness of his coming] More exactly, **and
shall bring to nought with the manifestation of his coming** (or
presence: Greek *parousia*; see note on this word, 1 Ep. ii. 19).

The Greek verb signifies *to make inoperative, destroy in effect*; it is a

9 his coming: *even him*, whose coming is after the working of

favourite word with St Paul: comp. 2 Tim. i. 10, "having *abolished* death;" and Gal. iii. 17, "to *make* the promise *of none effect*." The effect of the manifestation of the Lord Jesus will be to paralyse the Lawless One and strip him of his power. See note on ch. i. 9, "destruction (coming) from the presence of the Lord."

The word rendered "manifestation" (*epiphaneia*, our *Epiphany*) is not found in St Paul again till we come to his latest Epistles, where it is applied to the Second, and once to the First Coming: 1 Tim. vi. 14; 2 Tim. i. 10; iv. i. 8; Tit. ii. 13. It signifies by usage an extraordinary, commonly a *superhuman, divine appearance*. Similarly the corresponding adjective, rendered "notable" in Acts ii. 20 (from Joel ii. 31: Hebrew, "terrible"). *Prima ipsius adventus emicatio* (Bengel).

In *vv.* 9—12 we are told (1) of *the agency* which brings about the coming of the Man of Lawlessness and *the means* employed for the purpose, (2) of *the victims* of his ascendancy (ver. 10), and (3) of *the issue* for which in the sovereignty of Divine judgement his power is overruled (*vv.* 11, 12).

9. even him, *whose coming is after the working of Satan*] Rather, **even he, whose coming is according to the working of Satan** (R.V.); for this sentence does not qualify the last clause of ver. 8 by itself, it looks back to the principal subject of the paragraph,—"then shall be revealed the lawless one...whose coming," &c.

The two "comings" (*vv.* 8, 9)—the *parousia* of the Lord Jesus and that of the Man of Lawlessness—are set in contrast. The second forms the dark background to the glory of the first. "According to the working of Satan" is not, therefore, subordinate to the clause that follows, but forms a chief predicate. It is *Satan* that inspires and directs the advent of the Lawless One; hence the "powers and signs" which attend it: "who comes as one empowered by Satan, attended by all kinds of lying miracles." For "Satan" comp. 1 Ep. ii. 18, and "he that opposeth" in ver. 4 above.

"Working" (Greek *energeia*, *energy*) is a word that St Paul uses elsewhere of the operation *of God:* comp. note on "manifestation" above; and see e.g. Col. ii. 12; Eph. i. 19; similarly the kindred verb, as in ver. 7 (see note, and on 1 Ep. ii. 13). With studied emphasis and precision he borrows for the coming of Antichrist the terms proper to the coming of Christ, making the one appear as a frightful mimicry and mocking prelude of the other. The Lawless One has his "mystery," his "revelation," his "parousia," and his "power and signs and wonders," in which the "working of Satan" in him apes the working of God in Christ. This systematic, and as one might suppose, calculated adoption by Antichrist of the attributes of Christ is a most appalling feature in the Apostle's representation. Satan himself, through his agent, usurps God's throne amongst men. And the Man of Lawlessness holds a relation towards Satan the counterpart of the relation of Christ to God.

with all power and signs and lying wonders] Lit., **in all power and signs and wonders of falsehood**. There is no reason in grammar

Satan with all power and signs and lying wonders, and with
all deceivableness of unrighteousness in them that perish;
because they received not the love of the truth, that they

why the concluding epithet should not be referred to the three synonyms alike; it suits them all. St Paul does not mean to say that the miracles in question are pretended miracles, but that they *aid and abet falsehood*. They come from "the father of falsehood" (John viii. 44), to whose realm all lies belong. Comp. Matt. xxiv. 24, and Rev. xiii. 13, for predictions of Satanic miracles.

The three terms by which these manifestations are designated, are precisely those used of *the miracles of Christ and the Apostles;* comp. Acts ii. 22; Rom. xv. 19; 2 Cor. xii. 12; Heb. ii. 4, where they are variously combined. Of the three, *signs* is the most frequent, unfortunately rendered "miracles" in the A.V. of the Fourth Gospel (corrected in R.V.); occasionally *signs and wonders* (never *wonders* alone) are combined; more frequently *power* is used, or *powers*, rendered in the Gospels "mighty works." The Greek word for *wonder*, nearest in sense to our "miracle," denotes the outward effect of such deeds, the astonishment or fear they excite; while *power* points to the Divine (in this instance *Satanic*) agency that effects them, and *signs* calls attention to the significance of the event, its spiritual import.

While the last clause delineates the nature of the operations of Antichrist and the means by which he is accredited, the next verse goes on to describe their fatal effect:—

10. *and with all deceivableness of unrighteousness in them that perish*] Both reading and rendering need to be amended; it is rather, **and in all deceit of unrighteousness for the perishing**—the opposite of "them that are being saved," or "the subjects of salvation" (1 Cor. i. 18; 2 Cor. ii. 15). They follow, alas, the guidance of "the son of perdition," and share his ruin (ver. 3).

"Deceit of unrighteousness" is a phrase compounded similarly to "good pleasure of goodness," ch. i. 11; it signifies such deceit as belongs to unrighteousness, that which it is wont to employ. These devices are "deceit for the perishing," for men without the life of God, whose spiritual perception is destroyed by sin and who therefore fall a prey to deceit. The children of God are not imposed upon by these means; they know how to "prove all things" (1 Ep. v. 21). Read carefully 1 John iv. 1—6, and compare with this context.

because they received not the love of the truth, that they might be saved] Placing himself amid the scenes of the triumph of Antichrist and viewing the sad fate of his victims, St Paul explains their ruin. They had no "love of the truth." This sentiment they never "entertained." And so—*in compensation for this*—they believe wicked lies, to their undoing: **in return for their refusal to entertain the love of the truth.** On *receive*, see note to 1 Ep. ii. 13 (second "received"); there is implied a want of *heart* to receive.

It is not "the truth" simply, but "*the love* of the truth" that these unhappy men repudiate. Their unbelief is not of the reason so much as

11 might be saved.   And for this cause God shall send them

of the heart. Those of whom the Apostle speaks resist "the truth" with an instinctive, invincible prejudice; for they have no desire to "be saved" from the sins it condemns. Christ found in this moral prepossession the reason why so many rejected His word. "Every one that doeth evil," He said, "hateth the light" (John iii. 20; comp. x. 26; &c.). So St Paul writes in 2 Cor. iv. 3, 4, "Our gospel is a veiled thing amongst them that perish. The god of this world has blinded their minds...that the light of the gospel of the glory of Christ may not shine upon them." It is a just, but mournful result, that rejecters of Christ's miracles become believers in Satan's, and that atheism should be avenged by superstition. So it has been, and will be.

11. *And for this cause God shall send them strong delusion*] Rather **sends to them**, the present standing for the future by anticipation of the predicted certainty; or better explained as the statement of *a principle already at work*. What will take place in those deceived by Antichrist, is seen on a smaller scale every day.

For *strong delusion* read, with R.V., **working of error**, parallel to "working of Satan," ver. 9 (see note on *working*); a superhuman force and fascination is implied, that of Satan's miraculous working in the Antichrist. "Delusion" is deceit accepted, falsehood taken for truth (*vv.* 9, 10). And "God sends" this effectual deceit, with the very purpose **that they should believe the lie.** "O LORD, why dost Thou make us to err from Thy ways?" (Isai. lxiii. 17).

Vv. **11, 12**, therefore, ascribe to *God* the great delusion that we have been all along regarding as the masterpiece of Satan. Three things must be borne in mind here: (1) that Satan is never represented in Scripture as an independent power, or rival deity of evil, like the Persian Ahriman. However large the activity allowed to him in this world, it is under Divine control (see Job i. ii.; 1 Cor. v. 5; x. 13; &c.). (2) St Paul teaches that *God makes sin work out its own punishment*. In Rom. i. 24, 25, he represents the loathsome vice of the Pagan world as a Divine chastisement for its long-continued idolatry: "*For this cause* God sends effectual delusion" is parallel to "*For this cause* God gave them up to vile passions." In each case the result is inevitable, and comes about by what we now call a natural law. That persistent rejection of truth destroys the sense of truth and results in fatal error, is an ethical principle and a fact of experience as certain as any in the world. Now he who believes in God as the Moral Ruler of the Universe, knows that its laws are the expression of His will. Since this Satanic delusion is the moral consequence of previous and wilful rejection of the truth, it is manifest that God is here at work; He makes Satan and the Lawless One His instruments in punishing false-hearted men. As they loved lies, God "sends them" lies for their portion. Comp. Ezek. xiv. 9, and 1 Kings xxii. "Righteous and true are Thy ways, Thou King of the ages!" (Rev. xv. 3). (3) The advents of Christ and of Antichrist are linked together (*vv.* 3, 9); they are parts of the same great process and drama of judgement. God sends "the strong delusion, that they should believe a lie: that they all might be damned who believed not the truth, but had pleasure in unrighteousness.

working of error" in the Lawless One, Who will quickly send His Son to be Judge of the lawless and Avenger of His elect.

For "a lie" the Greek reads "*the* lie" (same word as *falsehood*, ver. 9), which probably means here not falsehood in general, but this particular falsehood—"the lie" *par excellence*, in which all previous delusions of Satan are consummated, viz. that the Lawless One is himself God (*vv.* 4, 9, 10). Similarly Idolatry is called "the (great) lie," in contrast with "the truth of God" (Rom. i. 25).

12. *that they all might be damned who believed not the truth*] **that they may be judged** is what the Apostle says.

Here is the further, judicial purpose of the great imposture. God intends that men who are so disposed should "believe the lie," so that their false belief may be a touchstone and demonstration of their falseness. Men without love of truth naturally believe the lie when it comes; there is nothing else for them. And this is a terrible judgement upon them. As Christ came at first "for judgement into this world" (John ix. 39, &c.), by His presence discriminating the lovers of truth and falsehood, so it will be with Antichrist at his coming. He will attract his like; and this attraction will be the exposure of their hatred of the truth. Comp. Rom. ii. 8: "To those who obey not the truth, but obey unrighteousness...wrath and indignation."

This is not yet the Last Judgement, and it is possible that some under this retribution may yet repent, seeing how shameful is the delusion into which they have fallen by rejecting Christ.

all (probably **all together**, in the Greek) marks the universal range of this judgement; the delusion takes effect everywhere; it will be the one thing in which the enemies of Christ agree, and it furnishes a decisive test of their character. Comp. "the mark of the Wild Beast" in Rev. xiii. 3, 16: "The whole earth wondered after the beast.. All that dwell on the earth shall worship him, every one whose name hath not been written in the Lamb's book of life."

That they *had pleasure in unrighteousness* explains the readiness of these unhappy men to accept the "deceit of *unrighteousness*" (ver. 10). They are credulous of that which falls in with their evil inclination. Wicked men are the dupes of wickedness. Comp. Rom. i. 32, where the fact that men not only do the vilest things, but "*take pleasure in* those who do them," adds the finishing touch to the Apostle's black picture. Such an one does wrong not through force of passion or example or habit, but out of sheer delight in wrong. "The light that is in him has become darkness." He says with Milton's Satan,

> "Farewell remorse, all good to me is lost;
> Evil be thou my good!"

Men of this type will welcome eagerly the reign of Antichrist. But their triumph will prove shortlived.

13 But we are bound to give thanks alway to God for you,

SECTION IV. WORDS OF COMFORT AND PRAYER.
CH. II. 13—III. 5.

Passing from the last Section, we breathe a sigh of relief, and gladly join in thanksgiving for those who will "prevail to escape all these things that shall come to pass, and to stand before the Son of Man" (Luke xxi. 36).

Under the solemn feelings awakened by his contemplation of the image of Antichrist, the Apostle turns to his readers, blending thanksgiving with exhortation and renewed prayer on their account. (1) He renders thanks to God Who *had chosen and called them to salvation*, *vv.* 13, 14; (2) he urges them *to be steadfast*, ver. 15; (3) he prays that *God's love* may be *their comfort*, *vv.* 16, 17. In turn he (4) *requests their prayers* for himself, ch. iii. 1, 2; (5) he assures them of *God's faithfulness*, and of *his own confidence* in them, *vv.* 3, 4; and (6) prays once more for *Divine guidance* on their behalf, ver. 5.

13. *But we are bound to give thanks alway to God for you*] Comp. ch. i. 3, and notes. The strain of the opening thanksgiving of the two Epistles is here blended. For while this clause repeats the first words of 2 Ep., the sentence that follows echoes 1 Ep. i. 4.

Here the subject, **we**, bears emphasis: "*we*, with this sad prospect of apostasy and delusion in view." Those who see deeply into the evil of the world, its immense power and untold possibilities, turn with the greater satisfaction to that which "speaks better things."

brethren beloved by the Lord (R.V.) is parallel to "beloved by God" (1 Ep. i. 4: see note).

"The Lord" is surely *Christ*, as distinguished from "God" in the adjoining clauses. The Church assailed by persecution, and appalled by the thought of Antichrist, finds in the love of Christ her refuge (comp. Rom. viii. 35, 39). To the same Divine Protector the Apostle commits his "brethren," so dear to him (*vv.* 16, 17; ch. iii. 3, 5). He recalls in this expression the blessing pronounced on Benjamin, his own tribe, in Deut. xxxiii. 12: "The *beloved of the LORD* shall dwell in safety by Him; He covereth him all the day long, and he dwelleth between His shoulders." The two phrases correspond precisely in the Greek.

because God hath from the beginning chosen you to salvation] Better, **in that God chose you**; see note on ch. i. 3.

These words are partly borrowed from Deut. vii. 6, 7; x. 15; xxvi. 18: "Thou art a holy people unto the LORD thy God. He hath chosen you to be a peculiar people unto Himself...He set His love upon you;" &c.

The Apostle's thanksgivings in the First Epistle centred in the fact of the "election" of the Thessalonian believers in Christ. (See note on *election*, 1 Ep. i. 4; and context.) To this his grateful thoughts now revert. God deals with them far otherwise than He will do with those to whom He "sends effectual delusion...that they may be judged" (*vv.* 11, 12): He "chose you for salvation...*not for wrath*" (1 Ep. v. 9). How safe and high above fear are "God's elect" (Rom. viii. 33—39)!

brethren beloved of the Lord, because God hath from the beginning chosen you to salvation through sanctification of

"From the beginning" points to the time when the Gospel first visited the Thessalonians; so the "election" of 1 Ep. i. 4 is associated with the "coming of our gospel to you" (1 Ep. i. 5, 9). Then it was that, practically and in human view, God chose this people—i.e. *selected them for His own out of the world* in which they moved. In later Epistles this "beginning" is traced back, on its Divine side, to "the foundation of the world" (Eph. i. 4, &c.), and shown to be a part of that which was absolutely "from the beginning" (comp. 1 John i. 1). There is an absolute beginning of salvation, hidden in the nature and eternal counsels of God; this is its relative, historical and manifest beginning (comp. Phil. iv. 15; Acts xv. 7).

And this choice is "unto salvation," in the utmost sense of the word, extended in ver. 14 to "the obtaining of the glory of our Lord Jesus Christ;" comp. 1 Ep. ii. 12; iii. 13; v. 9 (see note).

This salvation rests on God's election; at the same time it has its *human conditions:* **salvation** (experienced) **in sanctification of spirit and faith in the truth.** God chooses none to salvation apart from these qualifications; the end implies the way. It is believing and sanctified men who wear "for a helmet the hope of salvation" (1 Ep. v. 8). Comp. 1 Pet. i. 2 : "Elect...in sanctification of spirit" (*or* the Spirit).

"Chosen *unto salvation*" stands in contrast with "son *of perdition*" and "the *perishing*" (*vv.* 3, 10); "sanctification of spirit" and "belief in truth" on the part of God's elect, with the "pleasure in unrighteousness" and "belief in the lie" that mark the dupes of Antichrist. These are the moral preconditions of final salvation and perdition respectively.

St Paul writes **sanctification of spirit**, without the definite article. No doubt "spirit" may grammatically denote "the (Holy) Spirit," but the Apostle can scarcely have so intended here. For (1) the intimate connection of this phrase with "belief of truth" inclines us to read the two (Greek) genitives alike—"truth" being the *object* of "faith," and "spirit" of "sanctification." (2) "Your spirit" is the primary object of the sanctification prayed for in 1 Ep. v. 23. That memorable prayer is probably in the mind both of writer and readers. (3) "Sanctification of spirit," understood as an inward state of the Thessalonians, is a condition of "salvation" the opposite of the disposition described in *vv.* 10—12 as marking "those who perish" at the coming of Antichrist. For this reason sanctification is put first; but it depends in turn upon *faith,—*"belief in the truth." See Acts xxvi. 18; Eph. i. 13. The normal order therefore is that of 1 Tim. ii. 15, "in faith and sanctification."—For *sanctification*, see note to 1 Ep. iv. 3.

Lit., **belief of truth.** The Apostle is not stating *what* the truth is that saves, but *that it is truth* which saves, and faith in it *as truth.* A truth-accepting faith is the root of salvation, while the disposition to "believe the lie" is the root of perdition (*vv.* 9—12). "Sanctify them *in the truth,*" prayed Jesus for His disciples; "Thy word is truth"

¹⁴ the Spirit and belief of the truth: whereunto he called you by our gospel, to the obtaining of the glory of our Lord ¹⁵ Jesus Christ. Therefore, brethren, stand fast, and hold the

(John xvii. 17). The trustful acceptance of the truth revealed by Christ brings with it the consecration of our spirit to God. In such faith and consecration our salvation lies.

14. *whereunto* (**to which end**, including the whole salvation described in ver. 13) *he called you by our gospel*] i.e., "through the good news we brought." On *our gospel* see note to 1 Ep. i. 5; and on the *call* of God, 1 Ep. ii. 12, 13 (where mark its connection with the Divine *glory*), iv. 7, v. 24. The connection of *vv.* 13 and 14 resembles that of *vv.* 3 and 4 in 1 Ep. i., and of Rom. viii. 29, 30: "whom He forcordained, He also called." God's *election* is the moving spring of human salvation; but His *call* came to the Thessalonians, when the good tidings first sounded in their ears. That summons declared God's good will toward them, and His loving choice of each believing heart.

to the obtaining of the glory of our Lord Jesus Christ] More freely rendered, **that you might win the glory of our Lord Jesus Christ.** This defines more closely the "whereunto" just above, and brings to a climax the "salvation" contemplated in ver. 13: "To which end God sent you through us the gospel message, that so you might have Christ's glory at last for your own."

In ch. i. 12 (see note) the glory of Christ and that of His saints were declared to be mutual. Here they are identified. In the glory which the exalted and perfect "Lord Jesus Christ" receives, the Thessalonians were called each of them finally to share. This is the goal of their salvation, "the prize of their high calling" (Phil. iii. 14).

"*Obtaining* of glory" is therefore synonymous with the "*obtaining* of salvation" of 1 Ep. v. 9, where the same rare verbal noun is used (see note). Christ's glory is already won in principle, in its ground and beginning, both for Himself and His people. So He said, leaving the world, "Now *was* the Son of Man *glorified*" (John xiii. 31); yet He prays further, "Now, O Father, glorify Thou Me;" while He says of His disciples, "The glory which Thou hast given Me, I have given them" (John xvii. 5, 22). His glory is ever advancing and, as it unfolds itself, ever anew imparting itself to men, till it is *consummated* in "the revelation of the Lord Jesus from heaven" (ch. i. 7—12, ii. 8; comp. Tit. ii. 13; Matt. xxiv. 30, &c.). Then the glory of His saints will be complete and secure, in the completeness of His: "with Him in glory" (Col. iii. 4; comp. Phil. iii. 20, 21; and His own words in John xvii. 24). "We shall be like Him, for we shall see Him as He is" (1 John ii. 2).

15. *Therefore, brethren, stand fast*] **So then** (R.V.), as in 1 Ep. v. 6 (see note): the practical conclusion in which the Apostle gathers up all he has been saying in this letter. "Since the Lord's return is delayed and its time uncertain, and in prospect of the coming of Antichrist, whose deceptive influence is already secretly at work,—inasmuch as God by our means has made you heirs of His glorious kingdom—

traditions which ye have been taught, whether by word, or by our epistle. Now our Lord Jesus Christ himself, and God, even our Father, which hath loved us, and hath given *us* everlasting consolation and good hope through grace,

16

STAND FAST." Comp. 1 Cor. xv. 58; Col. i. 23,—where, as in this place, *hope* is the incentive to steadfastness.

and hold the traditions which ye have been taught] "Hold" is an emphatic word: **stand firm and hold fast** (Ellicott) gives the Greek sense more adequately.

In **traditions which you were taught** there is no suggestion of the Romanist idea of Tradition, conceived as an authority distinct from the written Word of God; for the Apostle continues, **whether by word or letter of ours** (the pronoun belongs to both nouns). He bids them hold by what he had taught, whether it came through this channel or that, provided it were really from himself (comp. ver. 2, and ch. iii. 14, 17). He is now beginning to communicate with the Churches *by letter*, and stamps his Epistles with the authority of his spoken word. The sentence asserts the claim of the true Apostolic teaching, as against any who would "beguile" the Church away from it. Comp. 1 Cor. xi. 2: "I praise you that in all things you remember us, and *hold fast the traditions, even as I delivered them to you*."

The Apostle's "traditions" included, besides *doctrine*, also the "charges" (or "commands") he gave on matters of morals and practical life (ch. iii. 4; 1 Ep. iv. 2). The body of Christian doctrine, brought to its finished form, he calls in his last letters "the deposit" (1 Tim. vi. 20; 2 Tim. i. 12, 14); while his practical teaching is "the charge" (or "commandment"), 1 Tim. i. 5, 18.

16. *Now our Lord Jesus Christ himself, and God, even our Father*] This remarkable invocation corresponds both in form and place in the Epistle to that of 1 Ep. iii. 11 (see note). But here *Christ's* name comes first, a circumstance indicating the Divinity with which the writer invests it: "Where now are those who would lower the Son of God?" (Chrysostom). Comp. 2 Cor. xiii. 14.—Again the Subjects are united by the singular number of the following verbs (*comfort*, &c., ver. 17).

As in 1 Ep. iii. 11, we prefer to render the particle of transition **But** (rather than *Now*) **may our Lord Jesus Christ and God our Father.** On "Lord Jesus Christ," see note to 1 Ep. i. 1. St Paul invokes *our Lord Jesus Christ Himself* as their stablisher, with *God our Father*, in contrast with the efforts on their own part to which he has exhorted his readers (ver. 15); comp. the transition in 1 Ep. v. 22, 23 (see note).

St Paul prays with confidence for his emperilled brethren at Thessalonica, because of the grace which Christ and God had already bestowed both on them and him : **Who loved us and gave us eternal comfort** (or **encouragement**) **and good hope.**

"God *our Father*, Who *loved* us and *gave*," &c. There is the tenderest connection of thought in these words. God's Fatherly love prompts His great gifts. See the words of Christ in Matt. vii. 11; Luke xii.

17 comfort your hearts, and stablish you in every good word and work.

3 Finally, brethren, pray for us, that the word of the Lord may have *free* course, and be glorified, even as *it is* with

32: "Your Father who is in heaven shall give (you) good things," &c.; comp. John iii. 16; 1 John iii. 1; also Rom. v. 8. While the Thessalonians are "beloved of God" (1 Ep. i. 4), they are also "beloved by the Lord" (ver. 13); and this clause, though singular, may include *Christ* in its reference, He and the Father being one in *love* as in *comfort* (ver. 17).

In His love the Father had already given the readers gladness of heart in trouble (ch. i. 4; 1 Ep. i. 6), such as the Apostle often acknowledges in his own case (e.g. in 2 Cor. i. 4—6)—an "*eternal* comfort," which the sorrows of time will never waste. To know that God loves us is in itself a comfort infinitely rich. "Consolation" (A.V.) represents the Greek noun corresponding to the verb "comfort" of ver. 17. It is *comfort* in its older sense of *heartening, encouragement*, rather than *consolation*: see note on "comfort," 1 Ep. iii. 2.

A "*good* hope" is such a hope as it is good to have, that gives worth and joy to life. See note on "hope," 1 Ep. i. 3.

These kindred blessings flowing from the love of God, are given in **grace**—not out of merit, and as to the worthy; but in the way of bounty to the undeserving. See notes on "grace," ch. i. 12 and 1 Ep. i. 1.

17. *comfort your hearts*] Comp. ch. iii. 5; 1 Ep. iii. 13; and the similar expression in Col. ii. 2. The "heart" is the inward man, the seat of our thoughts and emotions (see note, 1 Ep. ii. 4); there doubt and fear arise, which can be allayed only by Divine comforting. For this verb, comp. note on "consolation" above, and on 1 Ep. iii. 2.

and stablish you in every good word and work] Rather, **establish them**, i.e. *your hearts*, understood from the last clause. This expression was previously used in 1 Ep. iii. 13, see note. The Apostle does not mean, "May God make you steadfast in saying and doing all that is good," for the "heart" neither speaks nor works; but rather, "May God give you courage and confidence of heart in all good that you say or do." He knows that they are busy in doing good (1 Ep. i. 3; iv. 10), and he would have them do it with a good and cheerful heart (comp. 1 Ep. v. 17, 18).

SECTION IV. (*continued*). CH. III. 1—5.

1. *Finally*] See note, 1 Ep. iv. 1. The chief topic of the letter is disposed of, and the wishes and hopes immediately arising out of it have been expressed. **For what remains:—**

brethren, pray for us] So in 1 Ep. v. 25 (see note): a frequent request with St Paul—addressed to "brethren," concerned in everything that concerns their Apostle and the Christian cause. Their prayers,

you: and that we may be delivered from unreasonable and *2* desired generally in 1 Ep., are now to have a more specific object,— viz., **that the word of the Lord may run and be glorified** (R.V.)

On "the word of the Lord," see note to 1 Ep. i. 8.

This singular metaphor of the *running word* is probably suggested by Ps. xix. 5, where the course of the sun is pictured in glowing poetic language—"rejoicing as a hero to run a race" (ver. 5), while the latter part of the Psalm sets "the law of the Lord" in comparison with his glorious career. St Paul applies ver. 4 of the Psalm in Rom. x. 18, with striking effect, to the progress of the Gospel. See also Ps. cxlvii. 15, "His word runneth very swiftly." Through "running" the word is "glorified," and that is true of it which Virgil writes in his splendid lines on *Fama* (*Aeneid* IV. 173 ff.):—

"Mobilitate viget viresque adquirit eundo."

even as it is *with you*] Lit., **even as also with you.** They are to pray that the work of the missionaries may be as successful in Achaia as it was in Macedonia: comp. 1 Ep. i. 5; ii. 1. From Thessalonica "the word of the Lord has sounded forth" over all the neighbouring region, and "in every place your faith is gone forth:" might it only be so in Corinth! Reading Acts xviii. 5—11, we gather that St Paul's work in the Achaian capital was at first discouraging in its results; and it was during the earlier period of his residence there that he wrote these letters (comp. 1 Ep. iii. 7, 8, and notes).

2. *and* (pray) *that we may be delivered from unreasonable and wicked men*] Better, **perverse and evil men.** The Apostle is thinking, no doubt, of the fanatical Jews at Corinth (see Acts xviii. 5—17), who stood in the way of the Gospel; when Gallio's judgement removed this obstacle, Christianity appears to have spread rapidly in this city. Comp. Rom. xv. 31, "that I may be delivered from the disobedient in Judæa." From Ephesus four years later he writes (1 Cor. xvi. 9), "A great and effectual door is opened" to me, notwithstanding "many adversaries." Through this open door the word gloriously *ran*; at Corinth it was not so as yet.

For "wicked" (or "evil"), see notes on 1 Ep. v. 22, and also ver. 3 below. For "delivered" (or *rescued*) comp. 1 Ep. i. 10 (note), where the same word is used. It points to enemies who seemed to have the writer in their power. Read 2 Cor. xi. 23—33 for a graphic description of the Apostle's perils.

for all men *have not faith*] Or, **not to all does the faith belong.** There are those, alas, with "no part nor lot in the matter" (Acts viii. 21). The Apostle puts his meaning in a pathetically veiled and softened way (see note on "not pleasing," 1 Ep. ii. 15). "It is not all who share our faith: many are its enemies, and bear us on its account a deadly hatred. Will you pray that we may be delivered from their power?" Their unbelief in Christ made the Corinthian opposers "perverse and evil." Not being *for* Him, they came to be furiously *against* Him (Matt. xii. 30). This is enough, in the Apostle's view, to explain their conduct; comp. ver. 10, "they received not the love of the truth, that they might be saved."

3 wicked men: for all *men* have not faith. But the Lord is faithful, who shall stablish you, and keep *you* from evil. 4 And we have confidence in the Lord touching you, that ye

With relief he turns from these perverse unbelievers to think of the safety and confidence that abide within the Church of Christ:—

3. *But the Lord is faithful*] In the Greek order, **But faithful is the Lord.** Man's *want of faith* suggests by contrast the *faithfulness* of our Divine Lord (Faith and Faithfulness are alike denoted by *pistis* in Greek; as Believing and Faithful—Trusting and Trusty—alike by *pistos*). Comp., for this contrast, Rom. iii. 3; 2 Tim. ii. 13.

"The Lord" appears to be throughout these Epistles *the Lord Christ*, Ruler and Defender of His people. Comp. 2 Tim. iv. 17, "The Lord stood by me...The Lord shall save me into His heavenly kingdom." So he continues: **who will establish you, and guard you from the Evil One.**

On "stablish," see notes to 1 Ep. iii. 2, 13, and ch. ii. 17 above. It denotes the *settled, steady confidence* which this young Church required, assailed by persecution from without and alarms from within.

While the unbelief of men made the Apostle think of the faith-keeping Lord, behind these "evil men" (ver. 2) he saw another and mightier enemy,—"the Evil One" (R.V.). The Greek adjective may be read either in the neuter (*the evil, evil in general*), as by A.V. and R.V. *margin;* or in the masculine, as by the R.V. *text.* There is the same ambiguity in the words of the Lord's Prayer, and in the Sacramental Prayer of Jesus (Matt. vi. 13; John xvii. 15); in which instances also the Revisers, rightly as we think, prefer the *personal* rendering. Both our Lord and the Apostle John, in passages where the termination of the adjective is unequivocal—Matt. xiii. 19; 1 John ii. 13, 14, v. 18—point out *the Evil One* as the enemy of Christ and His people and injurer of their work; and in Eph. vi. 16, while the grammatical form is ambiguous, it is "the Evil *One*" who shoots "the fire-tipped darts." So, surely, here; and in the two prayers of Jesus, echoed seemingly in this passage. The conflict of the Church and of the Christian life is not a matter of principles alone and abstract forces; it is a personal encounter, and behind all *forces* there are living *wills.* This is the plain teaching of Christ and the New Testament. The Evil One is "the Satan" of ch. ii. 9; 1 Ep. ii. 18; and "the Tempter" of 1 Ep. iii. 5.

"The Lord will guard you;" comp. the words of Jesus in John xvii. 12, "I *guarded* them (the disciples), and not one of them perished, except the son of perdition." Like *rescue* (ver. 2), *guard* is a military word, implying conflict and armed protection: Vulgate, *custodiet.* Though St Paul began by asking the Thessalonians to pray for him, yet "it is plain that he was more anxious for them than for himself" (Calvin).

Their safety is ensured by the Lord's fidelity: but it requires *their own obedience;* and this the Apostle counts upon:—

4. *And we have confidence in the Lord touching you, that ye both do*

both do and will do *the things* which we command you. And the Lord direct your hearts into the love of God, and 5 into the patient waiting for Christ.

and will do the things *which we command you*] "The Lord" is not, as the English phrase may suggest, the *object* of this confidence—ver. 3 declared the Apostle's trust in Him—but the ground on which rests his confidence in the Thessalonian Church. His relations with them and feelings towards them have the common relationship of both to Christ for their foundation and background, their vital underlying bond; comp. 1 Ep. iii. 2; iv. 1, 16; v. 12, and ver. 12 below. No idiom is more frequent or characteristic of St Paul than this—*in the Lord, in Christ*. But it is "to *you*" that his confidence is now directed; the construction of the Greek is identical with that of 2 Cor. ii. 3, "having confidence in you all." Let us accordingly read here, **in the Lord we have confidence in you.** Such is the trust that all true Christians should give to each other.

For *command* read **charge**, as in 1 Ep. iv. 2, 11 (see notes). The word is taken up again in ver. 6. The Apostle seems to have an eye already to the "charge" that he is about to give, which will put to the test his readers' obedience. The like satisfaction he has repeatedly expressed (ch. i. 3, 5; ii. 13; 1 Ep. i. 3; iii. 6—10; iv. 1, 9, 10; v. 11).

5. *And* (or *But*) *the Lord direct your hearts*] "The Lord" is still Christ: see note, ver. 3.

"May He *direct* (or *guide*) you *as Lord* of His people, Shepherd of the sheep" (John x.). The Apostle expects his Thessalonian flock to follow *his* directions (ver. 4); but above both himself and them is the Supreme Director of hearts, Whose guidance he invokes. For the transitional, contrastive **But**, comp. notes on ch. ii. 16 and 1 Ep. iii. 11. "Direct your hearts" is a Hebraism, used in the LXX to translate the words rendered "set" or "prepare the heart" in our Version (Ps. lxxviii. 8; 1 Chron. xxix. 18, &c.) It denotes giving *a fixed direction*, a steady purpose, as to "stablish the heart" (ch. ii. 17) signifies to give *a sure position*. On *direct* see also 1 Ep. iii. 11.

into the love of God, and into the patient waiting for Christ] A. V. margin and R. V., **patience of Christ.** *Patience* (or **endurance**) is what the Greek noun signifies in ch. i. 4; 1 Ep. i. 3 (see note), and in the other numerous examples of its use in the N.T. For the way in which "Christ's endurance" is made a model for our own, see 1 Pet. ii. 19—24; iii. 17, 18; iv. 1, 2, and Heb. xii. 2, 3. Elsewhere St Paul speaks of His *sufferings* as shared by His people (2 Cor. i. 5; Phil. iii. 10, &c.); and if the sufferings, surely *the patience*. The Thessalonians were eagerly awaiting His return (1 Ep. i. 10; 2 Ep. ii. 1, 2); let them wait for it in His patient spirit. Had the Apostle wished to speak of *waiting for* the glorified Christ, he would surely have called Him, as so often in these Epistles, "the Lord Jesus."

Christ is in this place the patient Christ, who "endured the cross" and the "contradiction of sinners," fulfilling the prophetic ideal of Jehovah's suffering Servant, Isai. liii.; comp. 1 Pet. ii. 21—25; Matt. xi.

6 Now we command you, brethren, in the name of our

29, 30, &c. The Greek article is therefore not otiose, but has its distinctive and graphic force—*Christ as the prophets foresaw Him, and we know Him:* **the patience of the Christ.** Comp. Rom. xv. 3, "*The Christ* did not please Himself;" Eph. iv. 20, "You did not so learn (get to know) *the Christ*,"—the great Ideal. We wish that the Revisers had seen their way to restore to us the expressive definite article in such passages.

To "love God" was the Lord's "great and first commandment" (Matt. xxii. 36—38); it is the soul of religion (see Rom. viii. 28; 1 Cor. viii. 1—3; and 1 John, *passim*). "God our Father has loved" the Thessalonian believers (ch. ii. 16); Christ must teach them to reciprocate the Divine love, and in the strength of this love to endure evil and sorrow even as He Himself endured.

SECTION V. DISCIPLINE FOR THE DISORDERLY.

CH. III. 6—15.

In his former letter St Paul had found it needful to exhort his readers to live a quiet life and to attend to their daily duties and pursuits. Some members of the Church were of an idle and improvident disposition. The Day of the Lord, they supposed, was imminent, and worldly occupations would therefore soon be at an end; the only business worth minding any longer, so they said, was to prepare for His coming. Their conduct was likely to bring discredit on the whole community; and they did it a material injury, by throwing the burden of their maintenance on their hard working and charitable brethren (see notes on 1 Ep. iv. 11, 12). These men were "the disorderly" of 1 Ep. v. 12—14 (comp. *vv.* 7, 8 below); they gave trouble to the officers of the Church, whom the Apostle in the First Epistle urges the Thessalonians loyally to support (ch. v. 12), while they united to "admonish" the offenders. This evil, which should have been checked by the reproofs of the first letter, had grown to larger proportions. The startling announcements that were made respecting the Second Advent, tended to aggravate the mischief. Indeed these rumours so unhinged the minds of some of the Thessalonian Christians, that it must have been difficult for them, however diligently inclined, to pursue their common avocations. And the Apostle, having calmed the agitation of his readers by what he has written in the second chapter, proceeds now in strong terms to rebuke the disorder which had thus been unhappily fostered and stimulated.

The chief points in St Paul's charge on this subject are the following:— (1) First, and last, he enjoins *the avoidance of those who persist in disorder, vv.* 6, 14 (whom notwithstanding he still, and pointedly, calls "brethren," *vv.* 6, 15); (2) he recalls *his personal example and teaching* in their bearing on this matter, *vv.* 7—10; and (3) he *solemnly charges the offenders to amend,* ver. 12.

Lord Jesus Christ, that ye withdraw yourselves from every brother that walketh disorderly, and not after the tradition which he received of us. For yourselves know how *ye* ought 7 to follow us: for we behaved not ourselves disorderly among

6. *Now we command you, brethren, in the name of our Lord Jesus Christ*] Or, **But we charge you, brethren.** See note, ver. 4.
St Paul has declared his confidence that the readers will do what he enjoins. Well! his injunction is this: **that you withdraw yourselves from every brother walking disorderly.** It is uttered "in the name of our Lord Jesus Christ,"—a solemn judicial sentence (comp. 1 Cor. v. 4, 5) pronounced by the Apostle who acts as judge in his Sovereign's name, and with the deepest sense of his responsibility; similarly, "through the Lord Jesus" in 1 Ep. iv. 2 (see note).
He does not wish these troublesome persons to be expelled; nor does he invoke supernatural penalties upon them, as in the vastly worse case of discipline at Corinth; he directs the loyal Thessalonians not to associate with them, nor lend countenance in any way to their proceedings. On "walk," see note to 1 Ep. ii. 12; and on "disorderly," ver. 7; 1 Ep. v. 14.
The rule of order or disorder in the case in question is thus laid down: **and not after the tradition which they received of us** (R. V.).
"*They* received" is the older reading, referring to the class of persons just described as "*every brother* walking disorderly." This slight grammatical discord the ancient copyists corrected, some by writing "*ye* received" (R. V. *margin*), and others "*he* received" (A. V.).
On *tradition* (or *instruction*), see note to ch. ii. 15. The nature of Paul's "tradition" at Thessalonica on Christian behaviour may be gathered from the verses that follow, and from 1 Ep. ii. 9—12; iv. 1—12; v. 12—24. It consisted of example equally with precept:—

7. *For yourselves know how ye ought to follow us*] Lit., **imitate us**: see note on 1 Ep. i. 6; and again, ch. ii. 14, and ver. 9 below. **you know of yourselves**—"without our needing to tell it all again." Such references are frequent in these Epistles; see note on 1 Ep. ii. 1.
"*How* you ought to imitate us" points beyond the mere duty to *the spirit and manner* of the imitation desired—"with what diligence and devotion."
for we behaved not ourselves disorderly among you] This "for" differs from that at the beginning of the verse; it is a *specifying for*—giving not a reason for what has just been said, but a definition of its meaning: **in that we did not play a disorderly part among you.** The readers' attention is called to this feature of the missionaries' conduct, and imitation is recommended. There is a *meiosis* (or *litotes*) in the expression, resembling that of ver. 2, and of 1 Ep. ii. 15 (see notes). "Far indeed was our walk from giving an example of disorder!" How far, the next line shows.
To-be-disorderly (a single verb in the Greek) is a word applied to *soldiers out of rank*. Officers in the army are as much subject to its discipline as the rank and file; and the Apostle Paul felt it to be due to

8 you; neither did we eat any *man's* bread for nought; but wrought with labour and travail night and day, that *we*
9 might not be chargeable to any of you: not because we

the Churches over which he presided, that he should set an example of a strictly ordered and self-denying life.

8. *neither did we eat any* man's *bread for nought*] This clause follows up and makes application of the last, showing by contrast in what lay the chief complaint against the "brethren walking disorderly." They would not work for their bread, and seemingly expected the Church to support them. The Church officers very properly resisted this demand, telling them to return to their occupations; so the Apostle himself had directed in 1 Ep. iv. 11, 12. This some of them refused to do; and they went up and down (ver. 11) retailing their supposed grievances, allying themselves with the false prophets of the Parousia, and making all kinds of mischief. Such is the picture of this unruly faction that we draw from the two Epistles. The fraternal spirit of the Primitive Church and the readiness of its members to put their goods at the common service (see Acts ii. 44, 45; iv. 32—35), were thus abused by idlers and fanatics—qualities not unfrequently united—by men impatient of the monotony of daily toil, and who found in spiritual excitement at once a diversion from irksome duty and an excuse for its neglect.

To correct this morbid tendency was one reason of many for which the Apostle practised manual labour. He tries to make these ill-conducted men feel by his own example the disgrace of living, without an effort, at the cost of others: **neither did we eat bread for nought at any man's hand** (R. V.) There was a manly pride about St Paul in this matter. Comp. 2 Cor. xi. 9, 10, and 1 Cor. ix. 15: "No man shall stop me of this glorying."—"To eat bread" is a Hebraistic synonym for *receive maintenance*; comp. 2 Sam. ix. 7.

but wrought with labour and travail night and day] Rather, **but in labour and travail, night and day working** (R.V.). Here are two clauses, the former standing in opposition to the foregoing sentence: "It was not for nought that we ate our bread, but in labour and travail;" then he continues, "working night and day." Dearly, and with hard labour did St Paul and his comrades earn their daily bread. The Thessalonians had seen him at his task. For the particular words of this clause see 1 Ep. ii. 9, which it repeats almost identically.

that we *might not be chargeable to any of you*] More lit., **that we might not put a burden on any of you.** Comp. again 1 Ep. ii. 9.

"The disorderly," without any right, were leaning heavily on their brethren and taxing their charity; the orderly apostles, with every right to do so, had never charged them anything.

9. *not because we have not power*] Better, **have not the right** (moral power, authority)—viz., "to lay the charge of our maintenance upon the Church;" see note on 1 Ep. ii. 6. In the other Epistle St Paul refers to this matter in order to prove his earnest care for the Thessalonian Church; but here, for the sake of making his behaviour

have not power, but to make ourselves an ensample unto you to follow us. For even when we were with you, this 10 we commanded you, that if any would not work, neither should he eat. For we hear that *there are* some which walk 11 among you disorderly, working not at all, but are busy-

an example to them. Similarly in 1 Cor. x. 33; xi. 1; and Acts xx. 34, 35; compare with 2 Cor. xii. 14, 15.

but to make ourselves an ensample unto you, &c.] Or, more freely rendered: **to furnish you with an example in ourselves, so that you might imitate us.** The apostles sacrificed their own rights and comfort for the benefit of the Thessalonians (comp. 1 Ep. ii. 8, also i. 5), wishing to supply them with the kind of example most suitable for their imitation; and we learnt from 1 Ep. i. 5—7, that this purpose had in most respects been realised.

On *example* (or *pattern*), see note to 1 Ep. i. 7; and on *imitate* (*follow*, A.V.), 1 Ep. i. 6, and ver. 7 above.

10. *For even when we were with you, this we commanded you*] Better, **For also**: St Paul's present charge on the subject repeats and reinforces what he said in his oral teaching; **this we used to charge you**—same *verb* as in *vv.* 4 and 6 (see note), and same *tense* as in ch. ii. 5 ("I was wont to tell you"), and 1 Ep. iii. 4 (see note). To this original "charge" the Apostle referred in 1 Ep. iv. 11, touching the same point; it formed part of "the tradition" which he and his fellow-missionaries "delivered" to the Thessalonians (ver. 6, ch. ii. 15).

that if any would not work, neither should he eat] In the Greek this is put vividly in direct narration: **If any will not work, neither let him eat.** A stern, but necessary and merciful rule, the neglect of which makes charity demoralising. But this law of St Paul's touches the idle rich, as well as the poor; it makes that a discredit which one hears spoken of as if it were a privilege and the mark of a gentleman,—to "live upon one's means," to live without settled occupation and service to the community—"natus consumere fruges."

The form of the Greek implies in this case a positive refusal to labour: the man *wont work* (Latin *nonvult operari*). Then it is God's law that he shall starve.

11. *For we hear that* there are *some which walk among you disorderly*] Rather, **we hear of some walking**, &c. It was not simply that the Apostle heard that there were such people at Thessalonica; he knew about them,—who they were, and how they were behaving. Further news had come since he wrote the First Epistle, in which he touched briefly, in mild and general terms, upon the subject (1 Ep. iv. 11, 12; v. 14). Now he is compelled to single out the offenders and to address them with pointed censure. For similar allusions to reports from a distant Church, comp. 1 Cor. i. 11; x. 18.

He writes, "some which *walk among you* disorderly" (not "*some among you* which walk," &c.), which implies that their public conduct and relations with the rest of the Church were irregular.

On "walk disorderly," see note to ver. 6.

12 bodies. Now *them that are* such we command and exhort by our Lord Jesus Christ, that with quietness they work, 13 and eat their own bread. But ye, brethren, be not weary

This disorder was not merely negative, consisting in refusal to work: mischief and idleness are proverbially companions; and we are not surprised to find the Apostle adding the further condemnation, **that work not at all, but are busybodies** (R.V.).

There is a play of words in the Greek, which gives to this reproach a keener edge, **whose one business is to be busybodies**; or rendered still more freely, **minding everybody's business but their own**,—*idly busy* with the concerns of others. These mischief-makers the Apostle had already bidden to "study to be quiet and to do their own work" (1 Ep. iv. 11); comp. the extended note on ver. 8 above. For the same disposition St Paul in 1 Tim. v. 13 reproves certain "younger widows"—"not only idlers, but tattlers also and busybodies."

For similar examples of paronomasia in St Paul, see *vv.* 2, 3 ("faith ...faithful"), Rom. i. 20 ("The unseen...clearly seen"); *Introd.* p. 33.

12. *Now* them that are *such we command and exhort by our Lord Jesus Christ*] The "exhort" of the first Epistle (iv. 10) is now **charge and exhort,** put with a new tone of sternness.

Not *by* but **in the Lord Jesus Christ** (R.V.); on this phrase—both as to the *preposition*, and the *triple name*—see notes to *vv.* 4, 5 above, also 1 Ep. iv. 1, i. 1 (p. 47). The appeal assumes a character of the most grave urgency.

These idle meddlers, a burden and scandal to the Church, the Apostle "charges, and appeals" to them, on the ground of their relationship to Christ and with all the weight of Christ's authority committed to him, that **working with quietness, they eat their own bread**—not the bread of their honest and laborious brethren. See notes to ver. 8, and 1 Ep. iv. 11.

In the *Teaching of the Twelve Apostles* (ch. i.), probably the oldest Post-Apostolic writing extant, there is a remarkable warning addressed both to givers and receivers of alms, which illustrates this passage: "Blessed is he that giveth according to the commandment, for he is guiltless. Woe to him that takes! For if indeed one takes out of necessity, he will be guiltless; but he who takes without need shall give account why he took, and for what purpose; and thrown into prison he will be examined respecting his conduct, and will not come out thence until he has paid the uttermost farthing. Moreover, concerning this matter it has been said: Let thine alms sweat into thy hands, until thou knowest to whom thou shouldst give."

13. *But ye, brethren, be not weary in well doing*] From this do-nothing, or ill-doing fraction of the Church the Apostle turns to the rest, who were busy in "well-doing," and bids them persevere. Comp. ch. ii. 17, and note; also 1 Ep. i. 3, iv. 1, 10, for the diligent and honourable character which in the main this Church bore.

The pronoun bears marked emphasis: **But as for you, brethren,**—in contrast with "them that are such," ver. 12.

in well doing. And if any *man* obey not our word by *this* 14
epistle, note that *man*, and have no company with him, that
he may be ashamed. Yet count *him* not as an enemy, but 15

On "well-doing," see note to 1 Ep. v. 21. The word rendered
"well" here is "good" there; it implies a *fine quality* of action.
The Greek verb for "be not weary" appears in other passages (e.g.
Luke xviii. 1; Gal. vi. 9) as "faint not," and signifies *failure of courage*
rather than of strength: **do not falter in well-doing**; comp. notes on
"stablish your hearts," ch. ii. 17 and 1 Ep. iii. 13. Perhaps the
Apostle's rebuke of "busy-bodies" and commendation of "quietness"
might have damped the ardour of some whose activity was praiseworthy,
had it remained unqualified. The misconduct of the unruly was of a
kind to disappoint and grieve all zealous friends of the Church.

14. *And if any* man *obey not our word by* this *epistle*] More strictly,
But if any one obeys not, &c. As the writer passes, by a contrasting
But in ver. 13, from the disorderly fraction to the well-conducted
majority of the Church, so he returns again from the latter to the
former, in order to give his final directions concerning them. "Obeys
not" (indicative): the Apostle is not providing for a contingency, but
dealing with the existing case. The matter is put, according to the
Greek epistolary idiom, from the standpoint of the readers. The letter
has been read to the assembled Church; the disorderly have received
the Apostle's message; some acknowledge their fault, and submit;
others—one or more—are still refractory; and he tells the Church how
it must now proceed.

"Our word through the Epistle,"—i.e. **what we say by this letter**.
Word and *Epistle* were distinguished in ch. ii. 2, 15, here identified; the
letter has the force and authority of the writer's spoken word (see note
on ch. ii. 15).

note that man, *and have no company with him*] Better reading: **note
that man, that ye have no company with him** (R.V.); i.e., "mark
him as a man with whom you are not to associate,"—literally, **not to
be mixed up with him**: comp. the use of the same verb in 1 Cor.
v. 9, 11. The "noting," one imagines, would be effected by publicly
naming the culprit in the Church as one disobedient to the Apostle's
command.

This "mark" set on the obstinate breaker of rule is intended for his
good—**to the end that he may be ashamed** (R.V.), or **abashed**. This
is all the punishment desired for him. If shame is awakened in him,
when he finds himself condemned by the general sentiment and left
alone, this may be the beginning of amendment. Compare the directions given in the extreme case of offence at Corinth, 2 Cor. ii. 6—8.
The door for repentance is left wide open.

15. *Yet count* him *not as an enemy, but admonish* him *as a
brother*] Lit., **And do not regard him as an enemy**, &c. The R.V.
retains "yet" in italics ("And *yet*"); but the contrast thus implied is
not in St Paul's thought, any more than in his language. The measure
which he directs to be taken in ver. 14 is a *saving* measure, designed

¹⁵ admonish *him* as a brother. Now the Lord of peace himself give you peace always by all means. The Lord *be* with you all.

to bring the intractable man to a better mind—"that he may be ashamed." Hence there must be no unkind feeling towards him, no bitter expression. This would provoke him to sullenness instead of shame, defeating the Apostle's purpose. In its sympathy with St Paul the assembly might easily be stirred, on reading this letter, to some hostile demonstration that would cause a decisive rupture; this he deprecates.

The instruction of ver. 6 was general in its terms, and would apply to any sort of disorder; so the direction of 1 Ep. v. 14, "Admonish the unruly." Those two injunctions are here combined, and enforced in this specific instance. For in such a case the disorder takes the form of open and avowed disobedience to the Apostle, such as the Church is bound to deal with publicly and to put an end to. But even now *expulsion* is not so much as named.

Conclusion of the Letter. Ch. III. 16—18.

16. *Now the Lord of peace himself give you peace always by all means*] Lit., **But may the Lord**, &c.; for there is a contrast between the directions just given and the *peace* for which the Apostle prays. Peace was disturbed by an irritating kind of disorder in the Church, by wild rumours and alarms respecting the Parousia (ch. ii. 1, 2), as well as by the unrelenting persecution from without. St Paul has done his best to tranquillize his readers' minds, and bring them all to a sober and orderly condition. But he looks to "the Lord of peace Himself" to shed on them His all-controlling and all-reconciling influence. Christ is invoked as *the Lord of peace* (comp. ver. 5), just as God was called "the God of peace" in 1 Ep. v. 23 (see note; and on the import of "peace" in St Paul, note to 1 Ep. i. 1). Christ is Lord and Disposer of the peace which the Gospel brings (comp. Col. iii. 15, R.V.). This St Paul asks, first (ch. i. 2) and last, for the troubled and harassed Thessalonians.

"Always" represents a different Greek adverb from that so often used in these letters (1 Ep. i. 2, &c.); it denotes not *on every occasion*, but *through all*,—"continually," as the same adverb is rendered in Luke xxiv. 53, Heb. xiii. 15: **the Lord...give you peace at all times in all ways** (R.V.).

Nor is it the Lord's sovereign peace alone, but *the Lord* Himself, in His personal presence and authority (comp. Matt. xxviii. 18, 20), Whom the Apostle invokes. **The Lord be with you all**, as in ver. 18,—not excluding the "brother walking disorderly," who even more than others needs the presence of *the Lord* and the virtue of His *peace*. Comp. 1 Cor. xvi. 24, 2 Cor. xiii. 14, where the "all" of the Benediction has a like pointed significance; also note on 1 Ep. v. 27.

The salutation of Paul with mine own hand, which is the 17 *token in every epistle: so I write. The grace of our Lord* 18 *Jesus Christ be with you all. Amen.*

¶ *The second epistle to the Thessalonians was written from Athens.*

17. *The salutation of Paul with mine own hand*] Lit., **The salutation with my own hand—of PAUL**. In the last word the Apostle's formal signature is attached. Pen in hand, he adds the brief concluding sentences to the letter, lying now all but complete before him.

The Apostle commonly employed one of his helpers as amanuensis. "I Tertius, who wrote this letter," e.g., in Rom. xvi. 22; comp. Gal. vi. 11, Philem. 19, where he notifies his writing *sua manu*. But it was needful that he should sign his name, with a few words of greeting written by himself, in order to authenticate the Epistle. In other Epistles we find the autograph conclusion without the final signature, which was not usual in ancient letters. There is no reference of this kind at the close of his First Epistle; but since that time his written authority had been alleged for statements he had never made (ch. ii. 2). He is careful to guard against this possibility in writing to Thessalonica a second time. He calls attention, as he pens this attestation, to his handwriting, and gives notice that no document bearing his name will be genuine without this seal: **which is the token in every epistle** ("Paul's mark," as one might say)—**thus I write**.

There was something peculiar and noticeable in the Apostle's penmanship, which could not be mistaken. Some infer from Gal. vi. 11 that St Paul's script was distinguished by its large and bold appearance; but it may be that he used large characters in that passage for the sake of emphasis. Further allusions to the autograph conclusion are found in 1 Cor. xvi. 21, and Col. iv. 18.

18. *The grace of our Lord Jesus Christ be with you all*] This sealing Benediction is identical with that of 1 Ep. v. 20 (see note), and is repeated in Rom. xvi. 20, and Rev. xxii. 21. Only the Apostle adds here, as in ver. 16 (see note), the "all" which is fitting where *some* had been objects of censure.

The *Amen* of the Received Text is absent in the oldest copies; comp. 1 Ep. v. 28.

On the subscription, see note in 1 Epistle, and *Introd.* p. 27.

APPENDIX.

THE MAN OF LAWLESSNESS (or MAN OF SIN).

2 Thessalonians ii. 1—12.

To give a full account of the interpretation of 2 Thess. ii. 1—12 would be almost the same thing as to write a history of Christendom. This is one of those dark passages of Scripture which in ordinary Christian teaching, and in peaceful and prosperous times, receive little attention; they are traversed with hasty step, and willingly dismissed as things hard to be understood. But in seasons of conflict and danger, such as those which gave them birth, and when some critical struggle arises between the kingdoms of God and Satan, the Church turns to these neglected prophecies; from their obscurity there breaks out a new and awful light; again she hears in them the "voices and thunders" that "proceed out of the Throne" and the shout of His coming Who "brings forth judgement unto victory." To such epochs we must look for the interpretation of these words of destiny. History is the expositor of Prophecy. For the seeds of the future lie in the past; and not the seeds alone, its buddings and beginnings, its leaves and blossomings are there, if we had eyes to see them. "First the blade, then the ear," said Jesus,—"then the full corn in the ear." The growth is continuous, until full ripeness.

Let us endeavour, therefore, to trace in its historical outline the development of the doctrine of Antichrist—*first*, as it appears in Scripture; and *secondly*, as it has been unfolded in the belief and teaching of the Church.

1. THE APOCALYPSE OF DANIEL.

We must go back to the Book of Daniel[1] for the origin of St Paul's conception of the Man of Lawlessness, as well as for that of the kindred visions of St John. Daniel's Apocalypse has its starting-point in the dream of Nebuchadnezzar (ch. ii.): *the Fourfold Metal Image*, with its feet of mixed iron and clay, broken in pieces by the "Stone cut out of the mountain without hands." This dream takes another and enlarged form in Daniel's first Vision, that of *the Four Wild Beasts* (ch. vii.).

---

[1] See the article in Smith's *Bible Dictionary*, by Bishop Westcott, on the Book of Daniel. There is nothing written on the subject, within our knowledge, more penetrating and suggestive.

Amidst the "ten horns" of the fourth Beast there springs up "a little horn," before which "three of the first horns were plucked up by the roots," having "eyes like the eyes of a man, and a mouth speaking great things" (ver. 8). In a moment the scene is changed: the "thrones" of the Last Judgement are placed; "the Ancient of Days" is beheld sitting; and there is "brought near before Him" the "One like unto a son of man, coming with the clouds of heaven," whom the Lord Jesus at the High Priest's tribunal identified with Himself. To Him the prophet assigns universal and everlasting dominion (*vv*. 9—14). As the judgement is proceeding, and before the appearance of the glorified Son of Man, the fourth Beast is slain and "his body destroyed, and given to be burned with fire" (ver. 11), "because of the voice of the great words which the little horn spake." The idea is here presented of a cruel, haughty and triumphant military power, to be overthrown suddenly by the judgement of God, whose fall, apparently, gives the signal for the establishment of the kingdom of heaven, which is to be ruled by one like unto a son of man yet sharing the Divine attributes.

In the next vision, ch. viii., of *the duel between the Ram and the He-goat* the Little Horn reappears, and takes on a distinct personal shape. He becomes "a king of fierce countenance and understanding dark sayings," who will "destroy (*or* corrupt) the people of the saints... and stand up against the Prince of princes; but shall be broken without hand" (*vv*. 22—25). The third vision, ch. xi.—of *the wars of North and South*—leads up to a further description of the great Oppressor, in which his atheism forms the most conspicuous feature: "Arms shall stand on his part, and they shall profane the sanctuary...and they shall set up the abomination that maketh desolate...And the king shall do according to his will; and he shall exalt himself, and magnify himself above every god, and shall speak marvellous things against the God of gods: and he shall prosper till the indignation be accomplished" (*vv*. 31—36). This series of tableaux gives a continuous view of a polity or empire evolved out of the warring kingdoms of this world, from which emerges at last a monster of wickedness armed with all earthly power and bent on the destruction of Israel's God and people, in whose person the realm of evil receives its decisive judgement.

2. THE MESSIANIC TIMES.

Antiochus Epiphanes[1], it is agreed, was the primary subject of Daniel's visions of judgement. In his overthrow, and in the Maccabean revival of the nationality of Israel, this Apocalypse had its verification; it received a fulfilment adequate and appropriate to the age. But when

---

[1] Antiochus IV., or Antiochus Epiphanes—i.e. the Brilliant, called also in mockery *Epimanes, the Madman*—was the seventh king of the Græco-Syrian dynasty of the Seleucids, and reigned from 175 to 164 B.C. His father was Antiochus III. (called the Great), after whose defeat by the Romans (188 B.C.) he was given to them as a hostage, and brought up at Rome. He returned to take his father's throne, full of wild ambition and of reckless impiety and prodigality. On the character and career of Antiochus Epiphanes see Stanley's *History of the Jewish Church*, vol. III., Ewald's *History of Israel*, vol. v. (Eng. Trans.); Smith's *Bible Dictionary*.

the period of the Maccabees was past, and no further sign appeared of the Messiah, it grew plain to believing readers that the revelation had a further import. In this faith the sufferings of the Jewish people under the Herodian and Roman oppression were endured, as "birth-pangs of the Messiah;" it was felt that Israel's hope was nigh at hand, even at the doors. Our Lord by assuming the title Son of Man appealed to and justified the expectations of those who in His day "looked for Israel's redemption,"—expectations founded to no small extent upon the Apocalypse of Daniel, and coloured by its imagery. Again "the abomination of desolation, spoken of by Daniel the prophet," was to "stand in the Holy Place" (Matt. xxiv. 15); and the "sign of the Son of Man" would be "seen in heaven," and at last the Son of Man Himself, "coming with the clouds of heaven" (Matt. xxiv. 30, xxvi. 64).

But the Messianic anticipations of our Lord's time, being drawn from this source, could hardly fail to be attended with their counterpart in the image of Daniel's *Antichrist*. In later Judaism Antichrist was known as *Armillus* (or *Armalgus*), under which name he figures largely in the Jewish fables of the Middle Ages, the Rabbinical conception being developed in forms partly analogous and partly hostile to the Christian doctrine. Armillus appears already in the *Targum of Jonathan* upon Isai. xi. 4, the passage quoted by our Apostle in ver. 8 above: "With the breath of His lips shall He (Messiah) slay Armillus, the wicked one." This interpretation was traditional, and may have been older than Christianity. The existence of an earlier Jewish doctrine of Antichrist, in however incipient a form, would make it easier to understand the rapid development which this conception receives in the New Testament, and the manner in which it appeals to the mind of the Apostolic Church.

The words of Christ fixed the attention of His first disciples upon Daniel's prophecies, and supplied the impulse and starting-point from which proceeded the revival of the O.T. Apocalypse in the teaching of SS. Paul and John. Besides His express citations of Daniel, there were other traits in our Lord's picture of the Last Things—the predictions of national conflict, of persecutions from without and defections within His Church (Matt. xxiv. 3—13)—which reproduced the general characteristics of this prophet's visions, and lent emphasis to the specific and most solemn references that He made to them. His use of this obscure and suspected Book has raised it to a position of high honour and importance in the regard of His Church.

3. ANTICHRIST IN THE BOOK OF REVELATION.

St Paul treats the subject in the passage before us in an incidental fashion, and nowhere in his extant Epistles does he again advert to it. His language, so far as it goes, is very positive and definite. There is scarcely a more matter-of-fact prediction in the Bible. While he refuses to give any chronological datum, his description of the personality of Antichrist is vividly distinct; and he asserts the connection between his appearance and Christ's return from heaven with an explicitness that leaves no room for doubt as to his meaning. But John's

Apocalypse was cast in a different mould. Like that of Daniel, his revelation came through *visions*, received apparently in a passive and ecstatic mental state, and clothed in a mystic robe of imagery through which it is difficult and indeed impossible altogether to distinguish the body and substance of truth, which one feels nevertheless to be everywhere present underneath it. St John's visions border upon those "unspeakable things" of "the third heaven," which it may be lawful for the human soul in rare moments of exaltation to see and hear, but not "to utter" in clear discourse of reason (2 Cor. xii. 2—4).

The visions of *the Wild Beast*, contained in Revelation xiii.—xx., do nevertheless present a tolerably distinct and continuous picture; and it is just in this part of John's Apocalypse that it comes into line with the Apocalypses of Daniel and Paul, and, as at least it seems to us, into connection with the course of secular history then proceeding. It accords with the nature of the two Revelations that St John's mind is possessed by the symbolic idea of the Horned Wild Beast of Daniel (chh. vii., viii.), while St Paul reflects in his Man of Lawlessness the later and more definite form which Daniel's conception of the great enemy of God assumes in ch. xi. But the representations of the two Apostles coincide in their essential features. The first Beast of St John, seven-headed and ten-horned, receives the "power and throne of the Dragon and great authority," from "him that is called Devil and the Satan, that deceives the whole world" (Rev. xii. 9, xiii. 1, 2), just as St Paul's Lawless One comes "according to the working of Satan" and "in all deceit of unrighteousness" (*vv.* 9, 10). He "opens his mouth in blasphemies against God, to blaspheme His name and tabernacle" and everything Divine; and "all that dwell in the earth worship him," whose names were "not written in the book of life;" and "torment" is promised to them, who "worship the Beast and his image" (Rev. xiii. 5—8; xiv. 11): so the Man of Lawlessness "exalts himself against all that is called God or worshipped," he "takes his seat in the temple of God, setting himself forth as God;" and men are found to "believe the lie," who will be "judged" for their "pleasure in unrighteousness" and are of "them that perish" (*vv.* 4, 10—12). Again, the authority of the Wild Beast is vindicated by means of "great signs," through which "they that dwell on the earth are deceived" (Rev. xiii. 13, 14): similarly, in our Apostle, Satan's great emissary "comes with all power and signs and wonders of falsehood" (*vv.* 9, 10). This token of false miracles was furnished by our Lord as the sign of "false Christs and false prophets" generally (Matt. xxiv. 24). Finally, having "come up out of the abyss," the Wild Beast "goes into perdition" (Rev. xvii. 8), like the Lawless One, with his Satanic coming, who is "the son of perdition" (*vv.* 3, 9).

The ten-horned Beast of John is set forth as the secular antagonist of the Man-child, son of the Woman[1], who was born "to rule all the nations," as His would-be destroyer and the usurper of His throne;

---

[1] Mr W. H. Simcox with good reason sees *the woman* who brings forth the Man-child, and then "flies into the wilderness unto her place" till the appointed time, in *the Jewish Church;* see his notes, in *Cambridge Bible for Schools,* on Rev. xii. Comp. Rom. ix. 5, "of whom is the Christ according to flesh."

by Whom at last when He appears as Conqueror upon the "white horse[1]," the Beast is taken and cast with his followers "into the lake that burneth with fire and brimstone" (comp. Rev. xii. with xiii., and then see ch. xix. 11—21). This conflict translates into an expanded picture the antagonism between the Lord Jesus and the Lawless One, Christ and Antichrist, which breathes in every syllable of St Paul's condensed and pregnant lines. The outlines etched in rapid strokes by Paul's sharp needle, are thrown out upon the glowing canvas of the Apocalypse in idealized and visionary shape; but the same conception dominates the imagination of the seer of Patmos which haunts the writer of this sober and calm Epistle.

The first Wild Beast of Rev. xiii. is the centre of a group of symbolic figures. There "comes up out of the earth another Beast," kindred to him, and called afterwards the "false prophet," who acts as his apostle, re-establishing his power after the deadly wound he received, and performing the "signs" by which his worship is supported and enforced. To this second actor, therefore, a *religious* part is assigned, resembling that of a corrupt Church serving a lawless, despotic State. The False Prophet supplies a necessary link between the Apostasy and the Lawless One of 2 Thess. ii. 3; by his agency the "lying miracles" of ver. 10 are provided, and superstition is enlisted in the service of atheism.

While the Beast has the False Prophet by his side for an auxiliary, he carries on his back the Harlot-woman, the antithesis of the Church, Christ's Bride. She is identified in the plainest manner with *the imperial city of Rome*. On her forehead stands written the legend, "Mystery, Babylon the Great, the mother of the harlots and the abominations of the earth." This is but Paul's "mystery of iniquity" writ large and illuminated. What Babylon was to O.T. prophecy, that Rome became to the prophets of the New, being the centre of the world's evil and the nidus of its future development. And *the imperial house of Rome—Nero* in particular for St Paul, and Domitian, probably, as *Nero redivivus* for St John—held to the prophetic spirit of the Apostles a relation similar to that of the Syrian monarchy and Antiochus Epiphanes toward the prophecy of Daniel, serving as a proximate and provisional goal of its anticipations, the object around which the secular forces of evil were about to gather and the fittest type of their further and ultimate evolution. But as history pursued its course and the Church passed beyond its Apostolic horizon, the new Apocalypse was found like the old to have a wider scope. The Wild Beast survived many wounds; it survived the fall of the great city, mistress of the earth,—the Woman whom John saw riding upon its back. The end was not yet; the word of prophecy must run through new circles of fulfilment.

It is only in the barest outline that we may pursue the subsequent history of the doctrine of Antichrist[2]. It has passed through four principal stages.

[1] In the Conqueror's name of Faithful and True, and in the "righteousness" with which "He judges and makes war," and "the righteous acts of the saints"—the "fine linen, clean and white" which clothes His army—we may see another antithesis to the moral picture given in 2 Thess. ii. 10—12.

[2] For the history of this question, see the Article *Antichrist*, Vol. i. (2nd ed.) of

4. ANTICHRIST IN THE EARLY CHURCH.

In the age of the early Church, ending with the conversion of the Empire and the Fall of Rome (410 A.D.), one consistent view prevailed upon this subject,—viz. that Antichrist was *an individual destined one day to overthrow the Roman Empire and to establish a rule of consummate wickedness, which would quickly be terminated by the appearing of the Lord Jesus from heaven.* Chrysostom probably represents the popular belief when he speaks of Nero as "a type of Antichrist," and "the mystery of iniquity already working." In the earliest times men associated with this tradition the expectation, long current in the East, of Nero's return and re-inthronement.

Many of the Fathers, after the manner of 1 John ii. 18—22, pointed out the workings of Antichrist in the various forms of *heresy*. It was frequently inferred from 2 Thess. ii. 4 that the Jewish Temple would in the last days be rebuilt in Jerusalem, and made the seat of Antichrist's empire and worship. In connection with this opinion, a *Jewish* origin (from the tribe of Dan, Gen. xlix. 17) was assigned to the Man of Sin. Others regarded the Church, either in a spiritual or local sense, as "the temple of God" signified by St Paul (see note on ver. 4).

"The withholder" was commonly understood to be the Roman Empire, with its fabric of civil polity,—*Romanus status*, as Tertullian says; its downfall imported the end of the world to the Church of the first three centuries. By some the withholding influence was seen in the Holy Spirit, or in His miraculous gifts.

5. ANTICHRIST IN THE MIDDLE AGES.

The Western Empire was submerged under barbarian invasions. But the fabric of society still held together; and out of the chaos of the early Middle Ages there gradually arose the modern polity of the Romanized European nations, with the Papal See for its spiritual centre, and the revived Roman Empire of Charlemagne—*magni nominis umbra*—holding the leadership of the new world (800 A.D.). Meanwhile the ancient Empire maintained a sluggish existence in the New Rome of Constantine on the Bosphorus, where it arrested for centuries the destructive forces of Mohammedanism, until their energy was comparatively spent. This change in the current of history, fol-

---

Smith's *Bible Dictionary*, also Herzog's *Real-Encyklopädie* (2nd ed.). There are valuable dissertations on "The Man of Sin" by Lünemann (Meyer's Handbook), Riggenbach (Lange's Commentary), and Olshausen *ad loc.*, also in Alford's *Prolegomena* to the Epp. Döllinger elucidates the subject with great learning and exactness in Appendix I. to his *First Age of the Church* (translated by Oxenham); and Eadie in the Appendix to his Commentary on *Thessalonians*. For the interpretation of the parallel texts in the Apocalypse, see Simcox's *Notes* in this Series and his most interesting and valuable *Introduction*. As to the bearings of the subject on the doctrines of Eschatology at large, see the profound remarks of Dorner in his *System of Christian Doctrine*, vol. IV., 373—401 (Eng. Trans). We find ourselves in general agreement with Dorner, Olshausen, Riggenbach, Alford, Ellicott, Eadie; and, to a large extent, with Hofmann.

lowing upon the union of Church and State under Constantine, disconcerted the Patristic reading of prophecy. And the interpretation of Scripture, along with the general cultivation of the human mind, fell into decline after the fourth century. Things present absorbed the energy and thought of the Church to the exclusion of things to come. The Western Church was occupied in converting and assimilating the Barbarian hordes, the Eastern Church was struggling for its very existence against Islam; while they contested with each other for supremacy. For the most part, the teaching of the Fathers respecting Antichrist was repeated by medieval divines, and embroidered with their fancies.

Gradually new interpretations forced themselves to the front. The Greeks naturally saw "the lawless one" in *Muhammad*, and "the apostasy" in the falling away of so many Eastern Christians to his delusions. In the West, the growing arrogance of the Bishops of Rome and the traditional connection of Antichrist with Rome united to suggest the idea of a *Papal Antichrist*. This view has high Papal authority in its favour; Gregory I. (or the Great, 590 A.D.), denouncing the assumptions of the contemporary Byzantine Patriarch, wrote as follows: "Ego autem fidenter dico quia quisquis se universalem sacerdotem vocat, vel vocari desiderat, in elatione sua *Antichristum præcurrit*;" he further styles the title of Universal Priest "erroris nomen, stultum ac superbum vocabulum...*nomen blasphemiæ.*" By this just sentence the later Roman Primacy is marked out as another type of Antichrist.

In the 13th century, when Gregory VII. (or Hildebrand, 1073—1085 A.D.) and Innocent III. (1198—1216 A.D.) had raised the power of the Roman See to its highest point, this doctrine was openly declared by the supporters of the Hohenstaufen Emperors; and the German State resumed the office of the Roman State as "the restrainer" of the Man of Sin. This century witnessed a general revival of religious zeal, of which the rise of the Waldenses, the theology of Thomas Aquinas, the founding of the Dominican and Franciscan orders, the immortal poem of Dante, and the widespread revolt and protest against the corruptions of Rome were alike manifestations. This awakening was attended with a renewal of Apocalyptic study. The numbers of Dan. xii. 6—13, Rev. xii. 6, &c., gave rise to the belief that the year 1260 would usher in the final conflict against Antichrist and the end of the world; while the invasion of the Mongols and the intestine divisions of Christendom threatened it with destruction. In the East, by adding 666, "the number of the Beast" (Rev. xiii. 18) to 622, the date of the Hejira, it was calculated that Mohammedanism was about to meet its doom. This crisis also passed, and the world went on its way. But it remained henceforth a fixed idea, proclaimed by every dissenter from the Roman See, that Antichrist would be found on the Papal throne. So the Waldenses, Huss, Savonarola, and our own Wickliff taught[1].

[1] We must distinguish, however, between *an* Antichrist and *the* Antichrist. A sincere Roman Catholic might assign to this or that unworthy Pope a place amongst the "many Antichrists," adopting St John's expression in 1 Ep. ii. 18; as indeed Romanists have done in the case of Luther and others of their opponents, without supposing the Apostle's prophecy to be in this way absolutely fulfilled.

6. THE LUTHERAN DOCTRINE OF ANTICHRIST.

Martin Luther's famous protest *adversus execrabilem bullam Antichristi* inaugurated the Protestant Reformation (1520 A.D.). It was one of his firmest convictions, shared by all the great Reformers, that the Papal system was the Antichrist of prophecy; Luther expected that it would shortly be destroyed by Christ in His second advent. This belief was made a formal dogma of the Lutheran Church by the standard Articles of Smalkald (1537 A.D.)[1]. It has a place in the English Bible; the translators in their address to King James I. credit that monarch with having given, by a certain tractate he had published, "such a blow unto that Man of Sin, as will not be healed." Bishop Jewel's Exposition of the Thessalonian Epistles, delivered in the crisis of England's revolt from Rome, gives powerful expression to the Lutheran view. In the 17th Century, however, this interpretation was called in question amongst English Divines. Amongst its recent advocates, the late Bishop Wordsworth, in his *Lectures on the Apocalypse* and *Commentary on the Greek Testament*, has supplied a learned and most earnest vindication.

This theory has impressive arguments in its favour, drawn both from Scripture and history. It contains large elements of truth. But many reasons forbid us to identify the Papacy with the Man of Lawlessness. Two must here suffice. (1) St Paul's words describe, as the early Fathers saw, *a personal Antichrist;* they cannot be satisfied by any mere succession of men, or system of Antichristian evil. (2) His Man of Lawlessness is to be *the avowed opposer and displacer of God*. Now, however gross the idolatry of which the Pope has been made the object, and however daring and blasphemous the arrogance of some occupants of the Papal Chair, one must seriously weaken and distort the words of the Apostle to adjust them to the Romanist pretensions. It is not true, in any strict sense of the words, that the Bishop of Rome "exalts himself against every one called God and every object of worship." The Roman Catholic system has *multiplied*, instead of abolishing objects of worship; its ruling errors have been those of superstition, not of atheism. At the same time, its exaltation of the Pope and the priesthood has debased the religious instinct of Christendom, and has nursed the spirit of *anthropolatry*—the man-worship, which St Paul believed was to have in the Man of Lawlessness its supreme object. Romanist teaching has prepared a fruitful soil for the seeds of atheism. It enervates the conscience, and loosens the bonds of moral obligation[2].

7. ANTICHRIST IN MODERN TIMES.

It would occupy several pages merely to state the various theories promulgated upon this mysterious subject in recent times.

---

[1] Melanchthon admitted a second Antichrist in Muhammad. He distinguished between the *Eastern* and *Western* Antichrists. The conjunction of Pope and Turk was common with our Protestant forefathers.

[2] Whatever is said in condemnation of the Romanist system, is said in remembrance and joyful recognition of the fact that within the Roman communion there are multitudes of sincere and exemplary Christians.

APPENDIX.

Not the least plausible is that which saw "the apostasy" in the later developments of the *French Revolution*, with its apotheosis of an abandoned woman in the character of Goddess of Reason, and which identified *Napoleon Buonaparte* with the Man of Sin. The Empire of Napoleon was essentially a restoration of the military Cæsarism of the first century. He came within a little of making himself, like Julius Cæsar, dictator of the civilized world. To our minds, this unscrupulous despot, with his superb genius and insatiable egotism—the offspring and the idol, till he became the scourge of a godless democracy—is in the true succession of Antiochus Epiphanes and Nero Cæsar. He has set before our times a new and commanding type of the Lawless One.

Nor is *godlessness* wanting in a bold and typical modern expression. Following upon the negative and destructive atheism of the last century, the scientific, constructive and humanistic atheism of this century has built up for itself an imposing system of thought and life. The theory of Positivism, as it was propounded by its great apostle, Auguste Comte, culminates in the doctrine that "Man is man's god." God and immortality, with the entire world of the supernatural, this philosophy abolishes in the name of science and modern thought. It sweeps them out of the way in order to make room for *le grand être humain*, or *collective humanity;* which is to command our worship through the memory of its heroes and men of genius, and in the person of woman, adored within the family. This scheme of religion Comte worked out with the utmost seriousness, and furnished with an elaborate hierarchy and ritual, based on the Roman Catholic model. Although Comte's religion of humanity is disowned by many of his followers, it is a phenomenon of great significance and interest. It testifies to the persistence of the religious instinct in our nature; and it shews the direction which that instinct is compelled to take when deprived of its rightful Object (see the Apostle's words in Rom. i. 23). Comte would carry us back, virtually, to the Pagan adoration of deified heroes and deceased Emperors, or to the Chinese worship of family ancestors. Moreover, Positivism provides in its Great Being an abstraction which, so far as it takes possession of the human mind, must inevitably tend to realise itself in concrete personal shape. It sets up a throne of worship which the man of destiny will be forthcoming "in his season" to occupy.

Since the time of Hugo Grotius (1583—1645 A.D.), the famous Dutch Protestant scholar, theologian, and statesman, numerous attempts have been made to demonstrate the fulfilment of N.T. prophecy within the Apostolic, or Post-apostolic age. This line of interpretation was adopted by Catholic theologians, as by Bossuet in the 17th century and Döllinger[1] in our own times, partly by way of return to the Patristic view, and partly in defence against Protestant exegesis. These *præterist* theories, restricting the application of St Paul's prediction to the first

---

[1] Döllinger sees "the Lawless One" in *Nero*, in the first instance; and "the Withholder"—or, as he prefers to render the word, "the Occupier" (viz. of the seat of power)—in *Claudius*, Nero's predecessor; the latter a very improbable identification. He does not suppose the meaning of the prophecy exhausted by this first fulfilment, but expects a second at the end of the world. All intermediate applications he regards as speculative and illegitimate.

age of the Church, in various ways strain and minimize his language, in attempting to make it square with actual events. Or else they assume, as rationalistic interpreters complacently do, that such prophecies were incapable of real fulfilment, and have been refuted by the course of history. Almost every Roman Emperor, from Caligula down to Trajan—some even of later times—has been adopted in turn for the Man of Sin or the Restrainer by one or other of the commentators. Nero figures in both characters; so does Vespasian. Others hold—and this view is partly combined with the last, as e.g. by Grotius—that *Simon Magus*, the traditional father of heresy, was the Lawless One; while others, again, see "the mystery of iniquity" in the *Jewish nation* of the Apostle's time. Outside the secular field, the *power of the Holy Spirit*, the *decree of God*, the *Jewish Law*, the *believing remnant* of Judaism, the *Christian Church*, and even *Paul himself* have been put into the place of "that which withholdeth," by earlier or later authors. But these fancies have never obtained much acceptance.

Like other great prophecies of Scripture, this word of the Apostle Paul has, it appears to us, a progressive fulfilment. It is carried into effect from time to time, under the action of Divine laws operating throughout human history, in partial and transitional forms, which prefigure and may contribute to its final realization. For such prophecies are inspired by Him Who "worketh all things after the counsel of His will;" and they rest upon the principles of God's moral government, and the abiding facts of human nature. We accept, with Chrysostom, an earnest of the accomplishment of St Paul's prediction in the person of Nero. We recognize, with the later Greek Fathers and Melanchthon, that there are plain Antichristian tokens and features in the polity of Muhammad. We recognize, with Gregory I. and the Protestant Reformers, a prelude of Antichrist's coming and conspicuous traits of his character in the spiritual despotism of the See of Rome; and we sorrowfully mark in the history of the Church how the tares ever grow beside the wheat, and in what manifold forms "the apostasy" which prepares the way of Antichrist and lays the foundations of his rule, has continued its baleful working. We agree with those who discern in the Napoléonic idea an ominous revival of the lawless absolutism and worship of human power that prevailed in the age of the Cæsars; while Positive and materialistic philosophy, with sensualistic ethics, unless we are much deceived, are making for the same goal[1].

[1] The following extract from Comte's *Catéchisme Positiviste* is a striking proof of the readiness with which scientific atheism may join hands with political absolutism: "Au nom du passé et de l'avenir, les serviteurs théoriques et les serviteurs pratiques de L'HUMANITÉ viennent prendre dignement la direction générale des affaires terrestres, pour construire enfin la vraie providence, morale, intellectuelle, et matérielle; en excluant irrévocablement de la suprématie politique tous les divers esclaves de Dieu, Catholiques, protestants, ou déistes, comme étant à la fois arrieres et perturbateurs."—The true Pontifical style! It is not a very long step from these words to that which the Apostles intimate in 2 Thess. ii. 4 and Rev. xiii. 16, 17, &c. It is significant that Comte issued this Catechism of the new religion just after the *coup d'état* of Louis Napoleon, whom he congratulates on "the happy crisis"! In the same preface he does homage to the Emperor Nicholas of Russia, as "the sole truly eminent chief of whom our century can claim the honour, up to the present time." Comte's

The history of the world is one; the first century lives over again in the nineteenth. All the factors of evil co-operate, as do those of good. There are, in truth, but two kingdoms, of Satan and of Christ; though to our eyes their forces lie scattered and confused, and we distinguish ill between them. But the course of time quickens its pace, as if nearing some great issue. Science has given an immense impetus to human progress in all directions, and moral influences propagate themselves with greater speed than heretofore. There is going on a rapid interchange and interfusion of thought, a unifying of the world's life, and a gathering together of the forces on either side to "the valley of decision," that seem to portend some world-wide spiritual crisis, in which the glorious promises, or dark forebodings of revelation, or both at once, will be anew fulfilled. But still Christ's words stand, as Augustine said, to "put down the fingers of all the calculators[1]." *It is not for us to know times or seasons.* What backward currents may arise in our secular progress, what new seals are to be opened in the book of human fate, and through what cycles the evolution of God's purpose for mankind has yet to run, we cannot guess.

The first disciples deemed themselves to live already in the dawn of the world's closing day. We in its later hours keep watch for the Lord Who said, "Behold, I come quickly,"—yet seems to tarry. Be it ours, none the less, with unwearied love and faith to repeat the cry which has never ceased from the lips of the Church, the Bride of Christ:

COME, LORD JESUS!

ignorance of politics is some excuse for these blunders; but the conjunction remains no less significant. Faith in God and faith in freedom are bound up together. See Arthur's *Physical and Moral Law*, pp. 231—237; and his *Religion without God*, on Positivism generally.

[1] "Omnes calculantium digitos resolvit;" on Matt. xxiv. 36.

INDEX.

Words specially defined or explained are printed in *italics*. Such references are omitted as are sufficiently indicated by chapter and verse of the two Epistles.

Achaia, 23, 55—7; see *map*
Acts of Apostles, comp. with 1 and 2 Thess., 13—6, 18—20, 22—3, 27, 34—6; other reff., 46, 62, 64, 66, 68, 75—7, 81, 98, 145, 148, 159, 164
address of ancient letters, 45
advent (see *coming*)
Ægean Sea, 10
affection of Paul for Thess., 35, 67—8, 78—80, 84—90, 128—9; of Thess. for Paul, 85—6
Alford, 54, 175
Amos, Book of, 110
analysis of the Epp., 37—8
Antichrist, 139—53; in Daniel, 170—1; in Messianic times, 171—2; in Revelation, 172—4; in 1 John, 175—6; in Early Church, 175; in Middle Ages, 175—6; in modern times, 177—80; Eastern and Western views of, 176—7; Lutheran doctrine of, 177; supposed Jewish origin of, 175
Antiochus Epiphanes, 144, 171, 174
Apocalypse, of Daniel (see *Daniel*); of John (see *Revelation*); of Paul, 26—31, 100—16, 129—53, 170—80
apostle, twofold meaning of, 66
Aristarchus, 11
Armillus, 172
atheism, 143—6, 178
Athens, 18—9, 22, 27, 79, 81—2
atonement, doctrine of, 17, 114
Augustine, 67, 180
Augustus, the imperial title, 145

Bashkirtseff, Marie, Journal of, 101
Baur, F. C., 26, 28—9
beast, the wild, of Revelation, 143; the first and second, 173—4; the four, of Daniel, 171
Bengel, 49, 59, 77, 150
Berœa, 16, 22, 81, 98
body, the human, 94, 123
Byzantine Empire, 12, 143, 175

Cæsarism, 20—1, 145—9, 178—9
Caligula, Emperor Caius, 21, 145
chastity, 21, 25, 93—7
CHRIST JESUS, the title, 74
Chrysostom, 56, 108, 146, 157; on Antichrist, 175
church, 47, 74, 115
Cicero, 11
Claudius, Emperor, 27, 178
clergy, 116—7
Colossians, Ep. to, 11, 46, 54, 91, 105, 115, 131, 137, 158
comfort, 82
coming, second, of the Lord Jesus, its place in the Epp., 18—21, 25—6, 29—31, 35—7; other reff., 59—60, 80, 90—1, 100—16, 123—4, 132—7, 149—50, 156, 170—80
Comte, his new religion, 178—9
conduct of Paul at Thess., 22—4, 60—72, 164—5
Constantinople, 175
conversion of Thess., 14—5, 53—9, 72—4, 155
Corinth, 22, 27, 56, 159
Corinthians, 1 Ep. to, on the Parousia, 36, 105—6; other reff., 31, 49—50, 58, 64, 66, 82, 94, 114, 120, 152, 157, 165
Corinthians, 2 Ep. to, 32, 36, 46, 66—9, 81, 86—7, 104, 106, 114, 121, 129, 131, 134, 152, 159, 164, 167, 173
cross of Christ, 48, 60, 114

Daniel, Book of, 31, 71, 105, 143—6, 170—2, 176; Christ's use of, 172
day of the Lord, in the O. T., 108—9; in the N. T. and Paul, 19, 21, 26, 60, &c.
Demas, 11
Demetrius, St, 11—2
Deuteronomy, Book of, 34, 132, 142, 154
diligence, 97—101
discipline, need of, 26, 31, 118, 162—8
Divinity of Christ, 47, 75, 88—9, 137, 160

Döllinger, on Man of Sin, 175, 178
Domitian, Emperor, 174
Dorner, 148, 175

ecclesia (see *church*)
edification, common office of Christians, 115—6, 167—8
election, by God, 51—3, 154—5
Ellicott, Bp., 51, 88, &c.
ellipsis, 33, 142, 147
Emperors, Roman, 15, 146, 174
Ephesians, Ep. to, 33, 71, 96, 100, 112—3, 115—6, 118, 138, 160, 162
epistles of Paul, their origin, 24; character, 32—3; arrangement, 45; authority, 157, 167; abuse of, 141; authenticity guarded, 169; reading enjoined, 125
eschatology (see *coming*, and *Antichrist*), 35—7, 175
ethics (see *morals*)
Eustathius, Bp. of Thess., 12
Exodus, Book of, 58
Ezekiel, Book of, 69, 109, 144

Fathers, the Early, on Antichrist, 175
Finlay, on Byzantine Empire, 148
French Revolution, and Antichrist, 178

Gabriel, the archangel, 105
Galatians, Ep. to, 13, 32, 47—8, 58, 66, 86, 97, 114, 131, 138
Gallio, 75—6, 148
Genesis, Book of, 34, 77, 175
Gentiles, Epp. addressed to, 17—8, 33—4, 58, &c.
GOD, doctrine of, 17—8, 48, 58, 64, 70—2, 122, 124, 133, 152, 157
gospel, the, how it came to Thess., 13—6; of Paul at Thess. 16—22, 114; a *gospel* to Paul from Thess., 85
grace, of God, 47—8, 138, &c.
Gregory I., on Antichrist, 176, 179
Grotius, Hugo, 26, 106; on Antichrist, 178—9

hapax legomena, 33
heart (figurative), 64, &c.
Hebrews, Ep. to, 45, 77, 95, 113, 117, 129, 132, 161
heresy and Antichrist, 175, 179
history and prophecy, 170, 180
Hofmann, 105, 175
Hohenstaufen Emperors, 176
holy, twofold meaning of (see also *sanctification*), 69—70, &c.
hopelessness of pagan world, 101
horn, the little, 171
humanity, worship of, 178

idleness, at Thess., 99—100, 164—6
idolatry, 17, 58, 133, 145, 153, 177, 179
Isaiah, Book of, 34, 58, 76, 93, 113, 134, 149, 152, 161, 172

James, Ep. of, 50, 80, 89
Jason of Thess., 15, 69
JEHOVAH, 58
Jeremiah, Book of, 58, 77, 142
JESUS, name of, 47, 102; union with, 103; *Jesus Christ*, 74
Jewel, Bp., on Antichrist, 177
Jews, the, in Thess., 10, 14—5, 23—4, 77; other reff., 46, 68, 72—7, 143, 172, 175
Job, Book of, 131, 152
Joel, Book of, 108, 150
John, the Apostle, 48, 78
„ Gospel of, 53, 58, 65—6, 80, 88, 97, 101, 105—6, 108, 110, 115, 133, 151—2, 156, 160—1
John, 1 Ep. of, 58, 89—90, 111, 121, 139, 143, 151, 160, 162, 175
Jowett, Dr, on Paul's style, 48; on persecution, 83—4; other reff., 50, 54, 78, &c.
Jude, Ep. of, 80, 120
Judenhasse, 76
judgement, the last, Paul's preaching of, 19—21; other reff., 60, 77, 103—14, 129—39, 147—53
Julius Cæsar, 145, 178

kingdom of God, 71—2, &c.
Kings, 1 Book of, 49, 152

law, the withholder, 148
lawlessness, the man of, 26, 30, 143—53, 170—80 (Appendix)
Leviticus, Book of, 94
life in Christ, 115
Lightfoot, Bp., 66
litotes, 76
LORD, the (Christ), 56, 88, 154, 160, 168
„ (Jehovah), 58
„ JESUS, 75, 80, 137, 149, &c.
„ „ CHRIST, 47, 51, 166, &c.
Luke, St, association with Paul, 13, 81; Latin name of, 46
Luke, Gospel of, 34, 59, 67, 71, 75, 80, 108—9, 111—2, 121, 124
Luther, on Antichrist, 177

Maccabean times, 143, 172
Maccabees, 1 Book of, 142
Macedonia, 9—11, 13, 81—2, &c.; see *map*
Macedonian churches, 34—6, 56, 68, 98
manifestation, 150
Mark, Gospel of, 75, 107, 132—4
marriage, 95—6
Matthew, Gospel of, 31, 34, 71, 77, 80, 104, 106, 109—10, 119, 130, 146, 168, 172—3
Melanchthon, on Antichrist, 177, 179
Micah, Book of, 71
Michael, the archangel, 105
military metaphors, 104—5, 112—3
miracles of Antichrist, 151, 174

Muhammadanism and Antichrist, 175—6
morals, Christian, 21—2, 91—100, 116—22

Napoleon Buonaparte and Antichrist, 178—9
Nehemiah, Book of, 74
Nero, Emperor, 148; the wild beast, 174; a type of Antichrist, 175
Numbers, Book of, 124

Old Testament, use of, 33—4
Olshausen, 145, 175
Olympus, Mt., 10; see *map*
Origen, 67

paganism, 17, 47, 58, 95, 101, 133, 145, 147
Papacy and Antichrist, 175—7, 179
paraphrase of the Epp., 38—43
paronomasia, 33, 166
parousia (see *coming*)
pauperism, danger of, 100, 166
persecution, causes of, 83—4; at Thess., 22—5, 35, 72—7, 129—31, &c.
Peter, 1 Ep. of, 46, 52, 60, 80, 83, 119, 123, 125, 155, 161
Peter, 2 Ep. of, 98, 132, 142
Pfleiderer, 28, 30
Philemon, Ep. to, 46, 57, 85, 169
Philippi, 13—4, 20, &c.
Philippians, Ep. to, resemblance to Thess. Epp., 32, 34—5, 46, 55, 68, 79; difference from Thess. Epp., 33, 36, 51, 117; other reff., 69, 91—2, 106, 109, 119, 122, 130, 136—7, 155
politarchs, 10, 15
Positivism and Antichrist, 178—9
preaching, Paul's, at Thess., 16—21, 62—3, 69—72
prophecy, 120; of Antichrist, 143—9, 170—4; of Christ's coming (see *coming*); progressive fulfilment of, 170, 179
proselytes, 14, 58
Psalms, Book of, 34, 52, 57—8, 71, 88, 93, 111, 123, 132, 134—5, 138, 159
purity, 63, 93—7

Rabbinical teaching, 71, 172
Reformers, the Protestant, on Antichrist, 177, 179
retaliation, 118—9
retribution, 95—6, 129—35
revelation, 132, 147; of the lawless one, 139—53
Revelation, Book of, 28, 30, 36, 79, 105, 109—10, 130, 134—6, 143, 148, 151, 169, 172—4, 176
right of maintenance, apostolic, 66—9, 164—5

Romans, Ep. to, 17, 32, 40, 52, 58, 60, 66, 72, 88, 95, 97, 102, 105, 111—2, 114—5, 119, 133, 137—8, 143, 143, 152—3, 15, 162, 178
Rome, 9, 11, 20, 57, 76, 174, 176

saints (see *holy*)
St Sophia, mosque of, 12
Samuel, 1 Book of, 93
„ 2 Book of, 71
sanctified life, rules for, 116
Saracens, 12, 148
self-defence of Paul, 23—4, 61, 63—70
Silas, or Silvanus, 13—5, 22, 46, 81—2
Simcox, W. H., on Revelation, 173, 175
Simon Magus, 179
Stephen, St, 77
subscription to Epp., 126
Suetonius, on life of Cæsars, 145
synagogue, the Jewish, 14, 17, 24

Tacitus, 76, 145
Tafel, 12
Targum of Jonathan, 172
Teaching of Twelve Apostles, 166
Tendency school of criticism, 28
Tertullian, 175
Theodosius, Emperor, 12
Thermaic Gulf, 10; see *map*
Thessalonians, their character, &c., 14—6, 23—9, 34—5, 49, 54—7, 68—9, 74, 79—80, 85—9, 97—101, 108, 117—21, 125, 128—30, 139—41, 160—8
Thessalonica, its position, 10—1, 14, 56—7, 98, see *map*; history, 9—12; Paul's experience there, 14—6, 53, 57, 60—74
Timothy, 22, 24, 46, 81—2
„ 1 Ep. to, 46, 64, 67, 93, 99, 100, 113, 117, 142, 147, 150, 155
Timothy, 2 Ep. to, 36, 46, 54, 63, 73, 97, 131, 137, 148, 150, 160
Titus, Ep. to, 36, 58, 70, 138, 150
Tobit, Book of, 105
Trench, on N. T. Synonyms, 50
Trinity, the Divine, 55

union of Christians with Christ, 103, 115

Vespasian, Emperor, 28, 145
Via Egnatia, 11, 14, 20, 62; see *map*

Westcott, Bp., on Daniel, 170
Westcott and Hort, N. T. in Greek, 67, 110, 143
withholder, the, 139, 146—9, 175, 179
woman, the scarlet, 174
Wordsworth, the late Bp., 177
worship, objects of, 144, 176

Cambridge:
PRINTED BY J. & C. F. CLAY,
AT THE UNIVERSITY PRESS.

THE PITT PRESS SERIES.
COMPLETE LIST.

1. GREEK.

Author	Work	Editor	Price
Aeschylus	Prometheus Vinctus	Rackham	*In the Press*
Aristophanes	Aves—Plutus—Ranae	Green	3/6 each
,,	Vespae	Graves	3/6
,,	Nubes	,,	*In the Press*
Demosthenes	Olynthiacs	Glover	2/6
Euripides	Heracleidae	Beck & Headlam	3/6
,,	Hercules Furens	Gray & Hutchinson	2/-
,,	Hippolytus	Hadley	2/-
,,	Iphigeneia in Aulis	Headlam	2/6
,,	Medea	,,	2/6
,,	Hecuba	Hadley	2/6
,,	Alcestis	,,	2/6
,,	Orestes	Wedd	4/6
Herodotus	Book V	Shuckburgh	3/-
,,	,, VI, VIII, IX	,,	4/- each
,,	,, VIII 1—90, IX 1—89	,,	2/6 each
Homer	Odyssey IX, X	Edwards	2/6 each
,,	,, XXI	,,	2/-
,,	Iliad VI, XXII, XXIII, XXIV	,,	2/- each
Lucian	Somnium, Charon, etc.	Heitland	3/6
,,	Menippus and Timon	Mackie	3/6
Plato	Apologia Socratis	Adam	3/6
,,	Crito	,,	2/6
,,	Euthyphro	,,	2/6
,,	Protagoras	J. & A. M. Adam	4/6
Plutarch	Demosthenes	Holden	4/6
,,	Gracchi	,,	6/-
,,	Nicias	,,	5/-
,,	Sulla	,,	6/-
,,	Timoleon	,,	6/-
Sophocles	Oedipus Tyrannus	Jebb	4/-
Thucydides	Book III	Spratt	5/-
,,	Book VII	Holden	5/-
Xenophon	Agesilaus	Hailstone	2/6
,,	Anabasis Vol. I. Text.	Pretor	3/-
,,	,, Vol. II. Notes.	,,	4/6
,,	,, I, II	,,	4/-
,,	,, I, III, IV, V	,,	2/- each
,,	,, II, VI, VII	,,	2/6 each
,,	,, II	Edwards	1/6
,,	,, III	,,	1/6
,,	Cyropaedeia I, II (2 vols.)	Holden	6/-
,,	,, III, IV, V	,,	5/-
,,	,, VI, VII, VIII	,,	5/-

I

THE PITT PRESS SERIES.
2. LATIN.

Author	Work	Editor	Price
Caesar	De Bello Gallico		
	Com. I, III, VI, VIII	Peskett	1/6 each
,,	,, II–III, and VII	,,	2/- each
,,	,, I–III	,,	3/-
,,	,, IV–V	,,	1/6
,,	De Bello Gallico I ch. 1–29	Shuckburgh	1/6
,,	,, ,, II Belgic War	,,	1/6
,,	De Bello Civili. Com. I	Peskett	3/-
,,	,, ,, Com. III	,,	In the Press
Cicero	Actio Prima in C. Verrem	Cowie	1/6
,,	De Amicitia	Reid	3/6
,,	De Senectute	,,	3/6
,,	Div. in Q. Caec. et Actio Prima in C. Verrem	Heitland & Cowie	3/-
,,	Philippica Secunda	Peskett	3/6
,,	Pro Archia Poeta	Reid	2/-
,,	,, Balbo	,,	1/6
,,	,, Milone	,,	2/6
,,	,, Murena	Heitland	3/-
,,	,, Plancio	Holden	4/6
,,	,, Sulla	Reid	3/6
,,	Somnium Scipionis	Pearman	2/-
Cornelius Nepos	Miltiades, Themistocles, &c.	Shuckburgh	1/6
,,	Hannibal, Cato, Atticus	,,	1/6
,,	Lysander, Alcibiades, &c.	,,	1/6
,,	Timotheus, Phocion, Agesilaus, Epaminondas, Pelopidas, Timoleon, Eumenes, Datames, Hamilcar	,,	1/6
Horace	Epistles. Bk I	,,	2/6
,,	Odes and Epodes	Gow	5/-
,,	Odes. Books I, III	,,	2/- each
,,	,, Book II, IV	,,	1/6 each
,,	Epodes	,,	1/6
Livy	Books IV, VI, IX, XXVII	Stephenson	2/6 each
,,	,, V	Whibley	2/6
,,	,, XXI, XXII	Dimsdale	2/6 each
Lucan	Pharsalia. Bk I	Heitland & Haskins	1/6
,,	De Bello Civili. Bk VII	Postgate	2/-
Lucretius	Book V	Duff	2/-
Ovid	Fasti. Book VI	Sidgwick	1/6
,,	Metamorphoses, Bk I	Dowdall	1/6
Plautus	Epidicus	Gray	3/-
,,	Stichus	Fennell	2/6
,,	Trinummus	Gray	3/6
Quintus Curtius	Alexander in India	Heitland & Raven	3/6
Tacitus	Agricola and Germania	Stephenson	3/-
,,	Hist. Bk I	Davies	2/6
Terence	Hautontimorumenos	Gray	3/-
Vergil	Aeneid I to XII	Sidgwick	1/6 each
,,	Bucolics	,,	1/6
,,	Georgics I, II, and III, IV	,,	2/- each
,,	Complete Works, Vol. I, Text	,,	3/6
,,	,, ,, Vol. II, Notes	,,	4/6

THE PITT PRESS SERIES.

3. FRENCH.

Author	Work	Editor	Price
About	Le Roi des Montagnes	Ropes	2/-
Biart	Quand j'étais petit, Pts I, II	Boïelle	2/- each
Corneille	La Suite du Menteur	Masson	2/-
,,	Polyeucte	Braunholtz	2/-
De Bonnechose	Lazare Hoche	Colbeck	2/-
,,	Bertrand du Guesclin	Leathes	2/-
,,	,, Part II (*With Vocabulary*) ,,		1/6
Delavigne	Louis XI	Eve	2/-
,,	Les Enfants d'Edouard	,,	2/-
D'Harleville	Le Vieux Célibataire	Masson	2/-
De Lamartine	Jeanne d'Arc	Clapin & Ropes	1/6
De Vigny	La Canne de Jonc	Eve	1/6
Dumas	La Fortune de D'Artagnan	Ropes	2/-
Erckmann-Chatrian	La Guerre	Clapin	3/-
Guizot	Discours sur l'Histoire de la Révolution d'Angleterre	Eve	2/6
Lemercier	Frédégonde et Brunehaut	Masson	2/-
Mme de Staël	Le Directoire	Masson & Prothero	2/-
,,	Dix Années d'Exil	,,	2/-
Malot	Remi et ses Amis	Verrall	2/-
Merimée	Colomba	Ropes	2/-
Michelet	Louis XI & Charles the Bold	,,	2/6
Molière	Le Bourgeois Gentilhomme	Clapin	1/6
,,	L'École des Femmes	Saintsbury	1/6
,,	Les Précieuses ridicules	Braunholtz	2/-
,,	,, (*Abridged Edition*)	,,	1/-
,,	Le Misanthrope	,,	2/6
,,	L'Avare	,,	2/6
Perrault	Fairy Tales	Rippmann	1/6
Piron	La Métromanie	Masson	2/-
Ponsard	Charlotte Corday	Ropes	2/-
Racine	Les Plaideurs	Braunholtz	2/-
,,	,, (*Abridged Edition*)	,,	1/-
Sainte-Beuve	M. Daru	Masson	2/-
Saintine	Picciola	Clapin	2/-
Scribe & Legouvé	Bataille de Dames	Bull	2/-
Scribe	Le Verre d'Eau	Colbeck	2/-
Sédaine	Le Philosophe sans le savoir	Bull	2/-
Souvestre	Un Philosophe sous les Toits	Eve	2/-
,,	Le Serf & Le Chevrier de Lorraine	Ropes	2/-
,,	Le Serf (*With Vocabulary*)	,,	1/6
Thierry	Lettres sur l'histoire de France (XIII—XXIV)	Masson & Prothero	2/6
,,	Récits des Temps Mérovingiens, I—III	Masson & Ropes	3/-
Villemain	Lascaris ou les Grecs du XVe Siècle	Masson	2/-
Voltaire	Histoire du Siècle de Louis XIV, in three parts	Masson & Prothero	2/6 each
Xavier de Maistre	La Jeune Sibérienne. Le Lépreux de la Cité d'Aoste	Masson	1/6

4. GERMAN.

Author	Work	Editor	Price
Andersen	Six Fairy Tales	Rippmann	2/6
	Ballads on German History	Wagner	2/-
Benedix	Dr Wespe	Breul	3/-
Freytag	Der Staat Friedrichs des Grossen	Wagner	2/-
	German Dactylic Poetry	,,	3/-
Goethe	Knabenjahre (1749—1761)	Wagner & Cartmell	2/-
	Hermann und Dorothea	,, ,,	3/6
,,	Iphigenie	Breul	In the Press
Grimm	Selected Tales	Rippmann	3/-
Gutzkow	Zopf und Schwert	Wolstenholme	3/6
Hackländer	Der geheime Agent	E. L. Milner Barry	3/-
Hauff	Das Bild des Kaisers	Breul	3/-
,,	Das Wirthshaus im Spessart	Schlottmann & Cartmell	3/-
,,	Die Karavane	Schlottmann	3/-
Immermann	Der Oberhof	Wagner	3/-
Klee	Die deutschen Heldensagen	Wolstenholme	3/-
Kohlrausch	Das Jahr 1813	,,	2/-
Lessing	Minna von Barnhelm	Wolstenholme *Nearly ready*	3/-
Lessing & Gellert	Selected Fables	Breul	3/-
Mendelssohn	Selected Letters	Sime	3/-
Raumer	Der erste Kreuzzug	Wagner	2/-
Riehl	Culturgeschichtliche Novellen	Wolstenholme	3/-
,,	Die Ganerben & Die Gerechtigkeit Gottes	,,	3/-
Schiller	Wilhelm Tell	Breul	2/6
,,	,, (*Abridged Edition*)	,,	1/6
,,	Geschichte des dreissigjährigen Kriegs Book III.	,,	3/-
,,	Maria Stuart	,,	3/6
,,	Wallenstein I. (Lager and Piccolomini)	,,	3/6
,,	Wallenstein II. (Tod)	,,	3/6
Uhland	Ernst, Herzog von Schwaben	Wolstenholme	3/6

THE PITT PRESS SERIES.

5. ENGLISH.

Author	Work	Editor	Price
Bacon	History of the Reign of King Henry VII	Lumby	3/-
,,	Essays	West	3/6 & 5/-
Cowley	Essays	Lumby	4/-
Earle	Microcosmography	West	3/-
Gray	Poems	Tovey	*In the Press*
Lamb	Tales from Shakespeare	Flather	1/6
Macaulay	Lord Clive	Innes	1/6
,,	Warren Hastings	,,	1/6
,,	William Pitt and Earl of Chatham	,,	2/6
Mayor	A Sketch of Ancient Philosophy from Thales to Cicero		3/6
More	History of King Richard III	Lumby	3/6
,,	Utopia	,,	3/6
Milton	Arcades and Comus	Verity	3/-
,,	Ode on the Nativity, L'Allegro, Il Penseroso & Lycidas	,,	2/6
,,	Samson Agonistes	,,	2/6
,,	Paradise Lost, Bks I, II	,,	2/-
,,	,, Bks III, IV	,,	2/-
,,	,, Bks V, VI	,,	2/-
,,	,, Bks VII, VIII	,,	2/-
,,	,, Bks IX, X	,,	2/-
,,	,, Bks XI, XII	,,	2/-
Pope	Essay on Criticism	West	2/-
Scott	Marmion	Masterman	2/6
,,	Lady of the Lake	,,	2/6
,,	Lay of the last Minstrel	Flather	2/-
,,	Legend of Montrose	Simpson	2/6
Shakespeare	A Midsummer-Night's Dream	Verity	1/6
,,	Twelfth Night	,,	1/6
,,	Julius Caesar	,,	1/6
,,	The Tempest	,,	1/6
,,	King Lear	,,	1/6
,,	Merchant of Venice	,,	*Nearly ready*
Shakespeare & Fletcher	Two Noble Kinsmen	Skeat	3/6
Sidney	An Apologie for Poetrie	Shuckburgh	3/-
Wallace	Outlines of the Philosophy of Aristotle		4/6
West	Elements of English Grammar		2/6
,,	English Grammar for Beginners		1/-
Carlos	Short History of British India		1/-
Mill	Elementary Commercial Geography		1/6
Bartholomew	Atlas of Commercial Geography		3/
Robinson	Church Catechism Explained		2/-

5

THE PITT PRESS SERIES.

6. EDUCATIONAL SCIENCE.

Author	Work	Editor	Price
Colbeck	Lectures on the Teaching of Modern Languages		2/-
Comenius	Life and Educational Works	Laurie	3/6
	Three Lectures on the Practice of Education		
Eve	I. On Marking		
Sidgwick	II. On Stimulus	} 1 Vol.	2/-
Abbott	III. On the teaching of Latin Verse Composition		
Farrar	General Aims of the Teacher	} 1 Vol.	1/6
Poole	Form Management		
Locke	Thoughts on Education	Quick	3/6
Milton	Tractate on Education	Browning	2/-
Sidgwick	On Stimulus		1/-
Thring	Theory and Practice of Teaching		4/6

7. MATHEMATICS.

Ball	Elementary Algebra		4/6
Euclid	Books I—VI, XI, XII	Taylor	5/-
,,	Books I—VI	,,	4/-
,,	Books I—IV	,,	3/-
	Also separately		
,,	Books I, & II; III, & IV; V, & VI; XI, & XII		1/6 each
,,	Solutions to Exercises in Taylor's Euclid	W. W. Taylor	10/6
	And separately		
,,	Solutions to Bks I—IV	,,	6/-
,,	Solutions to Books VI. XI	,,	6/-
Hobson & Jessop	Elementary Plane Trigonometry		4/6
Loney	Elements of Statics and Dynamics		7/6
	Part I. Elements of Statics		4/6
	,, II. Elements of Dynamics		3/6
,,	Solutions of Examples, Statics and Dynamics		7/6
,,	Mechanics and Hydrostatics		4/6
Smith, C.	Arithmetic for Schools, with or without answers		3/6
,,	Part I. Chapters I—VIII. Elementary, with or without answers		2/-
,,	Part II. Chapters IX—XX, with or without answers		2/-
Hale, G.	Key to Smith's Arithmetic		7/6

LONDON: C. J. CLAY AND SONS,
CAMBRIDGE UNIVERSITY PRESS WAREHOUSE,
AVE MARIA LANE.
GLASGOW: 263, ARGYLE STREET.

The Cambridge Bible for Schools and Colleges.

GENERAL EDITORS:
J. J. S. PEROWNE, D.D., BISHOP OF WORCESTER,
A. F. KIRKPATRICK, D.D., REGIUS PROFESSOR OF HEBREW.

Extra Fcap. 8vo. cloth, with Maps when required.

Book of Joshua. Rev. G. F. MACLEAR, D.D. 2s. 6d.
Book of Judges. Rev. J. J. LIAS, M.A. 3s. 6d.
First Book of Samuel. Prof. KIRKPATRICK, D.D. 3s. 6d.
Second Book of Samuel. Prof. KIRKPATRICK, D.D. 3s. 6d.
First & Second Books of Kings. Prof. LUMBY, D.D. 5s., and separately 3s. 6d. each.
Books of Ezra & Nehemiah. Prof. RYLE, D.D. 4s. 6d.
Book of Job. Prof. DAVIDSON, D.D. 5s.
Psalms. Book I. Prof. KIRKPATRICK, D.D. 3s. 6d.
Psalms. Books II and III. Prof. KIRKPATRICK, D.D. 3s. 6d.
Book of Ecclesiastes. Very Rev. E. H. PLUMPTRE, D.D. 5s.
Book of Isaiah. Chaps. I.–XXXIX. Rev. J. SKINNER, D.D. 4s.
—— **Chaps. XL.–LXVI.** Rev. J. SKINNER, D.D. *In the Press*
Book of Jeremiah. Rev. A. W. STREANE, D.D. 4s. 6d.
Book of Ezekiel. Prof. DAVIDSON, D.D. 5s.
Book of Hosea. Rev. T. K. CHEYNE, M.A., D.D. 3s.
Books of Joel and Amos. Rev. S. R. DRIVER, D.D. 3s. 6d.
Books of Obadiah and Jonah. Arch. PEROWNE. 2s. 6d.
Book of Micah. Rev. T. K. CHEYNE, M.A., D.D. 1s. 6d.
Nahum, Habakkuk & Zephaniah. Prof. DAVIDSON, D.D. 3s.
Books of Haggai, Zechariah & Malachi. Arch. PEROWNE. 3s. 6d.
Book of Malachi. Archdeacon PEROWNE. 1s.
First Book of Maccabees. Rev. W. FAIRWEATHER and Rev. J. S. BLACK, LL.D. 3s. 6d.
Gospel according to St Matthew. Rev. A. CARR, M.A. 2s. 6d.
Gospel according to St Mark. Rev. G. F. MACLEAR, D.D. 2s. 6d.
Gospel acc. to St Luke. Very Rev. F. W. FARRAR, D.D. 4s. 6d.
Gospel according to St John. Rev. A. PLUMMER, D.D. 4s. 6d.
Acts of the Apostles. Prof. LUMBY, D.D. 4s. 6d.
Epistle to the Romans. Rev. H. C. G. MOULE, D.D. 3s. 6d.
First and Second Corinthians. Rev. J. J. LIAS, M.A. 2s. each.
Epistle to the Galatians. Rev. E. H. PEROWNE, D.D. 1s. 6d.
Epistle to the Ephesians. Rev. H. C. G. MOULE, D.D. 2s. 6d.
Epistle to the Philippians. Rev. H. C. G. MOULE, D.D. 2s. 6d.
Colossians and Philemon. Rev. H. C. G. MOULE, D.D. 2s.
Epistles to the Thessalonians. Rev. G. G. FINDLAY, B.A. 2s.
Epistles to Timothy & Titus. Rev. A. E. HUMPHREYS, M.A. 3s.
Epistle to the Hebrews. Very Rev. F. W. FARRAR, D.D. 3s. 6d.
Epistle of St James. Very Rev. E. H. PLUMPTRE, D.D. 1s. 6d.
St Peter and St Jude. Very Rev. E. H. PLUMPTRE, D.D. 2s. 6d.
Epistles of St John. Rev. A. PLUMMER, D.D. 3s. 6d.
Book of Revelation. Rev. W. H. SIMCOX, M.A. 3s.

Other Volumes Preparing.

LONDON: C. J. CLAY AND SONS,
CAMBRIDGE UNIVERSITY PRESS WAREHOUSE,
AVE MARIA LANE.

The Smaller Cambridge Bible for Schools.

Now Ready. With Maps. Price 1s. each volume.

Book of Joshua. Rev. J. S. BLACK, LL.D.
Book of Judges. Rev. J. S. BLACK, LL.D.
First Book of Samuel. Prof. KIRKPATRICK, D.D.
Second Book of Samuel. Prof. KIRKPATRICK, D.D.
First Book of Kings. Prof. LUMBY, D.D.
Second Book of Kings. Prof. LUMBY, D.D.
Ezra & Nehemiah. Prof. RYLE, D.D.
Gospel according to St Matthew. Rev. A. CARR, M.A.
Gospel according to St Mark. Rev. G. F. MACLEAR, D.D.
Gospel according to St Luke. Very Rev. F. W. FARRAR, D.D.
Gospel according to St John. Rev. A. PLUMMER, D.D.
Acts of the Apostles. Prof. LUMBY, D.D.

The Cambridge Greek Testament for Schools and Colleges

GENERAL EDITOR: J. J. S. PEROWNE, D.D.

Gospel according to St Matthew. Rev. A. CARR, M.A. With 4 Maps. 4s. 6d.
Gospel according to St Mark. Rev. G. F. MACLEAR, D.D. With 3 Maps. 4s. 6d.
Gospel according to St Luke. Very Rev. F. W. FARRAR. With 4 Maps. 6s.
Gospel according to St John. Rev. A. PLUMMER, D.D. With 4 Maps. 6s.
Acts of the Apostles. Prof. LUMBY, D.D. 4 Maps. 6s.
First Epistle to the Corinthians. Rev. J. J. LIAS, M.A. 3s.
Second Epistle to the Corinthians. Rev. J. J. LIAS, M.A. 3s.
Epistle to the Hebrews. Very Rev. F. W. FARRAR, D.D. 3s. 6d.
Epistles of St John. Rev. A. PLUMMER, D.D. 4s.

GENERAL EDITOR: Prof. J. A. ROBINSON, D.D.

Epistle to the Philippians. Rev. H. C. G. MOULE, D.D. 2s. 6d.
Epistle of St James. Rev. A. CARR, M.A. 2s. 6d.
Pastoral Epistles. Rev. J. H. BERNARD, D.D. [*In Preparation*
Book of Revelation. Rev. W. H. SIMCOX, M.A. 5s.

London: C. J. CLAY AND SONS,
CAMBRIDGE WAREHOUSE, AVE MARIA LANE.
Glasgow: 263, ARGYLE STREET.
Leipzig: F. A. BROCKHAUS.
New York: THE MACMILLAN COMPANY.

CAMBRIDGE: PRINTED BY J. & C. F. CLAY, AT THE UNIVERSITY PRESS.

THE CAMBRIDGE BIBLE FOR SCHOOLS AND COLLEGES.

General Editors:
J. J. S. PEROWNE, D.D., *Bishop of Worcester.*
A. F. KIRKPATRICK, D.D., *Regius Professor of Hebrew.*

Opinions of the Press.

Guardian.—"*It is difficult to commend too highly this excellent series.*"

Academy.—"*The modesty of the general title of this series has, we believe, led many to misunderstand its character and underrate its value. The books are well suited for study in the upper forms of our best schools, but not the less are they adapted to the wants of all Bible students who are not specialists. We doubt, indeed, whether any of the numerous popular commentaries recently issued in this country will be found more serviceable for general use.*"

Baptist Magazine.—"*One of the most popular and useful literary enterprises of the nineteenth century.*"

Sword and Trowel.—"*Of great value. The whole series of comments for schools is highly esteemed by students capable of forming a judgment. The books are scholarly without being pretentious: and information is so given as to be easily understood.*"

Sunday School Chronicle.—"*There are no better books in exposition of the different parts of Scripture than those contained in the Cambridge Bible for Schools and Colleges. The series has long since established its claim to an honourable place in the front rank of first-rate commentaries; and the teacher or preacher who masters its volumes will be, like Apollos, 'mighty in the Scriptures.' All conscientious and earnest students of the Scriptures owe an immense debt to the Cambridge University Press for its Bible for Schools and Colleges. Take it for all in all, it is probably the most useful commentary alike on the Old Testament and on the New that has been given us in recent years.*"

II. Samuel. *Academy.*—"Small as this work is in mere dimensions, it is every way the best on its subject and for its purpose that we know of. The opening sections at once prove the thorough competence of the writer for dealing with questions of criticism in an earnest, faithful and devout spirit; and the appendices discuss a few special difficulties with a full knowledge of the data, and a judicial reserve, which contrast most favourably with the superficial dogmatism which has too often made the exegesis of the Old Testament a field for the play of unlimited paradox and the ostentation of personal infallibility. The notes are always clear and suggestive; never trifling or irrelevant; and they everywhere demonstrate the great difference in value between the work of a commentator who is also a Hebraist, and that of one who has to depend for his Hebrew upon secondhand sources."

I. Kings and Ephesians. *Sword and Trowel.*—"With great heartiness we commend these most valuable little commentaries. We had rather purchase these than nine out of ten of the big blown up expositions. Quality is far better than quantity, and we have it here."

Ezra and Nehemiah. *Guardian.*—"Professor Ryle's Commentary is quite the best work on these books accessible to the English reader."

Christian World.—"This book should be in the library of every Bible Student."

The Book of Job. *Spectator.*—"Able and scholarly as the Introduction is, it is far surpassed by the detailed exegesis of the book. In this Dr DAVIDSON's strength is at its greatest. His linguistic knowledge, his artistic habit, his scientific insight, and his literary power have full scope when he comes to exegesis."

Methodist Recorder.—"Already we have frequently called attention to this exceedingly valuable work as its volumes have successively appeared. But we have never done so with greater pleasure, very seldom with so great pleasure, as we now refer to the last published volume, that on the **Book of Job**, by Dr DAVIDSON, of Edinburgh....We cordially commend the volume to all our readers. The least instructed will understand and enjoy it; and mature scholars will learn from it."

Psalms. Book I. *Church Times.*—"It seems in every way a most valuable little book, containing a mass of information, well-assorted, and well-digested, and will be useful not only to students preparing for examinations, but to many who want a handy volume of explanation to much that is difficult in the Psalter........We owe a great debt of gratitude to Professor Kirkpatrick for his scholarly and interesting volume."

Literary Churchman.—"In this volume thoughtful exegesis founded on nice critical scholarship and due regard for the opinions of various writers, combine, under the influence of a devout spirit, to render this commentary a source of much valuable assistance. The notes are 'though deep yet clear,' for they seem to put in a concentrated form the very pith and marrow of all the best that has been hitherto said on the subject, with striking freedom from anything like pressure of personal views. Throughout the work care and pains are as conspicuous as scholarship."

Psalms. Books II. and III. *Critical Review.*—"The second volume of Professor KIRKPATRICK's Commentary on the Book of Psalms has all the excellent qualities which characterised the first....It gives what is best in the philology of the subject. Its notes furnish what is most needed and most useful. Its literary style is attractive. It furnishes all that is of real value in the form of introduction, and it has a studious regard for the devout as well as intelligent understanding of the Psalms."

Baptist.—"This volume of the Cambridge Bible for schools and colleges is a very valuable contribution to the expository literature of the Old Testament. The introduction, which occupies some 70 pages, is a compact compendium of explanatory and critical information upon the whole Psalter. The notes are brief, but full, and very suggestive."

Job—Hosea. *Guardian.*—"It is difficult to commend too highly this excellent series, the volumes of which are now becoming numerous. The two books before us, small as they are in size, comprise almost everything that the young student can reasonably expect to find in the way of helps towards such general knowledge of their subjects as may be gained without an attempt to grapple with the Hebrew; and even the learned scholar can hardly read without interest and benefit the very able introductory matter which both these commentators have prefixed to their volumes."

Isaiah. Chapters I—XXXIX. Professor W. H. Bennett in the *British Weekly*.—"Dr Skinner's name on the title-page of this book is a guarantee for extensive and exact scholarship and for careful and accurate treatment of the subject. This little volume will more than sustain the high reputation of the series in which it appears...readers will look forward with much interest to Dr Skinner's second volume on chapters xl—lxvi."

School Guardian.—"This last addition to 'The Cambridge Bible for Schools and Colleges,' is a most valuable one, and will go far to increase the usefulness of what we have no hesitation in calling the most useful commentary for school purposes. There ought to be two copies, at least, of this in every parish—one in the clergyman's and the other in the teacher's library."

Jeremiah. *Church Quarterly Review.*—"The arrangement of the book is well treated on pp. xxx., 396, and the question of Baruch's relations with its composition on pp. xxvii., xxxiv., 317. The illustrations from English literature, history, monuments, works on botany, topography, etc., are good and plentiful, as indeed they are in other volumes of this series."

Ezekiel. *Guardian.*—"No book of the Old Testament stands more in need of a commentator than this, and no scholar in England or Scotland is better qualified to comment upon it than Dr A. B. Davidson. With sound scholarship and excellent judgement he combines an insight into Oriental modes of thought which renders him a specially trustworthy guide to a book such as this....His commentary may be safely recommended as the best that has yet appeared. Nor is it unlikely that it will remain the best for some time to come."

Nahum, Habakkuk and Zephaniah. *Literary World.*—"An admirable little book, worthy of Dr A. B. Davidson's high scholarship and of the excellent series to which it belongs. The introductions are so comprehensive and thorough, and the notes so entirely useful, that one feels the book is all that can be required for the study of these prophecies by most biblical students, and by many Christian ministers."

Guardian.—"Prof. Davidson has laid all students of the Old Testament under a fresh debt of gratitude by the publication of this scholarly little volume. It is quite the best commentary on these books that has yet appeared....Small as it is, the volume is well worthy to take its place by the side of the same author's invaluable commentaries on Job and Ezekiel."

Spectator.—"We may say without hesitation that Professor Davidson's guidance is amply satisfactory. The theological student or the preacher who may have to deal with the subject cannot do better than consult him."

Malachi. *Academy.*—"Archdeacon Perowne has already edited

Jonah and Zechariah for this series. Malachi presents comparatively few difficulties and the Editor's treatment leaves nothing to be desired. His introduction is clear and scholarly and his commentary sufficient. We may instance the notes on ii. 15 and iv. 2 as examples of careful arrangement, clear exposition and graceful expression."

The Gospel according to St Matthew. *English Churchman.*—"The introduction is able, scholarly, and eminently practical, as it bears on the authorship and contents of the Gospel, and the original form in which it is supposed to have been written. It is well illustrated by two excellent maps of the Holy Land and of the Sea of Galilee."

St Mark. *Expositor.*—"Into this small volume Dr Maclear, besides a clear and able Introduction to the Gospel, and the text of St Mark, has compressed many hundreds of valuable and helpful notes. In short, he has given us a capital manual of the kind required—containing all that is needed to illustrate the text, i.e. all that can be drawn from the history, geography, customs, and manners of the time. But as a handbook, giving in a clear and succinct form the information which a lad requires in order to stand an examination in the Gospel, it is admirable......I can very heartily commend it, not only to the senior boys and girls in our High Schools, but also to Sunday-school teachers, who may get from it the very kind of knowledge they often find it hardest to get."

St Luke. *Spectator.*—"Canon FARRAR has supplied students of the Gospel with an admirable manual in this volume. It has all that copious variety of illustration, ingenuity of suggestion, and general soundness of interpretation which readers are accustomed to expect from the learned and eloquent editor. Anyone who has been accustomed to associate the idea of 'dryness' with a commentary, should go to Canon Farrar's **St Luke** for a more correct impression. He will find that a commentary may be made interesting in the highest degree, and that without losing anything of its solid value....But, so to speak, it is *too good* for some of the readers for whom it is intended."

The Gospel according to St John. *English Churchman.*—"The notes are extremely scholarly and valuable, and in most cases exhaustive, bringing to the elucidation of the text all that is best in commentaries, ancient and modern."

Acts. *School Guardian.*—"We do not know of any other volume where so much help is given to the complete understanding of one of the most important and, in many respects, difficult books of the New Testament."

Epistle to the Romans. *Expositor.*—"The 'Notes' are very good, and lean, as the notes of a School Bible should, to the most commonly accepted and orthodox view of the inspired author's meaning; while the Introduction, and especially the Sketch of the Life of St Paul, is a model of condensation. It is as lively and pleasant to read as if two or three facts had not been crowded into well-nigh every sentence."

Galatians. *Modern Church.*—"Dr PEROWNE deals throughout in a very thorough manner with every real difficulty in the text, and in this respect he has faithfully followed the noble example set him in the exegetical masterpiece, his indebtedness to which he frankly acknowledges."

English Churchman.—"This little work, like all of the series, is a scholarly production; but we can also unreservedly recommend it from a doctrinal standpoint; Dr E. H. PEROWNE is one who has grasped the distinctive teaching of the Epistle, and expounds it with clearness and definiteness. In an appendix, he ably maintains the correctness of the A. V. as against the R. V. in the translation of ll. 16, a point of no small importance."

Ephesians. *Baptist Magazine.*—"It seems to us the model of a School and College Commentary—comprehensive, but not cumbersome; scholarly, but not pedantic."

Guardian.—"It supplies matter which is evidently the outcome of deep study pursued with a devotional mind."

Philippians. *Record.*—"There are few series more valued by theological students than 'The Cambridge Bible for Schools and Colleges,' and there will be no number of it more esteemed than that by Mr H. C. G. MOULE on the *Epistle to the Philippians.*"

Colossians. *Record.*—"Those who have already used with pleasure and profit Mr Moule's volumes of the same series on Ephesians and Philippians will open this little book with the highest expectations. They will not be disappointed.......No more complete or trustworthy volume has been contributed to this series."

Expository Times.—"This is now the Commentary on Colossians and Philemon to have at your hand, whether you are schoolboy or scholar, layman or clergyman."

Thessalonians. *Academy.*—"Mr FINDLAY maintains the high level of the series to which he has become contributor. Some parts of his introduction to the Epistles to the Thessalonians could scarcely be bettered. The account of Thessalonica, the description of the style and character of the Epistles, and the analysis of them are excellent in style and scholarly care. The notes are possibly too voluminous; but there is so much matter in them, and the matter is arranged and handled so ably, that we are ready to forgive their fulness....Mr FINDLAY'S commentary is a valuable addition to what has been written on the letters to the Thessalonian Church."

Baptist Magazine.—"Mr FINDLAY has fulfilled in this volume a task which Dr Moulton was compelled to decline, though he has rendered valuable aid in its preparation. The commentary is in its own way a model—clear, forceful, scholarly—such as young students will welcome as a really useful guide, and old ones will acknowledge as giving in brief space the substance of all that they knew."

Timothy and Titus. *The Christian.*—"The series includes many volumes of sterling worth, and this last may rank among the most valuable. The pages evince careful scholarship and a thorough acquaintance with expository literature; and the work should promote a more general and practical study of the Pastoral Epistles."

Hebrews. *Baptist Magazine.*—"Like his (Canon Farrar's) commentary on Luke it possesses all the best characteristics of his writing. It is a work not only of an accomplished scholar, but of a skilled teacher."

James. *Expositor.*—"It is, so far as I know, by far the best exposition of the Epistle of St James in the English language. Not schoolboys or students going in for an examination alone, but ministers and preachers of the Word, may get more real help from it than from the most costly and elaborate commentaries."

The Epistles of St John. *Churchman.*—"This forms an admirable companion to the 'Commentary on the Gospel according to St John,' which was reviewed in *The Churchman* as soon as it appeared. Dr Plummer has some of the highest qualifications for such a task; and these two volumes, their size being considered, will bear comparison with the best Commentaries of the time."

Revelation. *Guardian.*—"This volume contains evidence of much careful labour. It is a scholarly production, as might be expected from the pen of the late Mr W. H. SIMCOX....The notes throw light upon many passages of this difficult book, and are extremely suggestive. It is an advantage that they sometimes set before the student various interpretations without exactly guiding him to a choice."

Wesleyan Methodist Sunday-School Record.—"We cannot speak too highly of this excellent little volume. The introduction is of the greatest possible value to the student, and accurate scholarship is combined with true loyalty to the inspired Word. There is much more matter of practical utility compressed into this volume of pp. 174 than is contained in many a portentous tome."

The Smaller Cambridge Bible for Schools.

Sunday-School Chronicle.—"*We can only repeat what we have already said of this admirable series, containing, as it does, the scholarship of the larger work. For scholars in our elder classes, and for those preparing for Scripture examinations, no better commentaries can be put into their hands.*"

Record.—"Despite their small size, these volumes give the substance of the admirable pieces of work on which they are founded. We can only hope that in many schools the class-teaching will proceed on the lines these commentators suggest."

Educational Review.—"*The Smaller Cambridge Bible for Schools is unique in its combination of small compass with great scholarship.... For use in lower forms, in Sunday-schools and in the family, we cannot suggest better little manuals than these.*"

Literary World.—"*All that is necessary to be known and learned by pupils in junior and elementary schools is to be found in this series. Indeed, much more is provided than should be required by the examiners. We do not know what more could be done to provide sensible, interesting, and solid Scriptural instruction for boys and girls. The Syndics of the*

OPINIONS OF THE PRESS.

Cambridge University Press are rendering great services both to teachers and to scholars by the publication of such a valuable series of books, in which slipshod work could not have a place."

Christian Leader.—"*For the student of the sacred oracles who utilizes hours of travel or moments of waiting in the perusal of the Bible there is nothing so handy, and, at the same time, so satisfying as these little books..... Nor let anyone suppose that, because these are school-books, therefore they are beneath the adult reader. They contain the very ripest results of the best Biblical scholarship, and that in the very simplest form.*"

Joshua. *School Guardian.*—"This little book is a model of what editorial work, intended for the use of young students, should be; and we could scarcely praise it more highly than by saying that it is in every way worthy of the volumes that have gone before it."

Schoolmistress.—"A most useful little manual for students or teachers."

Judges. *Educational News* (Edinburgh).—"The book makes available for teaching purposes the results of ripe scholarship, varied knowledge, and religious insight."

Schoolmaster.—"The work shows first-rate workmanship, and may be adopted without hesitation."

Samuel I. and II. *Saturday Review.*—"Professor KIRKPATRICK'S two tiny volumes on the First and Second Books of Samuel are quite model school-books; the notes elucidate every possible difficulty with scholarly brevity and clearness and a perfect knowledge of the subject."

Kings I. *Wesleyan Methodist Sunday-School Record.*—"Equally useful for teachers of young men's Bible classes and for earnest Bible students themselves. This series supplies a great need. It contains much valuable instruction in small compass."

St Mark. St Luke. *Guardian.*—"We have received the volumes of St Mark and St Luke in this series....The two volumes seem, on the whole, well adapted for school use, are well and carefully printed, and have maps and good, though necessarily brief, introductions. There is little doubt that this series will be found as popular and useful as the well-known larger series, of which they are abbreviated editions."

St Luke. *Wesleyan Methodist Sunday-School Record.*—"We cannot too highly commend this handy little book to all teachers."

St John. *Methodist Times.*—"A model of condensation, losing nothing of its clearness and force from its condensation into a small compass. Many who have long since completed their college curriculum will find it an invaluable handbook."

Acts. *Literary World.*—"The notes are very brief, but exceedingly comprehensive, comprising as much detail in the way of explanation as would be needed by young students of the Scriptures preparing for examination. We again give the opinion that this series furnishes as much real help as would usually satisfy students for the Christian ministry, or even ministers themselves."

THE CAMBRIDGE GREEK TESTAMENT
FOR SCHOOLS AND COLLEGES
with a Revised Text, based on the most recent critical authorities, and English Notes.

Expositor.—"*Has achieved an excellence which puts it above criticism.*"

Expository Times.—"*We could not point out better handbooks for the student of the Greek.*"

St Luke. *Methodist Recorder.*—"It gives us in clear and beautiful language the best results of modern scholarship....For young students and those who are not disposed to buy or to study the much more costly work of Godet, this seems to us to be the best book on the Greek Text of the Third Gospel."

St John. *Methodist Recorder.*—"We take this opportunity of recommending to ministers on probation, the very excellent volume of the same series on this part of the New Testament. We hope that most or all of our young ministers will prefer to study the volume in the *Cambridge Greek Testament for Schools.*"

II. Corinthians. *Guardian.*—"The work is scholarlike, and maintains the high level attained by so many volumes of this series."

London Quarterly Review.—"Young students will not easily find a more helpful introduction to the study of this Epistle than this....There is everything that a student of the Epistle needs in this little volume. It deals clearly and thoroughly with every point, and is written in a style that stimulates attention."

St James. *Athenæum.*—"This is altogether an admirable textbook. The notes are exactly what is wanted. They shew scholarship, wide reading, clear thinking. They are calculated in a high degree to stimulate pupils to inquiry both into the language and the teaching of the Epistle."

The Epistles of St John. *Scotsman.*—"In the very useful and well annotated series of the Cambridge Greek Testament the volume on the Epistles of St John must hold a high position....The notes are brief, well informed and intelligent."

Revelation. *Journal of Education.*—"Absolute candour, a feeling for Church tradition, and the combination of a free and graceful style of historical illustration with minute scholarship characterise this work. We wish we had more work of the same kind in the present day, and venture to think that a mastery of this unpretentious edition would prove to many a means of permanently enlarging the scope of their studies in sacred literature."

Guardian.—"The volume is well worthy of its place in the admirable series to which it belongs."

www.ingramcontent.com/pod-product-compliance
Lightning Source LLC
Chambersburg PA
CBHW020926230426
43666CB00008B/1585